George Ord, William Guthrie

A Reprint of the North American Zoology

George Ord, William Guthrie

A Reprint of the North American Zoology

ISBN/EAN: 9783743332478

Manufactured in Europe, USA, Canada, Australia, Japa

Cover: Foto ©Andreas Hilbeck / pixelio.de

Manufactured and distributed by brebook publishing software
(www.brebook.com)

George Ord, William Guthrie

A Reprint of the North American Zoology

Important Notice.

ORD'S ZOOLOGY.

The subscriber would announce that he has discovered a perfect copy (2 vols.) of the long lost "Second American Edition" of Guthrie's Geography, published in 1815. As is well known, this edition is of peculiar interest, as being the only one containing the part on American Zoology by the celebrated naturlist, George Ord. In it, Mr. Ord imposed, for the first time, binomial scientific names on several species of American Mammals and Birds, in some instances giving detailed descriptions of the same, quoted from the History of the Lewis and Clark Expedition.

The only copy of Ord's Zoology known to Bibliographers was an author's separate, probably presented by Mr. Ord, in the Library of the Academy of Natural Sciences of Philadelphia. This copy disappeared several years ago in a very mysterious manner.

The value of the present copy is greatly enhanced by the fact that is not only intact within the second volume of Guthrie's Geography, but that it is *Mr. Ord's private annotated copy* and was presented at his death to the Philadelphia College of Physicians.

A Reprint of the part on Zoology is now being prepared for publication and will probably be ready for distribution in February, 1894. It will include the entire part beginning, (Vol. II, p. 290.) at the word "Zoology," and ending, (p. 361,) at paragraph entitled "Natural Curiosities." This will be preceded by a frontispiece plate of Mr. Ord, with fac-simile signature and a brief introduction. An Appendix, treating briefly questions relating to nomenclature, history, etc., which remains unsettled owing to the disappearance of the work, or have arisen in the *renaissance* of American Mammalogy, will be added. As nearly as possible the reprint will be an exact reproduction of the size, paging, paragraphing, typography and mistakes of the original. The marginal annotations, in lead-pencil, made beyond reasonable doubt by Mr. Ord himself, will be fully commented upon. It is almost useless to add that no one with scientific, bibliographic or popular interest in American Literature can afford to be without this reprint of a strangely extinct work, the first systematic Zoology of America by an American.

Price per copy, prepaid, bound in cloth, ~~$1.50.~~

Address all orders to the author and publisher,

SAMUEL N. RHOADS,

Haddonfield, New Jersey.

George Ord

A REPRINT

OF THE

NORTH AMERICAN ZOOLOGY,

BY

GEORGE ORD.

BEING AN EXACT REPRODUCTION OF THE PART ORIGINALLY COMPILED
BY MR. ORD FOR JOHNSON & WARNER, AND FIRST
PUBLISHED BY THEM IN THEIR

SECOND AMERICAN EDITION

OF

GUTHRIE'S GEOGRAPHY,

IN

1815

TAKEN FROM MR. ORD'S PRIVATE, ANNOTATED COPY.

TO WHICH IS ADDED AN APPENDIX ON THE MORE IMPORTANT
SCIENTIFIC AND HISTORIC QESTIONS INVOLVED.

BY

SAMUEL N. RHOADS.

PUBLISHED, BY THE EDITOR,
HADDONFIELD, NEW JERSEY.
1894.

GEORGE STOKLEY, PRINTER,
Haddonfield, N. J.

INTRODUCTION.

The history of the "Second American Edition" of Guthrie's Geography, the only edition containing the complete part relating to North American Zoology prepared by George Ord, is involved in strange obscurity. Strictly speaking, this edition is *not* the "Second American," but is third. It is, however, the second of the three editions published by Johnson and Warner, the first appearing in 1809 and the last in 1820. The first of all the American editions of Guthrie's Geography that I can discover is a quarto in two volumes, the first bearing date February 1st, 1794, the second, April 27th, 1795. This edition was also published in Philadelphia, the title page stating it was 'printed for Mathew Carey." The edition of 1794 and 1809 contain no attempt at systematic zoology beyond desultory notices of the more striking animal productions of the world. I have been able to find seven volumes of the edition of 1794 and one volume of the edition of 1809 in our principal Philadelphia libraries. Of the edition of 1820, I have been able to find one copy. It was known to Prof. Baird, and Dr. Coues gives its full title in the Bibliographical Appendix to his Birds of the Colorado Valley and remarks that the zoological portion "consists of that given in the *second* ed., 1815, *q. v.*, but with the omission of the systematic list, which represented the whole of the technical value of the matter. Ord's name does not appear in connection with this performance."

Complete titles of these editions and the bibliographic references thereto, made by Prof. Baird and Dr. Coues, will be found in the Appendix to this work. It is hoped that the above facts will stimulate all interested persons in the search for copies of the editions of 1815 and 1820. A strange fatalilty seems to have overtaken all the Johnson and Warner editions when it is considered that the only known copy of the second edition has just come to light. There is only one copy of the third edition in four of the most important Philadelphia libraries and only half a copy of the first edition. The Carey quarto edition does not seem to be rare.

As long ago as 1857, Prof. Baird characterized the so-called Second American Edition of Guthrie's Geography as "exceedingly rare," adding, "I have never, even in Philadelphia, been able to see a perfect copy. The Library of the Philadelphia Academy has the natural history portion, separate."

It is probably to this copy that Dr. Coues refers in the Bibliographic Appendix to his Birds of the Colorado Valley. After giving part of the title of this specimen, Dr. Coues notes, "above title defective after the first two lines, the only copy I ever handled, having part of the title page torn off."

The all-around desirability of such a rare work, and the well known activity of Dr. Coues in his bibliographic researches, seem to have failed in revealing another copy, and, what is more unfortunate, to have resulted in the mysterious disappearance of the copy belonging to the Library of the Academy of Natural Sciences.

The numerous applications from scientists, both at home and abroad, for citations from this historic copy evidenced the extreme scarcity, if not extinction, of this edition of Guthrie's Geography and inspired certain workers at the Academy to renewed diligence in the search for it. In a casual conversation with Dr. Edward J. Nolan, librarian of the Academy, last November, he suggested to me that Mr. Ord, having presented a quantity of his private books and papers to the Philadelphia College of Physicians, it would be well to ask the College Librarian if they had a copy of the long-lost work. On application, I was informed that their library did not contain it, but as I was leaving, the librarian remarked that I might inquire of Dr. J. Solis Cohen, that gentleman having purchased a number of books and papers not coming within the scope of their library. I visited Dr. Cohen and after a delay of two days received a letter announcing that he had a perfect copy of the book I was after, containing marginal pencil notes on the zoological portion. On comparing these notes with Mr. Ord's letters written at that period, I feel no hesitation in attributing their authorship to him, not only from the chirographic resemblance but from the character of the notes themselves.

As a reward for having identified the work, Dr. Cohen has kindly placed the same in my custody until the present reprint could be satisfactorily completed. For this courtesy Dr. Cohen deserves not only the sincere gratitude of the editor, but of the scientific world, for to his interest in these matters we owe the rescue of an invaluable work from the musty chaos of some old book-store, or a fate even more obscure.

Owing to the worn and imperfect condition of the type and its very
small size as used in the tabulated lists, many of the characters are to
be distinguished only by closest scrutiny. On this account is was con-
cluded that a photographic reprint was impracticable. As stated in
my circular of announcement, as nearly as possible the reprint is an
exact reproduction of the style, form, size, paging, paragraphing, typography and inaccuracies of the original. The tables, which contain,
with their foot notes, that part of the reprint most requiring absolute
accuracy, have, (if that were possible), received greater care than
the text.

Apart from its technical value, the work before us has great
historic and literary interest. The name of George Ord was long ago
immortally associated with that of Alexander Wilson. If the latter
is the Father of North American Ornithology, Mr. Ord, in a humbler
sense, may be characterized Father of North American Zoology, his
contribution to Guthrie's Geography being the first systematic Zoology
of America by an American. The limited and concise nature of this
production gives only a casual glimpse at the personality of its author:
when, however, it does reveal itself, the same lofty and sacred animus
which inspired the noblest writings of Wilson and Audubon is
unmistakable.

The systematic zoologist of to-day, wearied with the modern techni-
calities of his profession, does well to recur to the heartfelt delineations
of nature by the old school masters, and to consider the present
scramble after names and novelties as a mere accessory to a clearer,
more spiritual insight and interpretation of life. George Ord was
quick to recognize in Wilson and others of his day the traits of true
genius for the study of nature, because he possessed these require-
ments in no small degree himself. To him the study of Natural History was not merely a delight or a hobby, but it became a sacred trust;
by it he not only sought to please but to instruct, to correct the crude
misrepresentations of foreign naturalists, to truthfully portray the
zoological productions of his native land and divert the reader from an
abstract view of created things to contemplate the omniscient plan of
the Creative Mind.

The modesty of George Ord is noteworthy. In neither edition of
Guthrie's Geography containing the North American Zoology does his
name appear. In the "Advertisement" preface to the edition of 1815
(vol. 1.) the editor refers to it in the following words:–

"The article on the Zoology of North America, is, for it extent, by far the most accurate which has ever appeared. The modesty of its author forbids a personal acknowledgement, which the editors would have the highest satisfaction in making."

Only through the recognition of his associates, and, in larger measure, by the citations of Prof. Baird in his work on the Mammals of North America, is the scientific world enabled to accord to the author of Ord's Zoology the honor and distinction which he humbly sought to avoid.

May the following pages not only serve to establish more clearly Mr. Ord's title to a high place among the Zoologists of America, but further those loftier interests which he considered so essential to scientific progress.

ACADEMY OF NATURAL SCIENCES, PHILADELPHIA,
NEW YEAR'S DAY,
1894.

A NEW

GEOGRAPHICAL, HISTORICAL,

AND

COMMERCIAL GRAMMAR;

AND PRESENT STATE OF THE

SEVERAL KINGDOMS OF THE WORLD.

CONTAINING,

1. The Figures, Motions, and Distances of the Planets, according to the Newtonian System, and the latest Observations.

2. A general View of the Earth considered as a Planet; with several useful Geographical Definitions and Problems.

3. The Grand Divisions of the Globe into Land and Water, Continents, and Islands.

4. The Situation and Extent of Empires, Kingdoms, States, Provinces, and Colonies.

5. Their Climate, Air, Soil, Vegetable Productions, Metals, Minerals, Natural Curiosities, Seas, Rivers, Bays, Capes, Promontories and Lakes.

6. The Birds and Beasts peculiar to each Country.

7. Observations on the Changes that have been any where observed upon the Face of Nature, since the most early Periods of History.

8. The History and origin of Nations, their Forms of Government, Religion, Laws, Revenues, Taxes, Naval and Military Strength, Orders of Knighthood, &c.

9. The Genius, Manners, Customs and Habits of the People.

10. Their Language, Learning, Arts, Sciences, Manufacturers, and Commerce.

11. The Chief Cities, Structures, Ruins, and Artificial Curiosities.

12. The Longitude, Latitude, Bearings, and distances of principal places from London.

TO WHICH ARE ADDED,

1. A GEOGRAPHICAL INDEX WITH THE NAMES OF PLACES ALPHABETICALLY ARRANGED. 2. A CHRONOLOGICAL TABLE OF REMARKABLE EVENTS, FROM THE CREATION TO THE PRESENT TIME. 3. A LIST OF MEN OF LEARNING AND SCIENCE.

BY WILLIAM GUTHRIE, ESQ.

THE ASTRONOMICAL PART BY JAMES FERGUSON, F. R. S.

TO WHICH HAVE BEEN ADDED,

THE LATE DISCOVERIES OF DR. HERSCHEL, AND OTHER EMINENT ASTRONOMERS,

ILLUSTRATED WITH TWENTY-EIGHT CORRECT MAPS.

THE SECOND AMERICAN EDITION IMPROVED.

IN TWO VOLUMES . . . . . . VOL. II.

PHILADELPHIA:

PUBLISHED BY JOHNSON & WARNER AND FOR SALE AT THEIR BOOK STORES ; IN PHILADELPHIA, AND RICHMOND VIRGINIA.

1815,

Zoology . . . . America, it is said, contains at least one half, and the United States about one fourth, of the Quadrupeds of the known world. The naturalists of Europe and America, with a commendable zeal, have directed their attention to the zoology of the western hemisphere; and their labours in this interesting and useful branch of natural science have been rewarded with success. But still their nomenclatures of the Quadrupeds of North America are very imperfect. The following catalogue is the best that we can at present obtain. In the sketches which follow, we have been greatly indebted to the works of the ingenious Mr. Pennant. The arrangement of the Orders and Genera, is that of the last edition of Linnæus by Dr. Turton.

ZOOLOGY OF NORTH AMERICA.

CLASS *MAMMALIA*.

ORDER *PRIMATES*.

GENUS *SIMIA*.

Horned Sapajou	-	**Simia fatuellus.**
Brown Sapajou	-	**Simia apella.**
Capucin Monkey	-	**Simia Capucina.**
*Ludicrous Monkey	Simia——

GENUS *VESPERTILIO*.

New-York Bat	-	*Vespertilio noveboracensis.*
Black Bat	-	*Vespertilio Americanus.*
Brown Bat	-	*Vespertilio fuscus.*
Vampyre Bat	-	*Vespertilio spectrum.*
Hang-lip Bat	-	*Vespertilio labialis.*
†Red Bat	-	*Vespertilio rubra.*

ORDER *BRUTA*.

GENUS *MYRMECOPHAGA*.

Least Ant-eater	-	*Myrmecophaga didactyla.*
Striped Ant-eater	-	*Myrmecophaga pentadactyla.*

GENUS *DASYPUS*.

Three-banded Armadillo	*Dasypus tricinctus.*
Eight-banded Armadillo	*Dasypus octocinctus.*
Nine-banded Armadillo	*Dasypus novemcinctus.*

GENUS *TRICHECHUS*.

Arctic Walrus or Morse	*Trichechus rosmarus.*
Manati	-	*Trichechus australis.*
Siren or Sea Ape	-	*Trichechus siren.*

ORDER *FERÆ*.

GENUS *PHOCA*.

Maned Seal	-	*Phoca jubata.*
Sea Calf	-	*Phoca vitulina.*
Harp Seal	-	*Phoca Groenlandica.*
Rough Seal	-	*Phoca hispida.*
Crested Seal	-	*Phoca cristata.*
Hooded Seal	-	*Phoca monachus.*

GENUS *CANIS*.

Indian Dog	-	*Canis Americanus.*
Common Wolf	-	*Canis lupus.*
Black Wolf	-	*Canis niger.*
Mexican Wolf	-	*Canis Mexicanus.*
‡Large Prairie Wolf	*Canis ——*
‡Small Prairie Wolf	*Canis ——*
‡Large Red Fox	*Canis ——*
‡Small Red Fox	*Canis ——*
‡Varied Fox	-	*Canis alopex?*
Silvery Fox	-	*Canis cinereo-argenteus?*
Black Fox	-	*Canis lycaon.*
Gray Fox	-	*Canis Virginianus.*
Common Red Fox	-	*Canis vulpes.*
Arctic Fox	-	*Canis lagopus.*
Cross Fox	-	*Canis crucigera.*
Corsak Fox	-	*Canis Corsac.*

GENUS *FELIS*.

‡American Panther	*Felis conguar.*
§Brown Tiger	*Felis concolor.*
Black Tiger	*Felis discolor.*

Brasilian Tiger	-	*Felis onca.*
Mountain Lynx	-	*Felis montana.*
Bay Lynx or Wild Cat	*Felis rufa.*
Common Lynx	-	*Felis lynx.*
Mexican Cat	-	*Felis pardalis.*
Mexican Tiger-Cat	-	*Felis Mexicana.*

GENUS *VIVERRA*.

Vulpecula **Weasel or** Squash	-	*Viverra vulpecula.*
Mexican Weasel	-	*Viverra prehensilis.*
Striated Weasel or Skunk	*Viverra putorius.*
‖White Weasel	-	*Viverra albus.*

GENUS *MUSTELA*.

Sea Otter	-	*Mustela lutris.*
Common Otter	-	*Mustela lutra.*
Canada Otter	-	*Mustela Canadensis.*
Minx	-	*Mustela minx.*
Tawny Weasel	-	*Mustela vison.*
Fisher Weasel	-	*Mustela nigra.*
Common Weasel	-	*Mustela vulgaris.*
Pekan	-	*Mustela Hudsonius.*
Pine Martin	-	*Mustela martes.*
Sable	-	*Mustela zibellina.*
American Sable	-	*Mustela Americanus.*
Ermine or Stoat	-	*Mustela erminea.*

GENUS *URSUS*.

Polar Bear	-	*Ursus maritimus.*
Grizzly Bear	-	*Ursus horribilis.*
American Bear	-	*Ursus Americanus.*
Badger	-	*Ursus meles.*
American Badger	-	*Ursus Labradorius.*
Raccoon	-	*Ursus lotor.*
¶Wolverene	-	*Ursus luscus.*
¶Glutton	-	*Ursus gulo.*

GENUS *DIDELPHIS*.

Virginian Opossum	-	**Didelphis opossum.**
Mexican Opossum	-	**Didelphis cayopollin.**

GENUS *TALPA*.

Long-tailed Mole	-	*Talpa longicaudata.*
Red Mole	-	*Talpa rubra.*

GENUS *SOREX*.

**Crested Shrew	-	**Sorex cristatus.**
††Aquatic Shrew or Common Mole	-	*Sorex aquaticus.*
Fetid Shrew	-	*Sorex araneus.*
Black Shrew	-	*Sorex niger.*
Mexican Shrew	-	*Sorex Mexicanus.*
Pigmy Shrew	-	*Sorex exilis.*

ORDER *GLIRES*.

GENUS *HYSTRIX*.

Brasilian Porcupine	-	*Hystrix prehensilis.*
Canadian Porcupine	-	*Hystrix dorsata.*
Mexican Porcupine	-	*Hystrix Mexicana.*

GENUS *CAVIA*.

Gibconite or Spotted Cavy	*Cavia paca.*
Long-nosed Cavy	-	*Cavia aguti.*

---

*Henderson's Honduras, p. 104.
†Described by Mr. Wilson. See American Ornithology, vol. vi. p. 60.
‡These animals are described in the history of Lewis and Clark's expedition.
§Supposed to be the same.
‖Discovered by Lewis and Clark. This animal is of a yellowish white colour; its feet and end of its tail are dusky. Whether it is a new species, or a variety of one already known, we cannot determine. It is preserved in Peale's Museum.
¶Supposed by some writers to be the same.
**Radiated Mole of Pennant.
††Brown Mole of the same author.

GENUS CASTOR.

Common Beaver	-	Castor fiber.
Muskrat	- -	Castor zibethicus.

GENUS MUS.

Norway Rat	-	Mus decumanus.
Black Rat	-	Mus rattus.
American Rat	-	Mus Americanus.
Water Rat	-	Mus amphibius.
*Sand or Earth Rat	-	Mus talus.
Louisiana Earth Rat or Gopher	-	Mus Ludovicianus.
†Ash-coloured Rat	-	Mus cinereus.
Common Mouse	-	Mus musculus.
Rustic Mouse	-	Mus agrarius.
Mexican Mouse	-	Mus Mexicanus.
Virginian Mouse	-	Mus Virginianus.
Hudson's Mouse	-	Mus Hudsonius.
American Wandering Mouse	-	Mus Canadensis.
Meadow Mouse	-	Mus arvalis.
‡Pennsylvania Meadow Mouse	-	Mus Pennsylvanica.

GENUS ARCTOMYS.

Maryland Marmot or Ground Hog	-	Arctomys monax.
Canadian Marmot	-	Arctomys empetra.
Hoary Marmot	-	Arctomys pruinosa.
Tailless Marmot	-	Arctomys Hudsonius.
Earless Marmot	-	Arctomys citillus.
Louisiana Marmot or Prairie-dog	-	Arctomys Ludoviciana.
Columbia Marmot	-	Arctomys Columbianus.

GENUS SCIURUS.

Large Black Squirrel		Sciurus niger.
§Small Black Squirrel	-	Sciurus Pennsylvanica.
Cat or Fox Squirrel	-	Sciurus vulpinus.
Gray Squirrel	-	Sciurus cinereus.
Louisiana Gray Squirrel		Sciurus Ludovicianus.
Virginian Squirrel	-	Sciurus Virginianus.
‖New Jersey Squirrel	-	Sciurus hiemalis.
Varied Squirrel	-	Sciurus variegatus.
Mexican Squirrel	-	Sciurus Mexicanus.
Hudson's Bay Squirrel	-	Sciurus Hudsonius.
¶Carolina or Chickaree Squirrel	-	Sciurus Carolinensis.
Ground Squirrel	-	Sciurus striatus.
Fair Squirrel	-	Sciurus flavus.
Flying Squirrel	-	Sciurus volucella.
Hudson's Bay Flying Squirrel	-	Sciurus Labradorius.
**Columbia Gray Squirrel		Sciurus ——
**Red-breasted Squirrel		Sciurus ——
**Rocky-mountain Ground Squirrel	-	Sciurus ——
**Brown Squirrel	-	Sciurus ——

GENUS DIPUS.

Labrador Jerboa	-	Dipus Labradorius.
Canada Jerboa	-	Dipus Canadensis.
American Jerboa	-	Dipus Americanus.

GENUS LEPUS.

Common Hare	-	Lepus timidus.
Varying Hare	-	Lepus variabilis.
American Hare or Rabbit	Lepus Americanus.	

ORDER PECORA.

GENUS CERVUS.

Moose	-	Cervus alces.
Greater Stag or Elk	-	Cervus major.
Common Deer	-	Cervus Virginianus.
Rein Deer	-	Cervus tarandus.
Mexican Deer	-	Cervus Mexicanus.
Spring-buck Deer	-	Cervus ——
††Mule Deer	-	Cervus ——
††Long-tailed Fallow Deer	Cervus ——	
††Black-tailed Fallow Deer	Cervus ——	

GENUS ANTILOPE.

American or prong-horned Antelope	-	Antilope Americanus.
‡‡Barbarian Antelope		Antilope dorcas.

GENUS OVIS.

Big-horned Sheep or Argali	-	Ovis ammon.
Rocky-mountain Sheep	Ovis montanus.	

GENUS BOS.

Bison or American Ox		Bos Americanus.
Musk Ox	- -	Bos moschatus.

ORDER BELLUÆ.

GENUS EQUUS.

Wild Horse	-	Equus caballus.

GENUS TAPIR.

Long-nosed Tapir	-	Tapir Americanus.

GENUS SUS.

Mexican Hog or Peccary		Sus tajacu.
Darien Hog or Warree	-	Sus ——

ORDER CETE.

GENUS MONODON.

Narwal.	- -	Monodon monoceros.

GENUS BALÆNA.

§§Common Whale	-	Balæna mysticetus.
Hump Whale	-	Balæna gibbosa.
‖Pike-headed Whale		Balæna boops.
Beaked Whale	-	Balæna rostrata.
Fin-fish	-	Balæna physalus.

GENUS PHYSETER.

Blunt-headed Cachalot or Spermaceti Whale	-	Physeter macrocephalus.
Sharp-nosed Cachalot		Physeter mular.
Lesser Cachalot	-	Physeter catodon.
High-finned Cachalot	-	Physeter tursio.

GENUS DELPHINUS.

Porpoise	- -	Delphinus phocæna.
Grampus	- -	Delphinus orca.
Dolphin	- -	Delphinus delphis.
Beluga	- -	Delphinus leucas.

*Called by some writers Georgian Hamster, though it differs materially from the Hamsters of Europe in its cheek pouches. The animal which follows has similar pouches; but we have not the means of ascertaining whether or no it is the same species.

†Discovered by Lewis and Clark. See history of the expedition, vol. i, p. 239.

‡Described by Mr. Wilson. See American Ornithology, vol. vi, p. 59.

‡This has always been confounded with the foregoing, but it is a different species. It abounds in those parts of Pennsylvania which lie to the westward of the Allegany ridge.

‡This is a nondescript. It is about the size of the Sciurus cinereus; of a mixed gray and tawny colour; and has bearded ears. Inhabits near Little Egg-harbour, New-Jersey.

¶The lower parts of the Chikaree are white; sides of a beautiful gray; along the top of the back a rusty line; its ears are slightly tufted.

**These have been described by Lewis and Clark; but we suspect that the Brown Squirrel is no other than the Sciurus Hudsonius, No. 4 of Pennant, Arct. Zool. sometimes called the Pine Squirrel, from the circumstance of it being found in the Pine Woods.

††Described by Lewis and Clark.

‡‡Called also the Gazelle. Vide Henderson's Honduras, p. 97. Thus it appears that there are two species of Antelope in North America, notwithstanding the opinions and determinations of the European naturalists, that the New World did not afford a single species of this genus.

§§A young Whale of this species was taken in the Delaware, in the vicinity of the Falls, in the latter part of the year 1814; and exhibited at Philadelphia.

‖A Pike-headed Whale was caught some years since in the Delaware, near Reedy island, and shown in Philadelphia and New-York.

The *Arctic Walrus*, sometimes called the Sea Cow, is a native of the Magdalene islands, St. John's and Anticosti, in the gulph of St. Lawrence. They are, when out of the water, very unwiedly, and move with great difficulty. They crawl upon the islands in fair weather; and if not disturbed will remain, it is said, for several days without food, basking in the sun. They weigh from fifteen hundred to two thousand pounds; and produce from one to two barrels of oil, which is boiled out of the fat that lies between the skin and the flesh. Immediately on their arrival at their summer residence, the females calve, and engender again in two months after; so that they carry their young about nine mouths. They never have more than two at a time, and seldom more than one. They are monogamous.

In the upper jaw of this animal there are two long tusks, bending downwards. These are used for the purposes of defence; and in the dreadful conflicts which sometimes happen between them and the Polar Bears, arising from the occupancy of the same piece of ice, the advantage is generally on the side of the Walrus.

They are gregarious, and sometimes have been found together in thousands; are very shy, and avoid the haunts of mankind. They are usually seen on the floating ice. They sleep both on the ice, and in the water, and snore excessively loud. They are harmless, unless provoked: but when wounded, or attacked, grow fierce, and are very vindictive.

Manati. "This animal forms the connecting link between the beasts and fishes. It is a very clumsy creature, with a head thicker than that of an ox; eyes small; and the two feet are placed near the head, for the purpose of swimming. It is of sufficient size to form a load for two oxen. They are about fifteen feet long, and six broad. As this animal has only fore feet, it has obtained the name of *Manati*, i. e. 'an animal with both hands.' This animal has been found in the rivers which run from Georgia into the Gulf of Mexico." *

"The *Manati*," says Captain Henderson, "which is described as forming the boundary between quadrupeds and fishes, is an inhabitant of the waters contiguous *to the shores of Honduras. The male and female are usually found together and, whilst sporting on the surface of the different lagoons, are frequently destroyed by the harpoon or dart, in the use of which the slaves of the settlement, and the Indians of the neighbouring Mosquito nation, are wonderfully dexterous. This singular animal sometimes exceeds a thousand pounds in weight. Its flesh, either fresh or salted, is particularly admired, and thought very closely to resemble veal. The tail, which forms the most valuable part of the manati, after laying some days in a pickle prepared for it with spices &c. and eaten cold, is a discovery of which Apicius might have been proud, and which the discriminating palate of Elagabalus would have thought justly entitled to the most distinguished reward." †

The *Wolf* has a long head, pointed nose, sharp and erect ears, long legs, and a bushy tail which bends down; its hair is pretty long, the colour usually of a pale brown, mixed with dull yellow and black. This destructive animal has fortunately become scarce in the cultivated parts of America. Formerly rewards were offered for killing them, as their ravages among the sheep, calves and hogs of the

* Morse's Geography, vol. i. p. 247.
† An account of the British Settlement of Honduras, p. 37, London 1809.

settlers, tended greatly to impede the progress of husbandry. In the Gennesee country, and the western parts of Pennsylvania, they yet occasionally make a sweep among the sheep. But such is the hostility of the inhabitants, that in a short time these animals will entirely disappear from those parts. In Louisiana they are numerous; and commit ravages amongst the Deer and Antelopes, hunting them, it is said, in packs, like hounds, and sometimes relieving each other during the chase, as the game are too swift to be run down by a single Wolf. It is even asserted that they will venture to attack a straggling Bison or Buffaloe They frequently kill each other in their contests for a carcass.

Indian Dog. Pennant is of the opinion that this animal is the Wolf in a domesticated state. "It still betrays," says he, "its savage descent, by uttering only a howl, instead of the significant bark of the genuine dog. It is singular that the race of European dogs shew as strong an antipathy to this American species, as they do to the Wolf itself. They never meet with them, but they shew all possible signs of dislike, and will fall on and worry them; while the wolfish breed, with every mark of timidity, puts its tail between its legs, and runs from the rage of the others. The aversion to the Wolf is natural to all genuine dogs; for it is well known that a whelp, which has never seen a Wolf, will at first sight tremble, and run to its master for protection: an old dog will instantly attack it." *

Almost all the northern and western Indians employ these dogs, yoked to sledges, for the purpose of transporting their game &c. Mackenzie, in his general history of the fur trade, says "that the Knisteneaux Indians in the winter, when the waters are frozen, make their journies, which are never of any great length, with sledges drawn by dogs. † Patrick Gass observes that "the Sioux Indians fasten their dogs to poles, and make them draw them from one camp to another, loaded with skins and other articles."‡ And again, that "they yoke them to a kind of car, which they have to haul their baggage from one camp to another. The dogs," continues he, "are not large, much resemble a wolf, and will haul about seventy pounds each." §

From the Journal of Lewis and Clark we learn that "dog meat is a great dish among the Sioux Indians, and used on all festivals." But it seems that the nations to the westward of the Rocky Mountains, though they posess numbers of these animals, yet they do not eat them. With the last mentioned travellers, dog meat became a favorite food, was found to be a strong healthy diet, preferable to lean Deer or Elk, and much superior to horse flesh in any state.‖

With all due deference to the opinion of the respectable Mr. Pennant, we must dissent from him with respect to the origin of the Indain Dog. We do not consider this animal the Wolf. If he be not, as some suppose he is, a collateral decendant of the European family, introduced by the early adventurers into the New World, we have strong reasons to conclude that he is an independent species. However, the result of our inquires into the history of this animal is very unsatisfactory.

In Barton's Medical and Physical Journal, vol. i, part ii, p. 3, we are

*Arctic Zoology, Art. Wolf.   § Gass's Journal p. 47.
†Mackenzie's Voyages, vol. i. p. 120.   ‖ Hist. of the Exp. vol. 2. p. 2 39.
‡Gass's Journal, p. 42.

presented with a highly interesting article on the subject of the *Native Dogs of North America*; from which it is evident that the origin of the Indian Dog is still a desideratum in natural history.

"We are not yet prepared," says the Doctor, "to give an exact genealogical history of the Indian Dog. We are compelled to mix conjecture with fact. The anatomical structure of the animal should be examined. But whatever may have been the origin of this breed of dogs, I am disposed to think, with Josselyn, that the savages found it in the woods, and that it has existed as a distinct species, or breed, for a very long period of time.

"It is highly probable, that the Indian Dog still exists, in a wild state, in the woods of many parts of North America. It is likely that when seen, he has been sometimes mistaken for the Wolf. A very intelligent Indian informed me, that, in the year 1792, when travelling toward the head-waters of the river Miami, which empties into Lake Erie, he had met with Wolves which barked like Dogs, though, in other respects, they appeared to be little different from Wolves. Perhaps, future researches will show, that these were the real Indian Dogs, in their wild state. The subject is worthy of further inquiry."

In the history of Lewis and Clark's expedition, we have an account of two animals, which are termed *Prairie Wolves*, the barking of which, (whether one, or both is not specified) "resembles precisely that of the common Cur Dog." *

Thus the story of the Indian is corroborated, and the conjecture of Professor Barton receives additional strength, by the respectable testimony of Lewis and Clark.

The *Arctic Fox* is smaller than the common Fox; its colour a bluish gray, and sometimes white; hair long, soft and silky; legs short; tail shorter than that of the common Fox, and more bushy.

These animals are found only in the Arctic regions, a few degrees within and without the polar circle. They are only migratory in Hudson's Bay, once in four or five years. They are the hardiest of animals, and even in Spitzbergen and Nova Zembla prowl out for prey during the severity of the winter. They live on young wild geese, and all kinds of water fowl; on their eggs; on hares and smaller animals. They are tame and inoffensive; are killed for the sake of their skins, both in Asia and Hudson's Bay. Their fur is light and warm, but not durable.

Gray, and *Red Foxes* are common throughout North America; but the former are more numerous, especially to the southward. Although universally detested and persecuted by man, yet these animals do not often commit depredations upon the farmer, and then only when urged by necessity. Sometimes the hen-roost will be robbed, or some vagrant turkey or chicken carried off. But in common, these wary animals are not fond of approaching too near the habitation of man, especially if there be a dog near the premises.

Along the coast of New Jersey, Foxes abound, harbouring among the green briars and myrtle bushes of the sea shore. They choose these retreats that they may have the advantage of the salt marshes, which are their principal hunting grounds. An immense number of birds of various kinds, particularly of the *Grallæ* order, breed in these marshes, and on the sand hills, on the eggs and young of which the

Foxes feed; and during the whole of the winter these animals are abundantly supplied with geese, brant and ducks, which, on being wounded by the gunners, either die or are caught by the Foxes. They likewise lie in ambush on the margins of the fresh water ponds, where the ducks came to drink and feed at night, and destroy numbers.

The *Couguar* or *Panther* inhabits Canada and Florida, and is sometimes seen in the states bordering on the lakes, and the Mississippi. It has become a rare animal. Pennant observes that "it is the most pernicious animal of North America. It lives in forests. Sometimes purrs, at others times makes a great howling. Is extremely destructive to domestic animals, particularly to hogs. It preys also upon the Moose and other Deer; falling on them from the tree it lurks in. It will feed even on beasts of prey. I have seen the skin of one which was shot just as it had killed a wolf." *

The *Lynx* has pale yellow eyes; erect ears, tufted with long black hair; its body is covered with soft and long fur, of a cinereous colour, tinged with tawny, and marked with dusky spots, more or less visible in different subjects, dependent on the age, or season in which the animal is killed; the legs are strong and thick; the claws large. This animal is about three times the size of a domestic Cat; the tail is only four inches long, tipt with black.

The *Lynx* inhabits the great forests of North America. It is called in Canada *le Chat, ou le Loup-cervier*, on account of its being so destructive to the deer. The English inhabitants call it the Wild Cat. It is very destructive to their young pigs, poultry, and all kinds of game. The skins are in high esteem for the softness and warmness of the fur; and great numbers are annually imported into Europe.†

Of that species of the Feline race, named *Catamount*, we have so imperfect an account, that nothing conclusive or satisfactory can be given. The animal described by Pennant under the name of the Mountain Lynx, he supposed was the *Cat-a-mountain* of Lawson. Its length from the nose to the tail was two feet and a half. But in Morse's Geography an account is given of an animal, which is there named *Catamount*, which is said to have been killed in New Hampshire, and measured as follows; the length of its body, including the head, six feet; circumference of the body two feet, six inches; length of its tail three feet, and of its legs about one foot. The colour along its back was nearly black; of its sides, dark reddish brown; its feet were black.

Pike speaks of having seen an animal resembling the Panther, though considerably larger. Is this the Brown Tiger?

Skunk. This justly abhorred, and universally dreaded animal is found over the chief part of North America. Its ears are small and rounded; its general colour is black, marked with lines of yellowish white; its tail is bushy and long.

Nature has provided the Skunk with a singular, and very efficacious means of defence. On being irritated or attacked, it emits from behind a fluid of so intolerably suffocating and fetid a nature, that the boldest assailant will find himself compelled to a precipitate retreat. Should the smallest drop of this fluid fall on one's clothes, no washing will remove the scent; in order to be purified they must be buried in the ground for several days. The stench of the Skunk may

---

* Arctic Zoology, art. *Puma*.　　　† Pennant Arc. Zool.

be smelt at the distance of a mile. By accurate dissection, which was made by Dr. Mitchell, it has been found that this ill-scented fluid is entirely distinct from the urine. It is contained in two bags, situate in the posterior parts of the body; and surrounded by the circular muscles in such a manner, that, by their constriction, the fluid is forced out with great velocity. The urinary organs are totally distinct from these bags.* A well bred dog, after several attempts, will succeed in destroying this filthy animal; but a common cur will generally run from it with every sign of terror. When the dog receives the fluid, he retreats, runs his nose into the ground, and barks with great earnestness. A sportsman's dog should never be permitted to attack the Skunk, as he will be thereby rendered unfit for hunting for some time: his powers of scent being impaired.

This animal takes up its abode in old logs, and in the holes made in the earth by the foxes and other animals. It feeds upon birds and their eggs: is very fond of a hen-roost, where it makes free with the poultry and eggs. Whenever it approaches the farm-house, the whole fraternity is in an uproar: the name of Skunk enkindles alarm in every breast: the women run, the children scream, the dogs bark. At length with the aid of poles, stones, or guns, the unhappy intruder pays for his temerity with his life.

The writer of this article once caught a Skunk in a steel-trap, and was nearly suffocated with its stench before he could succeed in despatching it by means of a long pole. This animal was roasted for the purpose of ascertaining its *agreeable* qualities: it tasted sweet; but the idea of its being a Skunk operated so powerfully as to produce an aversion to it.

The Striated Wensel, and that above described appear to be the same. Pennant says that it "is often tamed, so as to follow its master like a dog." This is certainly an error, for who ever thought of taming a Skunk?

Sea Otter. These valuable animals are found on the coast of the the north east parts of America: between the Kamtschatkan shores and the isles which intervene between them and America: on the Kurile isles, and on the whole western coast of America, from 28 as far as 60 degrees north latitude. Their skin is extremely thick, covered closely with long hair, remarkably black and glossy, and beneath that is a soft down. The hair sometimes varies to silvery. The hair of the young is soft and brown. Their hind feet resemble exactly those of a seal; their fore feet are covered with hair and webbed. The tail is depressed, full of hair in the middle, and sharp pointed. The length of one full grown, from the nose to the tip of the tail, is about five feet: that of the tail from ten to thirteen inches. The weight of the largest, between seventy and eighty pounds.

They are extremely harmless, and singularly affectionate to their young. It is supposed that they bring forth but one at a time. They run very swiftly: swim sometimes on their sides, on their backs, and often in an erect position.

They never make any resistance; but endeavour when attacked, to save themselves by flight. When they have escaped to some distance, they look back, and hold one of their fore feet over their eyes, to gaze, as men do their hands to see more distinctly in a sunny day; for they are very dull sighted, though remarkably quick scented. They

* Mease's United States.

are fond of those parts of the sea which abound most with weeds, where they feed on fish, sepiæ, lobsters and shell fish, which they comminute with their flat grinders.

These animals partake very much of the nature of seals, in their almost constant residence in the water, their manner of swimming, fin-like legs, and number of fore teeth. Their skins meet a ready market in China, and command high prices.

The *Common Otters* inhabit as far north as Hudson's Bay, Labrador and Canada; and as low south as Carolina and Louisiana. They also inhabit the western coast of North America. Some few are yet found on the Delaware, below Philadelphia; and on the banks of its tributary streams.

Their fur is fine; of a deep brown colour, with the exception of a white spot on each side of the nose, and another under the chin.

The Otters of North America are larger than those of Europe; and the furs of such as inhabit the colder parts are very valuable. Their food is commonly fish; but it is said that they will attack and devour the Beaver. Lewis and Clark found this animal on their whole route to the Pacific Ocean, even amid the inhospitable regions of the Rocky Mountains.

The *Minx* is a little animal of the shape of the foregoing, but much smaller; its length being only about twenty inches from head to tail; of the tail only four. It inhabits various parts of the United States, and Canada. It frequents the banks of rivers and creeks, dwelling in hollow trees, or holes which it forms near the water. It can swim and dive admirably; feeds upon fish, frogs, &c. and is often found under barns and out houses, sneaking after the poultry and the rats. Along the coast this animal abounds; and it is very destructive to those birds which breed in the salt marshes, surprising them on their nests and sucking their eggs. When irritated, the Minx emits an excessively fetid odour. Its common name, and that whereby it is best known, is Mink.

Weasels are common throughout North America. They are well known to our farmers, who bear them no good will in consequence of the depredations which they commit among the poultry. But notwithstanding their bad qualities, they are sometimes of great benefit to the husbandman in ridding his granaries of those destructive pests, the rats.

Ermine. This neat and clean little animal, is said to change in the winter, in northern countries, to a snowy whiteness, the end of its tail excepted, which still remains black. In its summer dress it is called a Stoat; it is then of a tawny brown colour above, and white below. It inhabits the northern parts of North America.

The *Polar Bear* almost entirely surrounds the neighborhood of the Polar circle. It is found within it as far as navigators have penetrated; in the island of Spitzbergen, and within Baffin's Bay; in Greenland and Hudson's Bay; in Terra de Labrador; and, by accident, wafted from Greenland, on islands of ice, to Iceland and Newfoundland. These animals affect the utmost severity of the Arctic zone. They are impatient of heat. One that was brought alive into England, some years since, was restless and furious during the warm weather; and its keeper was obliged to pour on it frequently pailfuls of cold water.

The Polar Bear has a long narrow head and neck; the tip of the nose is black; its teeth are of great magnitude; its hair is of great length, soft and white, and in part tinged with yellow.

Travellers vary about their size. One measured by order of Lord Mulgrave was as follows

				Feet.	Inches.
Length from the snout to the tail	-	-	-	7	1
from snout to shoulder bone	-	-	-	2	3
Height at the shoulder	-	-	-	4	3
Circumference near the fore legs	-	-	-	7	
of the neck near the ear	-	-	2	1
Breadth of the fore paw	-	-	-	-	7

Weight of the carcass without the head, skin, or entrails 610 lbs.

These animals are very ferocious. They will attack, and attempt to board, vessels far distant from the shore; and in some instances, have been with difficulty repelled. They seem to give a preference to human blood. Their usual food is fish, seals, and the carcasses of whales. On land they prey on deer, hares, young birds and eggs, and often on whortleberries and crowberries. They are at constant enmity with the Walrus or Morse; the last, by reason of its vast tusks, has generally the superiority; but frequently both the combatants perish in the conflict.

Grizzly Bear. "This animal," says Mr. Brackenridge, "is the monarch of the country which he inhabits. The African Lion, or the Tiger of Bengal, are not more terrible or fierce. He is the enemy of man, and literally thirsts for human blood. So far from shunning, he seldom fails to attack; and even to hunt him. The Indians make war upon these ferocious monsters, with the same ceremonies as they do upon a tribe of their own species; and in the recital of their victories, the death of one of them gives the warrior greater renown than the scalp of a human enemy.

"He possesses an amazing strength, and attacks without hesitation, and tears to pieces, the largest Buffaloe. The colour is usually such as the name indicates, though there are varieties, from black to silvery whiteness. The skins are highly valued for muffs and tippets; and will bring from twenty to fifty dollars each.

"This Bear is not usually seen lower than the Mandan villages. In the vicinity of the Roche Jaune, and of the Little Missouri, they are said to be most numerous. They do not wander much in the prairies, but are usually found in points of wood, in the neighbourhood of large streams.

"In shape, he differs from the common Bear in being proportionally more long and lank. He does not climb trees, a circumstance which has enabled hunters, when attacked, to make their escape."|

In the history of the expedition under the command of Lewis and Clark, we have much interesting information relating to this dreadfully ferocious animal. These enterprising travellers made many narrow escapes from the attacks of this monster, who in some instances was not brought to the ground until he had received seven or eight balls through his body. As a wonderful proof of the tenacity of life of this animal, one that was killed the nineteenth of May, 1805, ran at his usual pace nearly a quarter of a mile, after having been *shot through the heart.*

* Views of Louisiana, by H. M. Brackenridge, Esq. p. 55.

The Grizzly Bear has been long known to naturalists; but the above mentioned travellers were the first to give us a particular account of this monarch of the American forests. One killed by them near the Porcupine river measured as follows:

	Feet.	Inches.
Length from the nose to the extremity of the hind feet, ...	8	7½
Circumference near the fore legs . . .	5	10½
of the neck . . .	3	11
of the middle of the fore leg .	1	11 .
Length of the talons		4⅜

His weight, on conjecture, was between five and six hundred pounds. But this was not the largest Bear that was killed by the party. They give an account of one which measured *nine* feet from the nose to the extremity of the tail; and the talons of another were six and a quarter inches in length. It is said that this animal when full grown and fat will exceed a thousand pounds.

The *American*, or common *Black Bear* is found all over the unsettled parts of North America. Its cheeks and throat are of a yellowish brown colour; the hair of its body and limbs is glossy and black.

They are inoffensive to mankind, provided they are not irritated; but if wounded, they will turn on their assailant with great fury, and, in case they can lay hold, seldom fail of hugging him to death. They cautiously avoid the hunters; and the smallest dog will fill them with alarm. They climb trees with great dexterity.

The long time which these animals subsist without food is amazing. They will continue in their retreat for six weeks without the least provision, remaining either asleep or totally inactive. It is pretended that they live by sucking their paws; but this is a vulgar error. The fact is, they retire immediately after autumn, when they have fattened themselves to an excessive degree by the abundance of the fruits which they find at that season. But when this internal support is exhausted, and they begin to feel the call of hunger, on the approach of the severe season they quit their dens in search of food.

In the lower parts of New Jersey a few of these animals are yet found. Their places of retreat are the thick solitary cedar swamps; through which it is extremely difficult for the hunters to pass, owing to the great quantity of fallen timber, the ruins of ancient forests; and the situation of the soil, which is low and wet. Now and then one of these Bears is brought to the Philadelphia market, and the lovers of good eating are indulged with a delicious repast. The fat of the Bear, like that of the Green Turtle, never cloys or lies heavy on the stomach, though one eats to excess.

Opossum. This species is found as far north as Canada, where it is called by the French inhabitants *Le Rat de bois*, or the Wood Rat; thence it extends southward, even to the Brasils and Peru.

The Opossum is condsidered by naturalists as one of the most curious animals yet discovered. On the lower part of the belly of the female is a large pouch, in which the teats are placed, and wherein the young lodge as soon as they are born. She produces from four to twelve at time. As soon as they come into the world they retreat into the false belly, blind, naked and exactly resembling little fœtuses. They fasten closely to the teats, as if they grew to them. Here they remain, adhering as though inanimate, till they arrive at some degree of perfection in shape, and obtain their sight, strength and hair, after which they undergo a sort of second birth. From that time, they use the pouch as an asylum from danger. The female carries them about with the utmost affection, and they may frequently be seen sporting in and out of this false belly.

The Opossum is both carnivorous and frugivorous. It is a great enemy to poultry, of which it is said to suck the blood, leaving the flesh untouched. It climbs trees very expertly; feeds on wild fruits, and also on various roots. Its tail, which is long and round, has the same prehensile quality as that of some species of Monkeys. It will hang from the branches by it, and, by swinging its body, fling itself among the boughs of the adjacent trees. It is a very sluggish animal; and makes scarcely any efforts to escape. When it finds itself on the point of being taken, it counterfeits death; and will endure very severe usage without giving signs of life.

This animal is very fond of ripe persimmons; and in the autumn it is frequently detected, at night, feasting upon this palatable fruit. At such times, if the tree be shaken, the Opossum will drop, and suffer itself to be borne off without a struggle. They become excessively fat; are common in the Philadelphia markets; and when roasted, or baked in the manner of a sucking pig, are an excellent and wholesome dish.

The history of the *Beaver* is so well known, and has been incorporated into such a variety of publications, that it seems not necessary, in this place, to enter into detail on the subject.

Our enterprising travellers, Lewis and Clark, found this valuable animal during their whole route to the Pacific Ocean. Even amid the Rocky Mountains, they were observed in immense numbers; and greatly contributed to the support of the wearied and half famished pilgrims, in those barren regions, where Nature assumes her wildest and most uninviting form. "The Beaver of this country," says the historian of the journey, "is large and fat: the flesh is very palatable and at our table was a real luxury."* The tail, when boiled, was esteemed the most delicate part; was said to resemble in flavour the tongues and sounds of codfish; and was generally so large as to afford a plentiful meal for two men.

"The Beaver on the upper parts of the Missouri are in greater quantities, larger and fatter, and their fur is more abundant, and of a darker colour than those below. Their favourite food seems to be the bark of the cotton wood and willow, as no other species of tree appeared to have been touched by these animals, and these trees they gnaw to the ground through a diameter of twenty inches."†

The junction of the Rochejaune or Yellowstone river with the Missouri has been recommended as a judicious position for the purposes of trade: the former river and its branches abounding in Beavers and Otters; and the circumjacent country being the grand pasturage of those innumerable herds of Buffaloe, Elk, Deer and Antelopes which have excited the astonishment of the inquisitive and intelligent voyagers of the Missouri.‡

"The Beaver," says Mr. Umfreville, "is of a very docile disposi-

* History of the Expedition, vol. ii. p. 170.
† Idem, vol. i. p. 191.
‡ Id. vol. ii. p. 397.

tion, and when taken young and properly brought up, may be made
to discover a very faithful and affectionate regard for his keeper. I
once possessed a young male which, after a month's keeping, would
follow me about like a dog; and when I had been absent from him for
a couple of hours, he would shew as much joy at my return, as one
of the canine species could possibly do." *

Muskrat. This well known animal is found all over North America. Its length from the nose to the end of the tail is about twenty-four inches; its eyes are small and dark; ears large, and hid in the fur; upper parts reddish brown; lower fore parts ferruginous; abdomen reddish drab; its feet are five-toed; the hind feet are semipalmate. The weight of one full grown is upwards of three pounds.

Pennant has with great propriety classed the Muskrat with the Beaver; but Turton has arranged it with the genus *Mus.* It is unquestionably a Beaver in its habits. It is never found remote from water: the margins of mill-ponds, brooks, creeks and meadow-ditches are its dwelling places. It feeds on various vegetable substances; on fruit; and, it is said, fresh water muscles.

Great quantities of this animal are caught every year in the United States, by those skilled in trapping; notwithstanding which multitudes yet remain, and occasion much trouble and damage to the proprietors of the meadows and mill-seats, in the embankments and dams of which, the Muskrats are continally burrowing.

In the summer, the Muskrat smells strongly of musk; but in the winter this odour is not perceptible, until the animal is handled.

The *Louisiana Marmot,* commonly called *Prairie Dog* or *Barking Squirrel,* is found in considerable numbers in the vicinity of the Missouri, and throughout the greater part of Louisiana. This animal commonly weighs three pounds. The colour is an uniform bright brick red and grey, the former predominates; the under side of the neck and belly are lighter than the other parts of the body; the legs are short, and the breast and shoulders wide; the head is stout and muscular, and terminates more bluntly, wider and flatter than that of the common squirrel; the ears are short, and have the appearance of amputation; the jaw is furnished with a pouch to contain his food, but not so large as that of the common squirrel; the nose is armed with whiskers on each side, and a few long hairs are inserted on each jaw, directly over the eyes; the eyes are small and black; each foot has five toes, and the two outer ones are much shorter than those in the centre. The two inner toes of the fore feet are long, sharp, and well adapted to digging and scratching. From the extremity of the nose to the end of the tail this animal measures one foot, five inches, of which the tail occupies four inches. Notwithstanding the clumsiness of his form, he is remarkably active, and burrows in the ground with great rapidity. These animals burrow, and reside in their little subterraneous villages like the Burrowing Squirrel. To these apartments, although six or eight usually associate together, there is but one entrance. They are of great depth, and Captain Lewis once pursued one to the depth of ten feet, and did not reach the end of the burrow. He likewise poured into one of the holes five barrels of water without filling it. The Prairie Dogs occupy, in this manner, several hundred acres of ground. They generally select a southeasterly exposure, on the side of a hill, for their villages; and they sit with

* Umfreville's Hudson's Bay, p. 171.

much confidence at the mouth of their burrows, barking at the intruder as he approaches, with a fretful and harmless intrepidity. Their note resembles that of the little toy-dog: the yelps are in quick and angry succession, attended by rapid and convulsive motions, as if they were determined to sally forth in defence of their freehold. When at rest, their position is generally erect on their hind feet and rump; and when alarmed they retreat into their subterraneous apartments. They feed on the grass of their village, the limits of which they never venture to exceed. As soon as the frost commences, they shut themselves up in their caverns, and remain in a torpid state until the spring. The flesh of this animal is not unpleasant to the taste.*

The Wolves are said to be the enemies of the Marmots, and to commit great havock among them.† The Rattle Snakes likewise frequent their villages to devour the inhabitants. Pike says: "It is extremely dangerous to pass through their towns, as they abound with Rattle Snakes, both of the yellow and black species: and strange as it may appear, I have seen the *Wisstonwish, (Prairie Dog)* the Rattle Snake, the Horn Frog (Horned Lizard)‡ and a land Tortoise all take refuge in the same hold. I do not pretend to assert, that it was their common place of resort, but I have witnessed the fact more than in one instance." §

It is said that the Horned Lizard and a small snake live habitually with the Marmot: the Indians call the snake the Dog's guard, and entertain many superstitious notions respecting these animals.||

Columbia Marmot. From the description which follows, taken from the History of Lewis and Clark's expedition, vol. ii, p. 173, we are inclined to consider the animal a *Marmot*, and have named it accordingly. We have not learnt whether or no a specimen of this animal has been preserved. A stuffed skin of the Louisiana Marmot, is in the Museum of Mr. Peale.

"There is a species of Squirrel, which we have denominated the Burrowing Squirrel. He inhabits the plains of the Columbia, and somewhat resembles those found on the Missouri.** He measures one foot and five inches in length, of which the tail comprises two and a half inches only; the neck and legs are short; the ears are likewise short, obtusely pointed, and lie close to the head and the aperture larger than will generally be found among burrowing animals; the eyes are of a moderate size, the pupil black, and the iris of a dark sooty brown; the whiskers are full, long and black; the teeth, and, indeed, the whole contour, resemble those of the Squirrel: each foot has five toes: the two inner ones of the fore feet are remarkably short, and are equipped with blunt nails, the remaining toes on the front feet are long, black, slightly curved, and sharply pointed; the hair of the tail is thickly inserted on the sides only, which gives it a flat appearance, and a long oval form: the tips of the hair forming the outer edges of the tail are white, the other extremity of a fox red, the under part resembles an iron gray, the upper is of a reddish brown; the lower part of the jaws, the under part of the neck, legs

* History of Lewis and Clark's expedition, vol. i, p. 68—ii, p. 175.
† Brackenridge's Views of Louisiana, p. 58.
‡ Lacerta orbicularis.
§ Pike's Journal, p. 156.
|| Description of Ohio, &c. p. 168, Boston. 1812.
** Prairie Dog.

and feet, from the body and belly downward, are of a light brick red; the nose is of a darker shade of the same colour; the upper part of the head, neck and body is of a curious brown gray, with a slight tinge of brick red: the longer hairs of these parts are of a reddish white colour at their extremities, and falling together give this animal a speckled appearance. These animals form in large companies, like those of the Missouri, occupying with their burrows sometimes two hundred acres of land: the burrows are separate, and each possesses, perhaps, ten or twelve of these inhabitants. There is a little mound in front of the hole, formed of the earth thrown out of the burrow, and frequently there are three or four distinct holes, forming one burrow, with these entrances around the base of these little mounds. These mounds, sometimes about two feet in height, and four in diameter, are occupied as watch-towers by the inhabitants of these little communities. The Squirrels, one or more, are irregularly distributed on the tract they thus occupy, at the distance of ten, twenty, or sometimes from thirty to forty yards. When anyone approaches, they make a shrill whistling sound, somewhat resembling *tweet, tweet, tweet*; the signal for their party to take the alarm, and to retire into their intrenchments. They feed upon the roots of grass &c."

North America abounds in *Squirrels* of various kinds; and there are doubtless several species which have not yet been noticed by Zoologists. We have lately discovered that a nondescript of this tribe, inhabits the eastern part of the State of New Jersey, near Tuckerton; as yet, we know not how far it extends. It has a characteristic mark in its greatly bearded ears; and, contrary to the practice of our common Squirrels, it is said not to dwell in hollow trees, but in nests, even during the severity of the winter. From this last mentioned circumstance, we have given it the specific denomination of *hiemalis*.

Our Catalogue, it will be perceived, is enriched with the names of those animals of this genus, which were discovered by Lewis and Clark, the stuffed skins of which have been deposited in Peale's Museum. The history of their journey gives an account of some others; but as this notice is a mere record of their existence, we are not enabled to determine whether or no they are nondescripts.

The Squirrels of the United States live chiefly upon forest nuts, of which the shellbark appears to be a favourite. The *Ground Squirrel*,* which is the most numerous of the genus, burrows in the earth, and lays up magazines of provisions for the winter, during the severity of which it is seldom seen. The rest chiefly dwell in hollow trees, where their provisions are deposited for the season of scarcity. The large Squirrels generally form their nests, of leaves, in the forks of trees, where they bring forth their young. In those parts of the country where these last mentioned are numerous, they commit great depredations upon the fields of Indian Corn, attacking it while it is in its milky state. In our western forests, partial migrations of these animals sometimes take place; and a few years since many thousands of them were drowned in attempting to cross the river Ohio.

The *Flying Squirrel* of the United States, is perhaps the most generally beloved of the whole tribe. It is a beautiful little animal, easily tamed, and becomes very familiar. It is likewise less mischievous than others. It is of a tender nature, loves warmth, and will creep

*Called by Pennant the *Striped Dormouse.* Arctic Zoology, vol. i, p. 146, edition 1792.

into the bosom, sleeve, or pocket of any one who will grant it that indulgence.

Squirrels when fat are good eating: their flesh is more juicy than that of the Rabbit, and in every respect it is preferable.

Moose. This celebrated animal has been described by the European naturalists, under the names of *Moose* and *Elk*, from its resemblance to the Elk of the old world. It is even said that it is the same species. Hence, many have supposed that the American animals called Moose and Elk have been confounded, which on due inquiry will be found to be otherwise, except in a few instances, wherein the name has created some confusion in the location of the subject of this article. The Deer known in America by the name of Elk, is very improperly designated, it having no resemblance to that animal.

The Moose has horns with short beams, spreading into a broad palm, furnished on the outward side with sharp snags, the inner side plain, no brow antlers; it has small eyes; long slouching asinine ears; large nostrils; the upper lip is square, great, and hanging far over the lower, and has a deep furrow in the middle, so as to appear almost bifid; under the throat there is a small excrescence, with a long tuft of coarse black hair pendant from it; the neck is shorter than the head; along the top there is an upright, short, thick mane of a light brown colour; withers elevated; tail short; the legs are long and those behind are the shorter; hoofs much cloven. The colour of the body is of a hoary brown; tail dusky above, white beneath. The vast size of the head, the shortness of the neck, and the length of the ears, give the beast a deformed and stupid look.

The greatest height of this animal, which Mr. Pennant had heard of, is seventeen hands; the greatest weight twelve hundred and twenty nine pounds. The largest horns which he had seen, are in the house of the Hudson's Bay Company: they weigh fifty-six pounds; their length is thirty-two inches, breadth of one of the palms thirteen inches and a half, space between point and point thirty-four. The female is less than the male, and wants horns.

The Moose inhabits the isle of Cape Breton, Nova Scotia, the western side of the Bay of Fundy and the Northern parts of Canada. In the territory of the United States, it is found at the headwaters of the Mountains of New Hampshire: that range having been formerly celebrated for the residence of these animals.

The Moose resides amidst forests, for the conveniency of browsing the boughs of trees, because they are prevented from grazing with any kind of ease, by reason of the shortness of their necks, and length of their legs. They have a singular gait: their pace is a shambling trot, but they go with great swiftness. In their common walk they lift their feet very high, and will, without any difficulty step over a gate five feet high. They feed principally in the night; and when they graze, it is always against an ascent, for the reason above assigned. They ruminate like the Ox.

They go to rut in Autumn, and are at that time very furious. They bring, in the month of April, two young at a birth, which follow the dam a whole year.

They are very inoffensive, except in the rutting season, or except they are wounded, when they will turn on the assailant, and attack him with their horns, or trample him to death beneath their great hoofs.

The flesh of the Moose is extremely sweet and nourishing. The Indians say that they can travel three times as far after a meal of this animal, as after any other food. The tongue is excellent, but the nose is perfect marrow, and esteemed the greatest delicacy in all Canada.

Greater Stag, or *Elk*. Under the name of *Stag*, Pennant has given an account of this animal, which somewhat resembles the Stag of Europe; though the materials whereof the ingenious naturalist composed its history were rather slender.

The early travellers in America mention this Deer, and call it a Stag. Kalm says that an Indian living in 1748 had killed many Stags on the spot where Philadelphia now stands.*

By what means this animal obtained the name of Elk, we are at present unable to determine; and it would be of no importance if the point were ascertained. It certainly was an improper appellation; but in compliance to long-standing custom, we shall retain it.

The Elk has an oblique slit or opening under the inner angle of each eye externally, of near an inch in length; which is said to communicate with the nostril. A like opening in the Cervine Antelope, *A. bubalis*, is noticed by Sparrman, and is supposed by him to answer the purpose of facilitating free respiration. The female has no horns. The males drop their horns annually in March, then leaving a pith about four inches in length, which is soon covered and protected by a substance resembling velvet. In eight weeks the horns begin to grow again: they are not palmated; the antlers are round and pointed; the lowermost antler forms a curve downward over each eye, to which it appears a defence.

The rutting season is from the 20th. September, to the 1st. of October. The female is gravid about eight months, and generally brings forth one, though sometimes she has twins.

The hoofs of the Elk are very much cloven; and like the Moose and Rein Deer he makes a great clattering with them in travelling. Though his gait is a trot, yet he is very fleet. The flesh is much esteemed, and the tongue is accounted delicious.

This species was seen by Lewis and Clark, in their route to and from the Pacific Ocean, in immense numbers, often herding in common with the Antelopes, Deer and Bisons. In describing the animals found to the westward of the Rocky Mountains, they say:

"The Elk is of the same species with that which inhabits much the greatest part of North America. They are common to every part of this country, as well the timbered lands as the plains, but are much more abundant in the former than in the latter. In the month of March we discovered several which had not cast their horns, and others where the new horns had grown to the length of six inches. The latter were in much the better order, and hence we draw the inference, that the leanest Elk retain their horns the longest."*

The above travellers killed a male Elk which measured five feet three inches from the point of the hoof to the top of the shoulder.

The *Common Deer* is too well known to require a description. They appear to be found over the chief parts of North America; and in the autumn and winter are quite common in the markets of Philadelphia. Their numbers decrease as population gains ground. In

‡ Kalm, vol. i, p. 336.   † History of the Expedition, vol. ii, p. 167.

the lower parts of the State of New Jersey many of these animals yet inhabit; they are found in the Pine barrens, among the Ground oaks, on the acorns of which they feed; and afford considerable diversion to the hunters every year. From being much persecuted by man, they have become extremely shy, and evince great sagacity in avoiding their pursuers.

The *Rein Deer* has large but slender horns, bending forward, with brow antlers broad and palmated, sometimes three feet nine inches long, two feet six from tip to tip, and weighing almost ten pounds. The body is thick and square; the legs shorter than those of the Stag. The height of a full grown Rein Deer is about four feet six inches.

The female is furnished with horns, but they are less, broader and flatter, and with fewer branches than those of the male. They bring forth two young at a time. The colour of the hair, at the first shedding. is of a brownish ash; it afterwards changes to a hoary whiteness.

The habitation of this interesting and valuable animal is more limited than that of the Moose it being confined to those parts where the Winter reigns with the utmost severity Its most southern residence is the northern parts of Canada, bordering on the territories of Hudson's Bay. Charlevoix mentions a single instance of one wandering as far as the neighbourhood of Quebec. Their true place is the vast tract which surrounds the Bay. They are met with in Labrador, and again in Newfoundland, originally wafted thither across the narrow straits of Belleisle, on islands of ice.

The Rein Deer are found in the neighbourhood of Hudson's Bay in great numbers, columns of eight or ten thousand being annually seen passing from north to south in the months of March and April, driven out of the woods by the moschetoes, seeking refreshment on the shore, and a quiet place to drop their young. They go to rut in September, and the males soon after shed their horns: they are at that season very fat, but so rank and musky as not to be eatable. The females produce their young in June, in the most sequestered spots they can find; and then they likewise loose their horns.

The attachment of the Laplanders to the Rein Deer, and the uses to which they apply this, to them, invaluable animal are well known.

The common name of this animal in Canada is *Le Caribou.*

Lewis and Clark describe three Deer, which they call *Mule Deer,* the *Common Red* or *Long-tailed Fallow Deer.* and *Black-tailed Fallow Deer.* Of the last they say: "The Black-tailed Fallow Deer is peculiar to this coast, (Pacific) and is a distinct species, partaking equally of the qualities of the Mule and Common Deer.* Their ears are longer, and their winter coat darker, than those of the Common Deer. The receptacle of the eye more conspicuous, their legs shorter, their bodies thicker and larger. The tail is of the same length with that of the Common Deer, the hair on the under side white, and on its sides and top of a deep jetty black. The hams resemble in form and colour those of the Mule, which it likewise resembles in its gait. The Black-tailed Deer never runs full speed, but bounds with every foot from the ground, at the same time. like the Mule Deer. He sometimes inhabits the woodlands, but more often the prairies and open grounds It may be generally said, that he is of a size larger

* That is, the Long-tailed Fallow Deer.

than the Common Deer, and less than the Mule Deer. The flesh is seldom fat, and in flavour it is far inferior to any other of the species."*

It is probable that the above described Deer has been introduced into Spain from California. In Bewick's History of Quadrupeds,† page 145, we have the following information: "The Fallow-Deer, with some variation, is found in almost every country of Europe.

Those of Spain are as large as Stags, but darker; their necks are also more slender; and their tails, which are longer than those of ours, are *black above,* and *white beneath.*"

The *Prong-Horned Antelope* is found in great numbers on the plains and the high-lands of the Missouri. It was to Messieurs Lewis and Clark that we were first indebted for a particular account of this beautiful animal. "Of all the animals we have seen," say they, "the Antelope seems to possess the most wonderful fleetness. Shy and timorous they generally repose only on the ridges, which command a view of all the approaches of an enemy. The acuteness of their sight distinguishes the most distant danger; the delicate sensibility of their smell defeats the precautions of concealment; and when alarmed, their rapid career seems more like the flight of birds than the movements of an earthly being. This fleet and quick-sighted animal is generally the victim of its curiosity. When they first see the hunter they run with great velocity: if he lies down on the ground and lifts up his arm, his hat, or his foot, the Antelope returns on a light trot to look at the object, and sometimes goes and returns two or three times till he approaches within reach of the rifle."‡

The Indians near the Rocky Mountains hunt these animals on horseback, and shoot them with arrows. "The Mandans' mode of hunting them is to form a large, strong pen or fold, from which a fence made of bushes gradually widens on each side. The animals are surrounded by the hunters, and gently driven towards this pen, in which they imperceptibly find themselves enclosed, and are then at the mercy of the hunters."§

The Antelopes go to rut about the 20th. of September; and bring forth two young about the 1st. of June. At this last mentioned season the females herd together, apart from the males.

The great body of the Antelopes spend the summer in the plains east of the Missouri, and in the autumn return to the Black Mountains, where they subsist on leaves and shrubbery during the winter, and resume their migrations in the spring.‖

Big-Horned Sheep or *Argali.* "Certain quadrupeds of this genus," says Pennant, "were observed in California by the missionaries in 1697; one as large as a calf of one or two years old, with a head like a Stag, and horns like a Ram. A second kind was larger, and varied in colour: some being white, others black, and furnished with very good wool. The Fathers called both Sheep, from their great resemblance to them."¶

In Venega's History of California, they are also noticed; and they were seen by Mr. M'Gillivray of Canada, who gives the dimensions of a male, taken on the spot where he was killed

---

* Vol. ii, p. 166.
† New-York edition.
‡ History of the Expedition, vol. i, p. 75. — Id. p. 202.
§ Idem, vol. i, p. 124.
‖ Id. p. 110.
¶ Arct. Zool. vol. i, p. 13.

	Feet.	Inches.
Length from the nose to the root of the tail	5	0
of the tail		4
of the horn	3	6
Circumference of the body	4	0
The stand	3	9

The horn is of the circular kind, proceeding in a triangle from the head like that of the ram. A pair of these horns have been known to weigh twenty-five pounds. In short, this animal appears to be a compound of the Deer and the Sheep, having the body and hair of the first, with the head and horns of the last.

But the animal above described was found in his summer dress, and we have no evidence that this species does not change its coat of hair for one of wool, which will better enable it to sustain the rigours of the Rocky Mountain winter. On the specimens which were brought by Lewis and Clark, and which are at present in Peale's Museum, the wool had made its appearance; and we have every reason to suppose that in the winter this animal exhibits all the appearance of the perfect sheep.

At the Yellowstone river, Lewis and Clark saw the first Argali; and they continued to see them until they left the Rocky Mountains on their journey to the west. These animals generally frequent the highest regions which produce any vegetation; though sometimes they descend to feed at the bottom of the valleys, whence, on the the least alarm, they retire to the most inaccessible precipices. They are extremely shy, and possess great speed and activity. They bound from rock to rock with all the facility and confidence of the Goat, and frequently disappoint the hunter by the celerity of their movements.

These animals must bring forth their young at a very early season; as on the 28th of May, on the upper parts of the Missouri, Lewis and Clark saw them in great quantities, with their young half grown.

In volume ii, page 359, they say, under the date of July 29th, "The Bighorns are in great numbers along the steep cliffs of the river, (Missouri) and being now in fine order, their flesh is extremely tender, delicate and well flavoured, and resembles in colour and flavour our mutton, though it is not so strong.

Lewis and Clark give us an account of another animal of the Ovis genus, which we have to lament that they had not the good fortune to see. In volume ii, p. 169, they say:

"The Sheep is found in many places, but mostly in the timbered parts of the Rocky Mountains. They live in greater numbers on the chain of mountains forming the commencement of the woody country on the coast, and passing the Columbia between the falls and rapids.

We have only seen the skins of these animals which the natives dress with the wool, and the blankets which they manufacture from the wool. The animal from this evidence appears to be of the size of our common sheep, of a white colour. The wool is fine on many parts of the body, but in length not equal to that of our domestic sheep.

On the back, and particularly on the top of the head, this is intermixed with a considerable proportion of straight long hairs. From the Indian accounts these animals have erect pointed horns: one of our engagees informed us that he had seen them in the Black hills, and that the horns were lunated like those of our domestic sheep.

We have nevertheless too many proofs to admit a doubt of their existing, and in considerable numbers, on the mountains near the coast."

This account was written while our American travellers wintered on the Pacific. But on their return up the Columbia, at Brant island, an Indian "offered two sheep skins for sale: one was the skin of a full grown sheep, was as large as that of a Common Deer; the second was smaller, and the head part, with the horns remaining, was made into a cap, and highly prized as an ornament by the owner. The horns of the animal were *black*, *smooth* and *erect*, and they rise from the middle of the forehead, a little above the eyes, in a *cylindrical* form, to the height of four inches, where they are *pointed*. The Clahelellahs informed us that the Sheep are very abundant on the heights, and among the cliffs of the adjacent mountains; and that these two had been lately killed out of a herd of thirty-six, at no great distance from the village."*

"The Indians assert, that there are great numbers of the White Buffaloe or Mountain Sheep, on the snowy heights of the mountains, west of Clark's river. They generally inhabit the rocky and most inaccessible parts of the mountain, but as they are not fleet, are easily killed by the hunters."†

The *Bison*, commonly called the Buffaloe, has short, black, rounded horns, with a great space between their bases; on the shoulders there is a gibbosity or bunch, composed of a fleshy substance; the fore part of the body is thick and strong; the hind part slender and weak; the tail is about a foot long, and naked to the end, which is tufted; legs short and thick.

The head and shoulders of the Bull are covered with long flocks of reddish wooly hair, falling over the eyes and horns, leaving only the points of the latter to be seen; on the chin, and along the dewlaps, there is a great length of shaggy hair; the rest of the body during Summer is naked, in the Winter it is clothed equally in all parts. The Cow is less, and wants the shaggy coat, which gives the Bull so tremendous an aspect.

Lawson says that the Buffaloe grows to the weight of sixteen hundred, or two thousand four hundred pounds.‡ But we think that there must be an error in this statement, as some of our late travellers represent it as weighing, when full grown, about one thousand pounds.

The European naturalists have been at considerable pains to ascertain the route by which these animals migrated from the Old to the New World: as it seems they are very unwilling to consider that the *Creator* has been as bountiful to the Americans, in the primeval distribution of his gifts, as He has been to the favoured of the ancient dominions.

"It is difficult to say," says Pennant, "in what manner these animals migrated originally from the old to the new world; it is most likely it was from the north of Asia, which in very ancient times *might have been* stocked with them to its most extreme parts, notwithstanding they are *now extinct*. At that period there is a probability that the old and the new Continents might have been united in the nar-

* History of the Expedition, vol. ii, p. 233.
† Idem, p. 331.—See also page 49 of the same volume.
‡ A voyage to Carolina, by John Lawson, p. 116.

row channel between *Tchutkinoss*, and the opposite headlands of America."

Admitting the fact, which Pennant and others have laboured to prove, that the two Continents formerly joined, what evidence have we that these animals did not migrate origionally from the New to the Old world? But our limits will not allow a disquisition on this subject; and in spite of all the ingenious hypotheses of the philosophers of Europe, some of whom consider the animals of the Western world mere varieties of their own "*more generous stock*," we are of the opinion that the American Bison differs essentially from that of Europe and Asia, and that it claims to be ranked as a distinct species.

These animals have an extensive range, being found in the countries six hundred miles west of Hudson's Bay, in Canada to the west of the lakes, and in New Mexico. They are not found in South America. The banks of the Ohio, within the memory of some of the present inhabitants of that country, were enlivened with herds of Buffaloes; and the plains of Indiana and Illinois were their places of favourite resort, but encroaching settlements have driven them west.

At the river Kanzas the party of Lewis and Clark saw the first Buffaloe, and they found them as high as near the dividing ridge, which separates the waters of the Columbia from those of the Missouri. To the westward of the Rocky Mountains they were not discovered.

At Big Dry-river the exploring party found these animals so tame, that they were obliged to drive them out of the way with sticks and stones. It is almost incredible what numbers of Bisons congregate: upwards of twenty thousand have been seen in a grove; and the noise they make in bellowing, and trampling on the earth, when such multitudes herd together, is said to be undescribable. In winding around the hills which border the Missouri, these animals contribute greatly to the picturesque effect of the scenery of that interesting river.*

The rutting season of the Bison commences about the first of August. When that period is past, the great body of females separate from the males, and it is not unusal to see many thousand together of one sex only. It has been particularly observed of the females, that when they calve they are removed at a considerable distance from the feeding ground of the other sex.† We may call this instinct, but it is something more. Nature has taught the female to be attentive to the wants of their offspring, to attend them while in a tender state, and to lead them no farther that their strength will admit. They are likewise taught, whether by experience or otherwise, that the ungovernable males are not influenced by the same feelings, and that amidst their overwhelming ranks the poor calves would be as clods of earth, or as the grass of the vallies.

The Indians have various ways of obtaining these animals, which afford them an esteemed food, and clothing of great value. They hunt them on horseback, killing the animals with spears and arrows; attack them in the Spring on the floating ice, and when the herds cross the rivers; and drive them down precipices, which last mode is sometimes attended with great slaughter. For a particular account of all these matters, we must refer the reader to the History of the expedition under the command of Lewis and Clark,‡ and Views of Louisiana by Mr. Brackenridge.§

* Views of **Louisiana**, p. 263.   ‡ Vol. i, p. 175, 235.
† Pike's Exp. **Appendix** to part ii, p. 5.   § Page 255.

The *Musk Ox* is numerous between the latitudes of 66 and 73 degrees north. It does not appear that they are found at the head waters of the Mississippi or the Missouri. They first appear on the western side of Hudson's Bay, and continue north. Mr. Hearne, in his journey to the Northern Ocean, saw many herds of these animals. They delight most in the rocky and barren mountains, and seldom frequent the woody parts of the country. They are found in droves of twenty or thirty. They run nimbly, and are very active in climbing the rocks. The flesh tastes strongly of musk; but it is considered wholesome and beneficial to convalescents. The hair of this animal is of a dusky red, extremely fine, and so long as to trail upon the ground, and render the beast a seeming shapeless mass, without distinction of head or tail: the legs and tail are very short; the shoulders are gibbous. In size, lower than a Deer, but larger as to belly and quarters. For a complete description of this animal, illustrated with a good plate, we refer the reader to Pennant's Arctic Zoology, London, 1792.

The *Long-nosed Tapir* has been, by some authors, mistaken for the *Hippopotamus*, which is not found in the New World. The Tapir is about the size of a small cow: its nose is long and slender, and extends far beyond the jaw, forming a kind of proboscis, which it can contract or extend at pleasure; its ears are small and erect; its body formed like that of a Hog: its hair short, and of a dusky brown colour. This animal inhabits the woods and rivers of Mexico: and extends through a considerable part of South America, as D'Azara describes it in his History of the Quadrupeds of Paraguay. It is a solitary animal, sleeps during the day, and goes out in the night in search of food, which consists of grass, sugar-canes, fruits, &c. It is quite inoffensive, avoids all hostilities with other animals, and flies from every appearance of danger.

"The Tapir," says Henderson, "is an inhabitant of the thickest and most retired woods in the neighbourhood of rivers and creeks. It swims, dives, and is considered to possess the property of walking beneath the water. As this animal cautiously avoids the day, it is but rarely met with. The meat of the Tapir, contrary to what has been pronounced of it, is in this country considered exceedingly coarse and rank.*

The *Pecary* is found in Louisiana, at the head waters of the Red River; and extends thence throughout Mexico, and the principal part of South America. In some places it is very numerous, herds of two or three hundred are said to be found together. They live chiefly in the higher parts of the country, and are not fond of wallowing in the mire like the common Hog. Their food consists of fruits, roots, seeds, &c. They likewise eat Serpents, Toads, and Lizards.

The Pecary resembles a small Hog of the common kind. Its body is covered with strong bristles, which, when the animal is irritated, rise up like the prickles of a Hedgehog, and are nearly as strong; they are of a dusky colour, with alternate rings of white; it has two tusks in each jaw; its ears are small and erect; and instead of a tail, it has a small fleshy protuberance, which does not cover its posteriors. This animal has a small glandular orifice on the lower part of the back, whence a thin watery humour flows. This humour has been represented by some, as of an extremely fetid smell; but Don

* Henderson's Honduras, p. 103.

D'Azara says that it is of an agreeable musky odour, though he
admits that the food of the animal, or other circumstances, may affect its sensible qualities.

Bewick says, "that although the European Hog is common in
America, and in many parts has become wild, yet the Pecary has
never been known to breed with it." "The Pecary is very prolific." *
This is contradicted by D'Azara, who says, that the female produces
her young once a year, and but two at a time.†

"The Pecary and the Warree," says Captain Henderson, "are
animals of the Hog kind. The former is the *Sus Tajassu* of Linnæus, or the Tajassu of other naturalists. On the back of this animal is placed a glandulous orifice, which has furnished a very common belief, that in this part of it the navel is situated. The flesh of
the Pecary is considered particularly good, either fresh or salted;
but on killing it, if the glands just mentioned be not instantly removed, the whole carcass becomes tainted with the most noxious and
fetid odour. The latter animal has not been so particularly described.
It has been denominated the Hog of the isthmus of Darien; and an
opinion has been suggested, that it may only be the European Hog run
wild. Both Pecary and the Warree usually go in large bodies;
and at such times it is not considered at all safe to wound or kill any
of the party, by firing on them, unless a retreat or place of security
be nigh: for those, which remain unhurt, commonly attack the of-
fender in the most desperate way. The approach of these animals
may be heard in the woods at a great distance, by the loud and clamorous noise they continually make; and like the domestic Hog, it
is asserted that they destroy and eat snakes and reptiles of different
kinds."‡

ORNITHOLOGY . . . The European naturalists, particularly Buffon in
his far-famed *Oiseaux*, have attempted to give an account of the Birds
of North America. But their works evince such a want of correct
information, or prejudice, or both, that the American reader who
takes them up with the expectation of amusement or improvement,
will be apt to find himself miserably disappointed; and will turn with
indifference or disgust from pages that generally exhibit merely a
dry detail of specific particulars, or what is worse, that are polluted
with injurious misrepresentations,§ the offspring of ignorance or
folly.

From the extent of this immense continent, so distinguished by
a variety of soil and climate, it is reasonable to conclude that a
rich harvest would reward the labours of him who should zealously
engage in the study of its natural history. In Europe, though now
grown gray in the arts and sciences, yet still retaining the pristine
vigour and inquisitiveness of youth, much had been done in this interesting class of animals. But it seemed reserved for America
to set the first example of a work, combining elegance of typogra-
phical execution and graphical illustration, with accuracy of detail,

* Bewick's Quadrupeds.
† Histoire Naturelle des Quadrupeds de la Province **du Paraguay, par Don**
Felix D'Azara, tome i, p. 38. Paris, 1801.
‡ Henderson's Honduras, p. 97.
§ We are free to explain, that it is principally against the Count de Buffon
that our censures are directed. It gives us pleasure to learn that the dog-
mata of this vain and whimsical philosopher, have lost much of that regard
which an imposing name has contributed to attract.

and scientific and moral utility. The "American Ornithology," by
the enterprising and ingenious Wilson, has not only immortalized its
author, but has greatly increased the stock of useful pleasures, by
forcibly directing our attention to a generally supposed unimportant
source of gratification; and claims our regard for rescuing a beautiful portion of animated nature from the rude hands of those to whom
it had been unfortunately committed.

Anterior to the appearance of the above mentioned magnificent
work, several nomenclatures of American birds had been published
by writers of America. "But these," says Mr. Wilson, "from the
nature of the publications in which they have been introduced, can
be considered only catalogues of names, without the detail of specific particulars, or the figured and coloured representations of the
birds themselves." It was the intention of Mr. Wilson to furnish a
description and coloured representation of every species of our native birds, from the shores of the St. Lawrence to the mouths of the
Mississippi, and from the Atlantic Ocean to the interior of Louisiana.
A task to which the inflexible mind of that remarkable individual
was fully competent. In the prosecution of his plan he had made
great progress, having published and prepared, an account of *two
hundred and sixty-five* species, *fifty-four* of which were nondescripts,
when the Almighty disposer of events saw fit to close his useful
labours by death.* May his noble example stimulate some zealous
naturalist to complete the design of our ornithologist: a task by no
means easy of execution, but if accomplished with the like success,
will be attended with honour and fame commensurate to the hazard
and difficulty of the undertaking. And may we not hope soon to be-
hold labourers in the other departments of natural history, equally
successful in defending the native productions of our country from
the attacks of prejudiced foreigners, who have made a merit of de-
priciating what in truth they do not understand!

"The Ornithology of the United States," says Mr. Wilson, "exhibits a rare display of the most splendid colours, from the green,
silky, gold-bespangled down of the minute Humming-bird, scarce
three inches in extent, to the black coppery wings of the gloomy
Condor of sixteen feet, who sometimes visits our northern regions;—
a numerous and powerful band of songsters, that for sweetness, variety and melody, are surpassed by no country on earth;—an ever-
changing scene of migration, from torrid to temperate, and from
northern to southern regions, in quest of suitable seasons, food and
climate; and such an amazing diversity in habit, economy, form, disposition and faculty, so uniformly hereditary in each species, and
so completely adequate to their peculiar wants and convenience, as
to overwhelm us with astonishment at the power, wisdom and bene-
ficence of the Creator.

"In proportion as we become acquainted with these particulars,
our visits to, and residence in, the country, become more and more
agreeable. Formerly, on such occasions, we found ourselves in so-
litude, or, with respect to the feathered tribes, as it were in a strange
land, where the manners, langauge, and faces of all were either totally overlooked, or utterly unknown to us: now, we find ourselves

---

*He left drawings of thirteen species more. These were given to the public
in a supplementary volume. The whole work consists of nine volumes, im-
perial quarto.

among interesting and well-known neighbours and acquaintance; and, in the notes of every songster, recognise with satisfaction the voice of an old friend and companion. A study thus tending to multiply our enjoyments at so cheap a rate, and to lead us, by such pleasing gradations, to the contemplation and worship of the *Great First Cause*, the Father and Preserver of all, can neither be idle nor useless, but is worthy of rational beings, and doubtless agreeable to the Deity."

ZOOLOGY OF NORTH AMERICA.

CLASS *AVES*.

LAND BIRDS.

ORDER *ACCIPITRES*.

GENUS *VULTUR*.

Condor Vulture	-	*Vultur gryphus.*
King V.	-	*V. papa.*
California V.	-	*V. Californianus.*
*Columbia V.	-	*V. Columbianus.*
Turkey-buzzard	-	*V. aura.*
Carrion Crow	-	*V. atratus.*

GENUS *FALCO*.

Bald Eagle	-	*Falco leucocephalus.*
Ring-tailed E.	-	*F. fulvus.*
Golden E.	-	*F. chrysaetos.*
White-tailed E.	-	*F. leucocephalus.*
Fish Hawk	-	*F. haliætus.*
Speckled Buzzard	-	*F. variegatus.*
American B.	-	*F. Leverianus.*
Ash coloured B.	-	*F. cinereus.*
Plain Falcon	-	*F. obsoletus.*
Gentle F.	-	*F. gentilis.*
Common F.	-	*F. communis.*
Chocolate F.	-	*F. spadiceus.*
St. John's F.	-	*F. S. Johannis.*
Sacre	-	*F. sacer.*
Newfoundland Falcon	-	*F. Novæ terræ.*
Hudson's Hawk	-	*F. Hudsonius.*
American H.	-	*F. fuscus.*
Dusky Falcon	-	*F. obscurus.*
Red-tailed Hawk	-	*F. borealis.*
Black cap H.	-	*F. atricapillus.*
Winter H.	-	*F. hiemalis.*
Rough-legged H.	-	*F. lagopus.*
Marsh H.	-	*F. uliginosus.*
Swallow-tailed H.	-	*F. furcatus.*
Mississippi Kite	-	*F. Mississippiensis.*
Black Hawk	-	*F. niger.*
Red-shouldered H.	-	*F. lineatus.*
Sharp-shinned H.	-	*F. velox.*
American Sparrow H.	-	*F. sparverius.*
Pigeon H.	-	*F. Columbarius.*
Slate-coloured H.	-	*F. Pennsylvanicus.*
Broad-winged H.	-	*F. latissimus.*
Great-footed H.	-	*F. peregrinus.*
Blue H.	-	*F. cœruleus.*

GENUS *STRIX*.

Great Owl	-	*Strix bubo.*
Mexican Owl	-	*S. Mexicana.*
American O.	-	*S. Americana.*
Sooty O.	-	*S. cinerea.*
Spotted O.	-	*S. nebulosa.*
Brown O.	-	*S. stridula.*
Canada O.	-	*S. funerea.*
New Spain O.	-	*S. tchichichactli.*
Tawny O.	-	*S. chichictli.*
Acadian O.	-	*S. Acadica.*
White-fronted O.	-	*S. albifrons.*
Snow O.	-	*S. nyctea.*
Great-horned O.	-	*S. Virginiana.*
Long-eared O.	-	*S. otus.*
Barred O.	-	*S. nebulosa.*

Mottled O.	-	*S. nævia.*
Barn O.	-	*S. flammea.*
Little O.	-	*S. passerina.*
Hawk O.	-	*S. Hudsonia.*
Short-eared O.	-	*S. brachyotus.*
Red O.	-	*S. asio.*

ORDER *PICÆ*.

GENUS *LANIUS*.

Crested Shrike	-	*Lanius Canadensis.*
Northern S.	-	*L. septentrionalis.*
American S.	-	*L. Americanus.*
Nootka S.	-	*L. Nootka.*
Great American S.	-	*L. excubitor.*
Loggerhead S.	-	*L. Carolinensis.*
Black capped S.	-	*L. pitangua.*

GENUS *PSITTACUS*.

White fronted Parrot	-	*Psittacus leucocephalus.*
Dusky P.	-	*P. sordidus.*
Mexican P.	-	*P. Mexicanus.*
Blue-headed P.	-	*P. menstruus.*
Yellow headed P.	-	*P. ochrocephalus.*
Red and Blue Macaw	-	*P. aracanga.*
Red and Yellow M.	-	*P. aracanga.*
Carolina Parrot	-	*P. Carolinensis.*

GENUS *RAMPHASTOS*.

Pavonine Toucan	-	*Ramphastos Pavoninus.*
Collared T.	-	*R. torquatus.*
Yellow T.	-	*R. luteus.*
Blue T.	-	*R. cœruleus.*

GENUS *CORVUS*.

Steller's Crow	-	*Corvus Stelleri.*
Mexican C.	-	*C. Mexicanus.*
Carthaginian C.	-	*C. perspicillatus.*
Zanoe C.	-	*C. Zanoe.*
Raven	-	*C. corax.*
Common Crow	-	*C. corone.*
Blue Jay	-	*C. cristatus.*
Canada J.	-	*C. Canadensis.*
Clark's Crow	-	*C. Columbianus.*
Fish C.	-	*C. ossifragus.*
Magpie	-	*C. pica.*

GENUS *CORACIAS*.

Mexican Roller	-	*Coracias Mexicanus.*

GENUS *ORIOLUS*.

Mexican Oriole	-	*Oriolus Novæ Hispaniæ.*
New Spain O.	-	*O. cærtold.*
Gray O.	-	*O. griseus.*
Red-breasted O.	-	*O. Americanus.*
Louisiana O.	-	*O. Ludovicianus.*
Black-crested O.	-	*O. Mexicanus.*
Bonana O.	-	*O. Bonana.*
Lesser Bonana O.	-	*O. Xanthornus.*

St. Domingo O.   -   O. Dominicensis.
Melancholy O.   -   O. melancholicus.
Olive O.   -   O. Cayanensis.
Yellow-throated O.   -   O. viridis.
Fork-tailed O.   -   O. furcatus.
Baltimore O.   -   O. Baltimorus.
Orchard O.   -   O. mutatus.

GENUS GRACULA.

Boat-tailed Grakle   -   Gracula barita.
Purple G.   -   G. quiscula.
Rusty G.   -   G. ferruginea.

GENUS TROGON.

Red-bellied Curucui   Trogon curucui.

GENUS CUCULUS.

Laughing Cuckoo   -   Cuculus vidibundus.
St. Domingo C.   -   C. Dominicus.
Yellow-billed C.   -   C. Carolinensis.
Black-billed C.   -   C. erythrophthalma.

GENUS PICUS.

Green Woodpecker   -   Picus viridis.
Varied W.   -   P. tricolor.
Canada Spotted W.   -   P. Canadensis.
Ivory-billed W.   -   **P.** principalis.
Pileated W.   -   P. pileatus.
Gold-winged W.   -   P. auratus.
Red-headed W.   -   P. erythrocephalus.
Hairy W.   -   P. villosus.
Downy W.   -   P. pubescens.
Yellow bellied **W.**   -   P. varius.
Red-cockaded W.   -   P. querulus.
Lewis's W.   -   P. torquatus.
Red-bellied W.   -   P. Carolinus.
Greater Spotted W.   -   P. major.
*Rocky-mountain W.   -   P. missouri.

GENUS ALCEDO.

Belted Kingfisher   -   Alcedo alcyon.
Cinereous K.   -   A. torquata.

GENUS SITTA.

White-breasted Nuthatch   Sitta Carolinensis.
Red-bellied N.   -   S. varia.
Brown headed N.   -   S. pusilla.

GENUS TODUS.

Dusky Tody   -   Todus obscurus.

GENUS MEROPS.

Cinereous Bee-eater   -   Merops cinereus.
California B.   -   M. Californicus.

GENUS UPUPA.

Mexican Hoopoe   -   Upupa Mexicana.

GENUS CERTHIA.

Red Creeper   -   Certhia Mexicana.
Brown C.   -   C. familiaris.
Black and white C.   -   C. maculata.
Great Carolina Wren.   -   C. Caroliniana.
Marsh W.   -   C. palustris.

GENUS TROCHILUS.

Paradise Humming-bird   Trochilus Paradiseus.
Blue-tailed H.   -   T. cyanurus.
Green-throated H.   -   T. maculatus.
Spotted H.   -   T. punctatus.
Crimson headed **blue H.**   -   T. transississimus.
Mango H.   -   T. mango.
Black-bellied H.   -   T. holosericus.
Ruby-throated H.   -   T. colubris.
Ruff-necked H.   -   T. rufus.
Least H.   -   T. minimus.
Little H.   -   T. exilis.

ORDER PASSERES.

GENUS STURNUS.

Louisiana Starling   -   Sturnus Ludovicianus.
Mexican S.   -   S. Mexicanus.
Brown Headed S.   -   S. obscurus.
Red-winged S.   -   S. praedatorius.

GENUS TURDUS.

Red-legged Thrush   Turdus plumbeus.
Spotted T.   -   T. aurius.
Hudsonian **T.**   -   **T.** Hudsonicus.
Labrador T.   -   T. Labradorus.
Mocking-bird   -   T. polyglottos.
Ferruginous Thrush   T. rufus.
Wood T, or Wood Robin   T. melodus.
Golden-crowned T.   -   T. aurocapillus.
Cat-bird   -   T. lividus.
Water Thrush   -   T. aquaticus.
Hermit T.   -   T. solitarius.
Tawny T.   -   T. mustelinus.
Robin   -   T. migratorius.

GENUS AMPELIS.

Cedar-bird or Chatterer   Ampelis Americana.

GENUS LOXIA.

Gray Grosbeak   -   Loxia grisea.
Mexican G.   -   L. Mexicana.
Yellow-headed **G.**   -   L. Nova Hispania.
Canada G.   -   L. Canadensis.
Brown-cheeked **G.**   -   L. canor.
Hudson's Bay G.   -   L. Hudsonica.
Black G.   -   L. nigra.
Cardinal **G.**   -   L. cardinalis.
Rose-breasted G.   -   L. Ludoviciana.
Blue G.   -   L. coerulea.
Pine G.   -   L. canicans.
Yellow-bellied G.   -   L. Virginiana.
Fan-tailed G.   -   L. flabellifera.
Dusky G.   -   L. obscura.

GENUS CURVIROSTRA.

American Crossbill   Curvirostra Americana.
White-winged C.   -   C. conoptera.

GENUS EMBERIZA.

Mexican Bunting   -   Emberiza Mexicana.
Black-crowned B.   -   E. atricapilla.
White-crowned B.   -   E. leucophala.
Blue B.   -   E. coerulea.
Louisiana B.   -   E. Ludoviciana.
Black-throated B.   -   E. Americana.
Towhee B.   -   E. erythrophthalma.
Reed Bird   -   E. oryzivora.
Cow B.   -   E. pecoris.
Snow B.   -   E. nivalis.
Painted B.   -   E. ciris.
Bay-winged **B.**   -   E. graminea.
Black B.   -   E. hiemalis.

GENUS TANAGRA.

Gray Tanager   -   Tanagra grisea.
Black and Blue **T.**   -   T. Mexicana.
Cerulean T.   -   T. coerea.
Scarlet T.   -   T. rubra.
Summer Red-bird   -   T. aestiva.
Louisiana Tanager   T. Ludoviciana.

GENUS FRINGILLA.

Lapland Finch   -   Fringilla Lapponica.
Carthagenian F.   -   F. Carthaginensis.
Variegated F. -   -   F. variegata.
Mexican Siskin   -   F. Mexicana.
Black Mexican S.   -   F. catotol.
Greater Red-poll   -   F. cannabina.
Lesser R.   -   F. linaria.
Black-faced Finch   -   F. cristata.
Carolina F.   -   F. Carolinensis.

---

* **History of Lewis and Clark's expedition, vol. 1, p. 395.**

Yellow-bird -	*F. tristis.*
Purple Finch -	*F. purpurea.*
Pine F. or Siskin -	*F. pinus.*
Sea-side F. -	*F. maritima.*
Sharp-tailed F. -	*F. caudacuta.*
Indigo-bird -	*F. cyanea.*
Snow-bird -	*F. Hudsonia.*
Field sparrow -	*F. pusilla.*
Tree S. -	*F. arborea.*
Song S. -	*F. melodia.*
Chipping S. -	*F. socialis.*
White-throated S. -	*F. albicollis.*
Swamp S. -	*F. palustris.*
Savannah S. -	*F. Savanna.*
Fox-coloured S. -	*F. ferruginea.*
Yellow-winged S. -	*F. passerina.*

GENUS MUSCICAPA.

Forked-tail Flycatcher -	*Muscicapa forficatus.*
Swallow-tailed F. -	*M. forficata.*
Louisiana F. -	*M. Ludoviciana.*
Solitary F. -	*M. solitaria.*
Red-eyed F. -	*M. olivacea.*
White-eyed F. -	*M. cantatrix.*
Tyrant F. or King-bird	*M. tyrannus.*
Great-crested F. -	*M. crinita.*
Pewee F. -	*M. nunciola.*
Wood-pewee F. -	*M. rapax.*
Small green F. -	*M. querula.*
Yellow-throated F. -	*M. sylvicola.*
Blue-gray F. -	*M. carulea.*
Canada F. -	*M. Canadensis.*
Hooded F. -	*M. cucullata.*
Warbling F. -	*M. melodia.*
Green black-capt F. -	*M. pusilla.*
Small-headed F. -	*M. minuta.*
American Redstart -	*M. ruticilla.*
Striped Flycatcher -	*M. striata.*
Rusty F. -	*M. ferruginea.*

GENUS ALAUDA.

Louisiana Lark -	*Alauda Ludoviciana.*
Meadow L. -	*A. magna.*
Shore L. -	*A. alpestris.*
Brown L. -	*A. rufa.*

GENUS SYLVIA.

Quebec Warbler -	*Sylvia leterocephala.*
Belted W. -	*S. cincta.*
Louisiana W. -	*S. Ludoviciana.*
Orange-throated W. -	*S. auricollis.*
Spotted-yellow W. -	*S. tigrina.*
Yellow-poll W. -	*S. aestiva.*
Hudson's W. -	*S. Hudsonica.*
Yellow-throat W. -	*S. tricoltis.*
Bay-breasted W. -	*S. castanea.*
Chestnut-sided W. -	*S. Pennsylvanica.*
Mourning W. -	*S. Philadelphia.*
Blue-winged yellow W. -	*S. solitaria.*
Golden-winged W. -	*S. chrysoptera.*
Blue-eyed W. -	*S. citrinella.*
Black-throated blue W. -	*S. Canadensis.*
Black-throated green W. -	*S. virens.*
Yellow rump W. -	*S. coronata.*
Cerulean W. -	*S. cerulea.*
Pine-creeping W. -	*S. pinus.*
Black and yellow W. -	*S. maculosa.*
Blackburnian W. -	*S. Blackburnae.*
Autumnal W. -	*S. Autumnalis.*
Prothonotary W. -	*S. protonotarius.*
Worm-eating W. -	*S. vermivora.*
Tennessee W. -	*S. peregrina.*
Kentucky W. -	*S. formosa.*
Blue-green W. -	*S. rara.*
Nashville W. -	*S. rubricapilla.*
Blue yellow-back W. -	*S. pusilla.*
Yellow red-poll W. -	*S. petechia.*
Black-poll W. -	*S. striata.*
Prairie W. -	*S. minuta.*
Connecticut W. -	*S. agilis.*
Blue-mountain W. -	*S. montana.*
Hemlock W. -	*S. parus.*
Pine-swamp W. -	*S. leucoptera.*
Cape May W. -	*S. maritima.*
Maryland yellow-throat	*S. Marylandica.*
Blue-bird -	*S. sialis.*
Ruby-crowned Wren -	*S. calendula.*
Golden-crested Wren -	*S. regulus.*

House Wren -	*S. domestica.*
Winter Wren -	*S. troglodytes.*

GENUS PIPRA.

Purple Manakin -	*Pipra cristata.*
Mexican M. -	*P. psicitti.*
New Spain M. -	*P. mincatatoti.*
Yellow-breasted Chat	*P. polyglotta.*

GENUS PARUS.

Hudson's Bay Titmouse	*Parus Hudsonius.*
Black-capt T. -	*P. atricapillus.*
Crested T. -	*P. bicolor.*

GENUS HIRUNDO.

Rock swallow -	*Hirundo rupestris.*
Ash-bellied S. -	*H. cinerea.*
Oonalaska S. -	*H. Oonalaskensis.*
Barn S. -	*H. Americana.*
Green white-bellied S. -	*H. viridis.*
Bank S. -	*H. riparia.*
Chimney S. -	*H. pelasgia.*
Purple Martin -	*H. purpurea.*

GENUS CAPRIMULGUS.

Chuck-will's-widow -	*Caprimulgus Carolinensis.*
Night-hawk -	*C. Americanus.*
Whip-poor-will -	*C. vociferus.*

ORDER COLUMBÆ.

GENUS COLUMBA.

White-crowned Pigeon	*Columba leucocephala.*
White-winged P. -	*C. leucoptera.*
Brown P. -	*C. fusca.*
Blue P. -	*C. cerulea.*
White-shouldered P. -	*C. badiati.*
Black-spotted P. -	*C. navia.*
Mexican P. -	*C. Mexicana.*
Passenger P. -	*C. migratoria.*
Canada Turtle -	*C. Canadensis.*
Turtle Dove -	*C. Carolinensis.*
Ground Dove -	*C. passerina.*

ORDER GALLINÆ.

GENUS MELEAGRIS.

Wild-Turkey -	*Meleagris gallipavo.*

GENUS PENELOPE.

Guan -	*Penelope cristata.*
Yacou -	*P. Cumanensis.*
Piping Curassow -	*P. pipile.*

GENUS CRAX.

Crested Curassow -	*Crax alector.*
Globose C. -	*C. globicera.*
Cashew C. -	*C. pauxi.*
Crying C. -	*C. vociferans.*

GENUS PHASIANUS.

Courier Pheasant -	*Phasianus Mexicanus.*
Crested P. -	*P. cristatus.*
*Columbian P. -	*P. columbianus.*

GENUS TETRAO.

*Sharp-tailed Grous -	*Tetrao phasianellus?*
Spotted G. -	*T. Canadensis.*
White G. -	*T. albus.*
Rock G. -	*T. rupestris.*
Pinnated G. -	*T. cupido.*
Ruffed G. or Pheasant	*T. umbellus.*
*Brown G. -	*T. fuscus.*
Ptarmigan -	*T. lagopus.*

GENUS PERDIX.

Mexican Partridge or Prairie-hen -	*Perdix varius.*
Virginia F. or Quail -	*P. Virginianus.*
Louisiana Q. -	*P. Mexicanus.*
California Q. -	*P. Californicus.*
Lesser Mexican Q. -	*P. expectes.*
Hudsonian Q. -	*P. Hudsonica.*
Crested Q. -	*P. cristatus.*

*Described by Lewis and Clark, **vol. II**, p. 180, 181, 182.

WATER BIRDS.

ORDER *GRALLÆ.*

GENUS *PLATALEA.*

Roseate Spoonbill	-	*Platalea ajaja.*

GENUS *PALAMEDEA.*

Horned Screamer	-	*Palamedea cornuta.*

GENUS *MYCTERIA.*

American Jabiru	-	*Mycteria Americana.*

GENUS *CANCROMA.*

Crested Boatbill	-	*Cancroma cochlearia.*

GENUS *ARDEA.*

Whooping Crane	-	*Ardea Americana.*
Night Heron or Qua-bird	*A. nicticorax.*	
Great White Heron	-	*A. egretta.*
Dry H.	-	*A. hoactli.*
Houhou H.	-	*A. hohou.*
Great H.	-	*A. herodias.*
Louisiana H.	-	*A. Ludoviciana.*
Yellow-crowned H.	-	*A. violacea.*
Blue H.	-	*A. cærulea.*
Rusty-crowned H. or		
Bittern	-	*A. minor.*
Least or Minute Bittern	*A. exilis.*	
Snowy Heron	-	*A. candidissima.*
Striated H.	-	*A. striata.*
Green H.	-	*A. virescens.*
Mexican H.	-	*A. apodicon.*
Streaked H.	-	*A. virgata.*
Ash-coloured H.	-	*A. cana.*
Gardenian H.	-	*A. Gardeni.*

GENUS *TANTALUS.*

Wood Ibis	-	*Tantalus loculator.*
Scarlet I.	-	*T. ruber.*
White I.	-	*T. albus.*
Lesser I.	-	*T. minutus.*
Mexican I.	-	*T. Mexicanus.*
White-necked I.	-	*T. albicollis.*

GENUS *NUMENIUS.*

Long-billed Curlew	*Numenius longirostra.*	
Esquimaux or short-		
billed C.	-	*N. borealis.*
Hudsonian C.	-	*N. Hudsonica.*

GENUS *SCOLOPAX.*

Black Snipe	-	*Scolopax nigra.*
Nodding S.	-	*S. nutans.*
Stone S.	-	*S. melanoleuca.*
Jack S.	-	*S. gallinula.*
Green-shank S.	-	*S. glottis.*
Red-shank S.	-	*S. calidris.*
Spotted S.	-	*S. totanus.*
White Red-shank S.	*S. candida.*	
Hudsonian Godwit	-	*S. Hudsonica.*
American G.	-	*S. fedoa.*
Red-breasted Snipe	*S. noveboracensis.*	
Semipalmated S.	-	*S. semipalmata.*
English S.	-	*S. gallinago.*
Tell-tale S.	-	*S. vociferus.*
Yellow-shanks S.	-	*S. flavipes.*
Woodcock	-	*S. minor.*

GENUS *TRINGA.*

Striated Sandpiper	-	*Tringa striata.*
Newfoundland S.	-	*T. Nova-terræ.*
Green S.	-	*T. ochropus.*
Knot S.	-	*T. canutus.*
Gray S.	-	*T. squatarola.*
Aberdeen S.	-	*T. Islandica.*
Ash-coloured S.	-	*T. cinerea.*
Boreal S.	-	*T. borealis.*

Bartram's S.	-	*T. Bartramia.*
Variegated S.	-	*T. variegata.*
Little S.	-	*T. pusilla.*
Red-breasted S.	-	*T. rufa.*
Ringed S.	-	*T. hiaticula.*
Semipalmated S.	*T. semipalmata.*	
solitary S.	-	*T. solitaria.*
Spotted S.	-	*T. macularia.*
Purre	-	*T. cinclus.*
Turnstone	-	*T. interpres.*

GENUS *CHARADRIUS.*

Black-bellied Plover	*Charadrius apricarius.*	
Golden P.	-	*C. pluvialis.*
Ringed P.	-	*C. hiaticula.*
Wilson's P.	-	*C. Wilsonia.*
Sanderling	-	*C. calidris.*
Kildeer	-	*C. vociferus.*

GENUS *HÆMATOPUS.*

Pied Oyster-catcher or		
Sea-pie	-	*Hæmatopus ostralegus.*

GENUS *RALLUS.*

Spotted Rail	-	*Rallus porzana.*
Little R.	-	*R. minutus.*
Clapper R.	-	*R. crepitans.*
Common R. or Sora	*R. Carolinus.*	
Red-billed R.	-	*R. Virginianus.*
Cayenne R.	-	*R. Cayennensis.*

GENUS *PARRA.*

Louisiana Jacana	*Parra Ludoviciana.*	
Chestnut J.	-	*P. jacana.*
Faithful J.	-	*P. chavaria.*
Black J.	-	*P. nigra.*

GENUS *GALLINULA.*

Purple Gallinule	*Gallinula porphyrio.*	
Moor-hen	-	*G. chloropus.*
Crowing Gallinule	*G. purpurea.*	
Favourite G.	-	*G. floricantis.*
Carthagena G.	-	*G. Carthagena.*
Black-bellied G.	-	*G. ruficollis.*
Yellow-breasted G.	*G. nova boraensis.*	

ORDER *PINNATIPEDES.*

GENUS *PHALAROPUS.*

Gray Phalarope	*Phalaropus lobata.*	
Plain P.	-	*P. glacialis.*
Brown P.	-	*P. fusca.*
Red P.	-	*P. hyperborea.*

GENUS *FULICA.*

Common Coot	-	*Fulica atra.*
Mexican C.	-	*F. Mexicana.*

GENUS *PODICEPS.*

Horned Grebe	-	*Podiceps cornutus.*
Little G.	-	*P. minor.*
Louisiana G.	-	*P. Ludovicianus.*
Dusky G.	-	*P. obscurus.*
Pied-bill G.	-	*P. podiceps.*

ORDER *PALMIPEDES.*

GENUS *RECURVIROSTRA.*

American Avoset	*Recurvirostra Americana.*	
White A.	-	*R. alba.*
Long-legged A. or Tilt	*R. himantopus.*	

GENUS *PHŒNICOPTERUS.*

Red Flamingo	-	*Phœnicopterus ruber.*

UNITED STATES OF AMERICA. 319

GENUS *DIOMEDEA.*

Wandering **Albatross**		*Diomedea exulans.*
Chocolate A.	-	*D. spadicea.*
Yellow-nosed A.	-	*D. chlororynchos.*

GENUS *ALCA.*

Labrador Auk	-	*Alca Labradora.*
Crested A.	-	*A. cristatella.*
Little A.	-	*A. alle.*
Pigmy A.	-	*A. pygmaea.*
Puffin	-	*A. arctica.*
Razor-bill	-	*A. torda.*
Penguin **or Great Auk**	-	*A. impennis.*

GENUS *URIA.*

Marbled Guillemot		*Uria marmorata.*
Black G.	-	*U. gentle.*
Foolish G.	-	*U. troile.*

GENUS *COLYMBUS.*

Striped Diver	-	*Colymbus striatus.*
Red-throated D.	-	*C. septentrionalis.*
Black-throated D.	-	*C. arcticus.*
Northern D. or Loon	-	*C. glacialis.*
Speckled D.	-	*C. stellatus.*
Imber D.	-	*C. immer.*

GENUS *RYNCHOPS.*

Black Skimmer or		
Shearwater	-	*Rynchops nigra.*

GENUS *STERNA.*

Sooty Tern	-	*Sterna fuliginosa.*
Cayenne T.	-	*S. Cayanensis.*
Surinam T.	-	*S. Surinamensis.*
Simple T.	-	*S. simplex.*
Great T.	-	*S. hirundo.*
Lesser T.	-	*S. minuta.*
Brown T.	-	*S. spadicea.*
Black T.	-	*S. fissipes.*
Marsh T.	-	*S. aranea.*
Short-tailed T.	-	*S. plumbea.*
*Banded-tail T.	-	*S. Philadelphia.*

GENUS *LARUS.*

Kittiwake Gull	-	*Larus tridactilus.*
Common G.	-	*L. canus.*
Black-backed G.	-	*L. marinus.*
Herring G.	-	*L. fuscus.*
Black-headed G.	-	*L. ridibundus.*
Arctic G.	-	*L. parasiticus.*
Skua G.	-	*L. cataractes.*
Esquimaux G.	-	*L. keensk.*
Ivory G.	-	*L. eburneus.*
†Toothed-bill G.	-	*L. Delawarensis.*

GENUS *PROCELLARIA.*

Dusky Petrel	-	*Procellaria obscura.*
Stormy P.	-	*P. pelagica.*
Forked-tailed P.	-	*P. furcata.*
Black-toed P.	-	*P. melanopus.*
Fulmar P.	-	*P. glacialis.*
Giant P.	-	*P. gigantea.*
Brazilian P.	-	*P. Braziliana.*
Glacial P.	-	*P. gelido.*
Shearwater P.	-	*P. puffinus.*

GENUS *MERGUS.*

Crested Merganser	*Mergus cucullatus.*

Red-breasted M.	-	*M. serrator.*
Brown M.	-	*M. fuscus.*
Blue M.	-	*M. cerrulous.*
White Nun or Smew	-	*M. albellus.*
Goosander or Sheldrake		*M. merganser.*

GENUS *ANAS.*

Wild Swan	-	*Anas cygnus.*
Whistling S.	-	*A. Columbianus.*
Snow Goose	-	*A. hyperborea.*
Gray G.	-	*A. anser.*
Canada G.	-	*A. Canadensis.*
Brant	-	*A. bernicla.*
Gray-headed **Duck**	-	*A. spectabilis.*
Velvet D.	-	*A. fusca.*
Scoter D.	-	*A. nigra.*
Blue-bill or Scaup D.	-	*A. marila.*
Eider D.	-	*A. mollissima.*
Muscovy D.	-	*A. moschata.*
Georgia D.	-	*A. Georgica.*
Bahera D.	-	*A. Bahamensis.*
Buffel-headed **D.**	-	*A. albeola.*
Western D.	-	*A. Stelleri.*
Surf D.	-	*A. perspicillata.*
Mexican D.	-	*A. Nova Hispania.*
Sprigtail D.	-	*A. acuta.*
Long-tailed D.	-	*A. glacialis.*
Red-headed D.	-	*A. ferina.*
Canvass-back D.	-	*A. valisineria.*
Harlequin D.	-	*A. histrionica.*
Barrow D.	-	*A. fuscescens.*
Spanish D.	-	*A. clatone.*
Red-billed D.	-	*A. Autumnalis.*
Pied D.	-	*A. Labradora.*
Summer D.	-	*A. sponsa.*
Black-billed **Whistling D.**	*A. arborea.*
Dusky or Common		
Black **D.**	-	*A. obscura.*
Tufted **D.**	-	*A. fuligula.*
Ruddy **D.**	-	*A. rubidus.*
Shoveller	-	*A. clypeata.*
Gadwall	-	*A. strepera.*
Spinous-tailed Teal	-	*A. spinosa.*
Green-winged T.	-	*A. crecca.*
Blue-winged T.	-	*A. discors.*
Golden-eye	-	*A. clangula.*
Widgeon or Bald-pate	-	*A. Americana.*
Mexican Pochard	-	*A. falco.*
Mallard	-	*A. boschas.*

GENUS *PELICANUS.*

Brown Pelican	-	*Pelicanus fuscus.*
Great White P.	-	*P. onocrotalus.*
Charleston P.	-	*P. Carolinensis.*
Rough-billed P.	-	*P. erythrorhynchos.*
Frigate P.	-	*P. aquilus.*
Saw-billed P.	-	*P. thagus.*
Gannet	-	*P. bassanus.*
Lesser G.	-	*P. piscator.*
Brown Booby	-	*P. fiber.*
Lesser G.	-	*P. piscus.*
Cormorant	-	*P. carbo.*
Shag	-	*P. graculus.*

GENUS *PHAETON.*

Common Tropic-bird	*Phaeton æthereus.*

GENUS *PLOTUS.*

Black-bellied **Darter**		*Plotus melanogaster.*
Surinam D.		*P. Surinamensis.*

*This is a nondescript. Its length is twelve inches, extent thirty-one; the lower parts pure white; above blue ash; below the auriculars there is a patch of dark slate; the tail is white, short, almost even, and crossed with a dark brown band; a line of brown passes from the shoulder of the wing to the tertials. Weight full five ounces avoirdupois.

†This is a beautiful Gull, and was discovered on the Delaware below Philadelphia; it is a nondescript. Length nineteen and a half inches, extent three feet ten inches; the up permandible has four indentations of blunt teeth, the lower three; corners of the mouth and the eyelids bright vermilion; head, neck, tail and lower parts pure white; wings, back and scapulars blue ash. Weight nineteen ounces avoirdupois.

‡See history of **Lewis and Clark's expedition,** vol. II p. 192.

Our limits will only allow us to give a succinct account of some of
the most interesting birds of the United States, for which we are
chiefly indebted to Mr. Wilson's Work. It is necessary to premise
that he follows, with some exceptions, the arrangement of Latham.

Turkey Vulture or *Turkey-buzzard.* This bird is found throughout
the United States, but is most numerous in the southern section of
the Union. The Turkey-buzzards are gregarious, peaceable and
harmless: never offering any violence to a living animal, or, like the
plunderers of the *Falco* tribe, depriving the husbandman of his stock.
Their food is carrion, of which they eat so immoderately, that frequently they are incapable of flying, until they disgorge the contents
of their stomach. The female lays from two to four eggs in a hollow tree, stump, or log; and brings forth her young in May. The
young are extremely filthy.

Black Vulture or *Carrion-crow.* Mr. William Bartram was the first
naturalist who indicated this bird as a distinct species from the preceding: notwithstanding which, all the Ornithologists of Europe have
confounded it with the Turkey-buzzard. In the Atlantic States, the
Black Vulture is seldom found to the northward of Newbern, North
Carolina: but inhabits the whole continent, to the southward, as far
as Cape Horn. In the towns and villages of the Southern States, particularly Charleston, Georgetown, and Savannah, they may be seen
sauntering about the streets, or sunning themselves on the roofs of
the houses, and fences; and may be said to be completely domesticated: being quite as familiar as the domestic poultry. They, as
well as the Turkey-buzzards, are protected by a law or usage; and
have a respect paid them as scavengers, whose labours are subser-
vient to the public good. They devour animal food of all kinds,
whether putrid or otherwise. They are highly useful birds. In those
parts of the continent where the Alligators abound, they attend these
dreadful amphibious animals, when they deposit their eggs in the
sand, and devour them the first opportunity. The destruction of these
birds ought to be prohibited under severe penalties.

White-headed or *Bald Eagle.* This distinguished bird, as he is
the most beautiful of his tribe in this part of the world, and the adopted
emblem of our country; is entitled to particular notice. He has been
long known to naturalists, being common to both continents, and occasionally met with from a very high northern latitude, to the borders of the torrid zone, but chiefly in the vicinity of the sea, and
along the shores and cliffs of our lakes and large rivers. Formed by
nature for braving the severest cold; feeding equally on the produce
of the sea, and of the land; possessing powers of flight capable of
out-stripping even the tempests themselves; unawed by anything but
man; and from the ethereal heights to which he soars, looking abroad,
at one glance, on an immeasureable expanse of forest, fields, lakes
and ocean, deep below him, he appears indifferent to the little loca-
lities of change of seasons; as in a few minutes he can pass from
summer to winter, from the lower to the higher regions of the atmosphere, the abode of eternal cold, and thence descend at will to the
torrid, or the arctic regions of the earth. He is therefore found at
all seasons in the countries he inhabits, but prefers such places as
have been mentioned above, from the great partiality which he has
for fish.

In procuring these he displays, in a very singular manner, the genius and energy of his character, which is fierce, contemplative, da-

ring and tyrannical: attributes not exerted but on particular occasions: but when put forth, overpowering all opposition. Elevated on the high dead limb of some gigantic tree, that commands a wide view of the neighbouring shore and ocean, he seems calmly to contemplate the motions of the various feathered tribes that pursue their busy avocations below:—the snow white Gulls slowly winnowing the air; the busy Tringæ coursing along the sands; trains of Ducks streaming over the surface; silent and watchful Cranes, intent and wading; clamorous Crows, and all the winged multitudes that subsist by the bounty of this vast liquid magazine of nature. High over all these hovers one, whose action instantly arrests all his attention. By its wide curvature of wing, and sudden suspension in air, he knows it to be the *Fish Hawk*, settling over some devoted victim of the deep. His eye kindles at the sight, and balancing himself, with half opened wings, on the branch, he watches the result. Down, rapid as an arrow from heaven, descends the distant object of his attention, the roar of its wings reaching the ear as it disappears in the deep, making the surges foam around. At this moment the eager looks of the Eagle are all ardour: and levelling his neck for flight, he sees the Fish Hawk once more emerge, struggling with its prey, and mounting in the air with screams of exultation. These are the signal for our hero, who, launching into the air, instantly gives chace, soon gains on the Fish Hawk, each exerts his utmost to mount above the other, displaying in these rencounters the most elegant and sublime aerial evolutions. The unincumbered Eagle rapidly advances, and is just on the point of reaching his opponent, when, with a sudden scream, probably of despair and honest execration, the latter drops his fish: the Eagle poising himself for a moment, as if to take a more certain aim, descends like a whirlwind, snatches it in his grasp ere it reaches the water, and bears his ill-gotten booty silently away to the woods.*

The Bald Eagle frequently destroys young lambs and pigs and will sometimes attack old sickly sheep, aiming furiously at their eyes. Ducks, Geese, Gulls and other sea fowl, are also seized with avidity. The most putrid carrion, when nothing better can be had, is acceptable. The nest of this species is generally fixed on a very large and lofty tree, often in a swamp or morass and difficult to be ascended. It is large, being added to and repaired every season, until it becomes a black prominent mass, observable at a considerable distance. It is formed of large sticks, sods, earthy rubbish, hay, moss &c. The eggs are often two to three in number, of a whitish colour; the young are hatched early in March. It has at length been ascertained that the Sea or Gray Eagle is the present species, in a different stage of colour.

Ring-tail Eagle. This noble bird, in strength, spirit and activity, ranks among the first of his tribe. It is found, though sparingly dispersed, over the whole temperate and arctic regions, particularly the latter; breeding on high precipitous rocks; always preferring a mountainous country. The tail feathers of this bird are highly valued by the various tribes of American Indians, for ornamenting their calumets or pipes of peace. Hence this bird has been called by some writers the Calumet Eagle.

* If Mr. Wilson had never written a line except the above, he would have deserved the highest eulogy for a description which is perhaps unrivalled by the whole tribe of naturalists, from the age of Pliny to the present day. The composition is not only excellent, but the accuracy of the detail transcends all praise.

Fish Hawk or *Osprey.* This formidable, vigorous-winged, and well known bird, subsists altogether on the finny tribes that swarm in our bays, creeks and rivers ; procuring his prey by his own active skill and industry ; and seeming no farther dependent on the land than as a mere resting place, or, in the usual season, a spot of deposit for his nest, eggs and young. The Fish Hawk is migratory ; arriving on the coasts of Newyork and Newjersey about the twenty-first of March, and retiring to the south about the twenty-second of September. Its nest is usually built on the top of a dead or decaying tree, sometimes not more than fifteen, often upwards of fifty feet, from the ground. About the first of May the female begins to lay her eggs, which are commonly three in number, sometimes only two, and rarely four. This species is considered the most numerous of its genus within the United States. There is one singular trait in the character of this bird, which is worthy of record. The Purple Grakles or Crow Blackbirds, are permitted by the Fish Hawk to build their nests among the interstices of the sticks of which his own is constructed. Several pairs of Grakles taking up their abode there, like humble vassals around the castle of their chief, laying, hatching their young, and living together in mutual harmony. We have seen no less than five of these nests so situated, and one or two on an adjoining tree. The Crows and Jays devour the eggs, and sometimes the young, of the Grakles ; and all the Hawks, except the generous and noble Fish Hawk, murder, at every opportunity, the birds themselves. Hence these birds, during the important periods of incubation and nutrition, have been directed to seek that protection which they can find nowhere else ; and under the guardianship of the Fish Hawk they are safe from every enemy, except the tyrant Man. How strikingly does this exemplify the superintending care of the God of Nature !

Marsh Hawk. This Hawk, and several others, particularly the White-breasted Hawk, *F. Leverianus,* are common in the winter season, among our meadows and marshes ; where they render an essential service, by destroying multitudes of the Mice, which are so injurious to the meadows and their embankments. Our Graziers and Farmers would do well to protect these birds ; for notwithstanding they now and then bear away a vagrant chicken, yet the good they do more than counterbalances their bad deeds.

Great-footed Hawk. This is the celebrated Peregrine Falcon, formerly so greatly esteemed for its use in Falconry. It is called along our coast the Duck Hawk, from its skill in knocking down the Ducks when on the wing. It flies with astonishing rapidity.

Snow Owl. This great northern hunter inhabits the coldest and most dreary regions of the northern hemisphere on both continents. He is often seen in the United States during the severity of winter. The usual food of this species is Hares, Grous, Rabbits, Ducks, Mice, and even Carrion. Unlike most of his tribe he hunts by day as well as by twilight. The female measures two feet in length, and five feet two inches in extent.

Great-horned Owl. This noted and formidable bird is found in almost every quarter of the United States. His favourite residence, however, is in the dark solitudes of deep swamps covered with a growth of gigantic timber ; and here, as soon as evening draws on, and mankind retires to rest, he sends forth such sounds as seem scarcely to belong to this world, startling the solitary pilgrim as he slum-

bers by his forest fire, "Making night hideous." He preys on Rabbits, Squirrels, Rats, Mice, Partridges, Small Birds and Chickens. The
nest of this species is generally placed in the fork of a tall tree, sometimes in the hollow of a tree. Eggs four in number of a pure white.
The Great-horned Owl is not migratory.

Red Owl. This is another of our nocturnal wanderers, well known
by its common name, the *Little Screech Owl*; and noted for its melancholy, quivering kind of wailing in the evenings particularly towards
the latter part of summer and autumn, near the farmhouse. They
roost during the day in the thick evergreens, such as the Pine, Cedar, &c.,
and sometimes will take up their abode in a vacant pigeon house, or
martin box, and occupy the same situation for several successive seasons. They construct their nest in the hollow of a tree, and lay four,
pure white eggs.

Great American Shrike or *Butcher-bird.* The character of this bird
is entitled to no common degree of respect. His activity is visible in
all his motions: his courage and intrepidity beyond every other bird
of his size, the King-bird excepted: and in affection for his young
he is surpassed by no other. He attacks the largest Hawk or Eagle
with a resolution truly astonishing: so that all of them respect him;
and on every occasion decline the contest. As the snows of winter
approach, he descends from the mountainous forests, and from the
regions of the north, to the more cultivated parts of the country,
hovering about the hedge-rows, orchards and meadows, and disappears again early in April. It breeds in the interior: the female lays
six eggs, and produces her young in June. This species preys occasionally on small birds, which he sticks on thorns that he may tear
them to pieces with greater ease; but his common feed, in the summer, appears to be the grasshoppers. The habit of the Shrike, of seizing
and impaling grasshoppers and other insects on thorns, has given rise
to an opinion, that he places their carcasses there by way of baits,
to allure small birds to them, while he himself lies in ambush to
surprise and destroy them. This is a mistake.

Carolina Parrot or *Parakeet.* Of one hundred and sixty-eight kinds
of Parrots enumerated by European writers as inhabiting the various
regions of the globe, this is the only species found native within the
territory of the United States. They are not often found to the east-
ward of the Allegheny ridge; but are numerous on the Great and Little Miami, and at Big-bone Lick, thirty miles above the mouth of
Kentucky river. In the fall, when their favourite cockle burrs are
ripe, they swarm along the high grounds of the Mississippi, above
New Orleans, for a great extent. They fly very much like the Wild
Pigeon, in close compact bodies, and with great rapidity, making a
loud and outrageous screaming, not unlike that of the Red-headed
Woodpecker. Their flight is sometimes in a direct line; but most
usually circuitous, making a great variety of elegant and easy serpentine meanders, as if for pleasure. They are particularly attached to
the large sycamores, in the hollow of the trunks and branches of which
they generally roost, thirty or forty, and sometimes more, entering at
the same hole. Here they cling close to the sides of the tree, hold-
ing fast by the claws, and also by the bills. They appear to be fond
of sleep, and often retire to their holes during the day, probably to
take their regular *siesta*. They regularly visit the salines or salt-
licks, to drink the salt water, of which they, as well as the Wild
Pigeons, are remarkably fond. The food of this species is ripe fruits,

the seeds of the Cypress tree and hackberry, beech nuts and cockle burrs. What is called by Europeans the Illinois Parrot, *P. pertinax*, is the young bird of this species, in its imperfect colours.

Raven. Found all over the habitable parts of America. Is more numerous in the interior, than on the coast. Along the Lakes they abound; and were seen in immense multitudes by Lewis and Clark's party on their whole route across the continent.

Common Crow. This is perhaps the most generally known, and least beloved, of all our land birds; having neither melody of song, nor beauty of plumage, nor excellence of flesh, nor civility of manners to recommend him; on the contrary, he is branded as a thief and a plunderer; a kind of black-coated vagabond, who hovers over the fields of the industrious, fattening on their labours; and by his voracity often blasting their expectations. Hated as he is by the farmer, watched and persecuted by almost every bearer of a gun, who all triumph in his destruction, had not heaven bestowed on him intelligence and sagacity far beyond common, there is reason to believe that the whole tribe, in these parts at least, would long ago have ceased to exist. The Crow is a constant attendant on agriculture, and a general inhabitant of the cultivated parts of North America.

It is in the month of May, and until the middle of June, that this species is most destructive to the corn-fields, digging up the newly planted grains of Maize, pulling up by the roots those that have begun to vegetate, and thus frequently obliging the farmer to replant, or lose the benefit of the soil; and this sometimes twice, and even three times, occasioning a considerable additional expense and inequality of harvest. No mercy is now shewn him. The myriads of worms, moles, mice, caterpillars, grubs and beetles which he has destroyed, are altogether overlooked on these occasions. Detected in robbing the hens' nests, pulling up the corn, and killing the young chickens, he is considered as an outlaw, and sentenced to destruction. But the great difficulty is how to put this sentence in execution. His watchfulness, and jealous sagacity in distinguishing a person with a gun, are notorious to every one.

Towards the close of summer, the parent Crows with their new families, forsaking their solitary lodgings, collect together, as if by previous agreement, when evening approaches. About an hour before sunset they are first observed, flying somewhat in Indian file, in one direction, at a short height above the tops of the trees, silent and steady, keeping the general curvature of the ground, continuing to pass sometimes till after sunset, so that the whole line of march would extend for many miles. The most noted Crow roost with which we are acquainted, is near Newcastle, on an island in the river Delaware, known by the name of the *Pea-patch.* This is a low flat alluvial spot of a few acres, elevated but a little above high water mark, and covered with a thick growth of reeds. This appears to be the grand rendezvous or headquarters, of the greater part of the Crows within forty or fifty miles of the spot. It is entirely destitute of trees, the Crows alighting and nestling among the reeds, which by these means are broken down and matted together. The noise created by these multitudes, both in their evening assembly, and re-ascension in the morning; and the depredations they commit in the immediate neighbourhood of this great resort, are almost incredible. Whole fields of corn are sometimes laid waste by thousands alighting on it at once, with appetites whetted by the fast of the preceding night; and the utmost vigilance is unavailing to prevent, at least, a partial destruction of this their favourite grain. Like the stragglers of an immense, undisciplined and rapacious army, they spread themselves over the fields, to plunder and destroy wherever they alight. It is here that the character of the Crow is universally execrated; and to say to the man who has lost his crop of corn by these birds, that *Crows are exceedingly useful for destroying vermin*, would be as consolatory as to tell *him* who has just lost his house and furniture by the flames, that *fires are excellent for destroying bugs*. Besides grain, insects and carrion the Crows feed on frogs, tadpoles, moles, mice, birds' eggs and their young, small fish, lizards and shell fish; with the last they frequently mount to a great height, dropping them on the rocks below, and descending after them to pick up the contents. The same habit is observable in the Raven, some species of Gulls and the Sea-side or Fish Crow

Fish Crow. This is another roving inhabitant of our coasts, ponds and river shores; pretty numerous in some districts; though always confounded with the foregoing, until Mr. Wilson introduced it as a distinct species. Though having a general resemblance to his brother, yet he appears not to possess his bad qualities. His food is chiefly fish, and the animal matter that is found along the shores. The voice of this species is very different from that of the Common Crow, being more hoarse and guttural, and uttered as if something stuck in their throat. They are smaller than the Common Crow, but of the same colour.

Magpie. This bird is much better known in Europe than in this country, where it has not been long discovered; although it is now found to inhabit a wide extent of territory, and in great numbers. The Magpie unites in its character courage and cunning, turbulence and rapacity. Not inelegantly formed, and distinguished by gay as well as splendid plumage, he has long been noted in those countries where he commonly resides; and his habits and manners are there familiarly known. He is particularly pernicious to plantations of young oaks, tearing up the acorns; and also to birds, destroying great numbers of their eggs and young, even young chickens, partridges, grous and pheasants. It is perhaps on this last account that the whole vengeance of the game laws has lately been let loose upon him, in some parts of Britain; as appears by accounts from that quarter, where premiums, it is said, are offered for his head, as an arch poacher; and penalties inflicted on all those who permit him to breed on their premises.

Lewis and Clark's party first met with the Magpie near the great bend of the Missouri, and found that the number of these birds increased as they advanced. Pike observed them in immense numbers, and was not a little incommoded by their pilfering and rapacity. "Our horses," says he, "were obliged to scrape the snow away to obtain their miserable pittance; and, to increase their misfortunes, the poor animals were attacked by the magpies, who, attracted by the scent of their sore backs, alighted on them, and in defiance of their wincing and kicking, picked many places quite raw. The difficulty of procuring food rendered these birds so bold as to light on our men's arms, and eat meat out of their hands."* This species build their nests in trees, and they are composed of small sticks, leaves, grass

*¹Pike's Journal, p. 170.

&c. lined with wool, hair and feathers. The eggs are usually five, of a bluish brown, freckled with reddish brown. Captain Lewis observes that the nests of the Bald Eagles, where the Magpies abound, are always accompanied by those of two or three of the latter, who are their inseparable attendants.*

The *Baltimore-bird*, as Catesby informs us, has been named from its colours, which are black and orange, being those of the arms or livery of Lord Baltimore, formerly proprietary of Maryland. From the singularity of its colours, and the construction of its nest, it is generally known, and, as usual, honoured with a variety of names, such as Hang-nest, Hanging-bird, Golden Robin, Fire-bird, &c. It is a beautiful bird, and adds much interest to the scenery of the American Farm.

The *Purple Grakle* or Crow Blackbird is well known to every farmer of the northern and middle states. About the twentieth of March the Grakles visit Pennsylvania from the south, fly in loose flocks, frequent swamps and meadows, and follow in the furrows after the plough; their food at this season consisting of worms, grubs and caterpillars, of which they destroy prodigious numbers, as if to recompense the husbandman before hand for the havock which they intend to make among his crops of Indian corn. Every industrious farmer complains of the mischief committed on his corn by the Blackbirds; though, were the same means used, as with Pigeons, to take them in clap nets, multitudes of them might thus be destroyed; and the products of them in market, in some measure, indemnify him for their depredations. As some consolation, however, to the cultivator, I can assure him, that were I placed in his situation, I should hesitate whether to consider these birds most as friends or enemies, as they are particularly destructive to almost all the noxious worms, grubs and caterpillars that infest his fields, which, were they allowed to multiply unmolested, would soon consume nine-tenths of all the production of his labour, and desolate the country with the miseries of famine. Is not this a striking proof that the Deity hath created nothing in vain; and that it is the duty of man to avail himself of their usefulness, and guard against their bad effects as securely as possible, without indulging in the barbarous, and even impious wish for their utter extermination?

Ivory-billed Woodpecker. This majestic and formidable species, in strength and magnitude stands at the head of the whole class of Woodpeckers hitherto discovered. He may be called the king or chief of his tribe; and nature seems to have designed him a distinguished characteristic in the superb carmine crest, and bill of polished ivory with which she has ornamented him. His eye is brilliant and daring; and his whole frame so admirably adapted to his mode of life, and method of procuring subsistence, as to impress on the mind of the examiner the most reverential ideas of the Creator. His manners have also a dignity in them superior to the common herd of Woodpeckers. Trees, shrubbery, orchards, rails, fence posts and old prostrate logs, are alike interesting to these, in their humble and indefatigable search for prey; but the royal hunter now before us, scorns the humility of such situations, and seeks the most towering trees of the forest; seeming particularly attached to those prodigious cypress swamps, whose crowded giant sons stretch their bare and blasted or

* History of the Expedition, vol. i, p. 198.

moss-hung arms midway to the skies. In these almost inaccessible recesses, amid ruinous piles of impending timber, his trumpet-like note and loud strokes resound through the dreary wilds, of which he seems the sole lord and inhabitant. Wherever he frequents he leaves numerous monuments of his industry behind him. We there see enormous pine trees with cart loads of bark lying around their roots, and chips of the trunk itself in such quantities as to suggest the idea that half a dozen of axe-men had been at work there for the whole morning. The body of the tree is also disfigured with such numerous and so large excavations, that one can hardly conceive it possible for the whole to be the work of a Woodpecker. With such strength, and an apparatus so powerful, what havoc might he not commit, if numerous, on the most useful of our forest trees! And yet with all these appearances, and much of vulgar prejudice against him, it may be fairly questioned whether he is at all injurious; or, at least, whether his exertions do not contribute most powerfully to the protection of our timber. Examine closely the tree where he has been at work, and you will soon perceive, that it is neither from motives of mischief nor amusement that he slices off the bark, or digs his way into the trunk. The sound and healthy tree is not the least object of his attention: the diseased, infested with insects, and hastening to putrefaction, are his favourites; there the deadly crawling enemy have formed a lodgement, between the bark and tender wood, to drink up the very vital juice of the tree. It is the ravages of these vermin which the intelligent proprietor of the forest deplores as the sole perpetrators of the destruction of his timber. Would it be believed that the larvæ of an insect or fly, no larger than a grain of rice, should silently, and in one season, destroy some thousand acres of pine trees, many of them from two to three feet in diameter, and a hundred and fifty feet high! Yet whoever passes along the highroad from Georgetown to Charleston, in South Carolina, about twenty miles from the former place, can have striking and melancholy proofs of this fact. In some places the whole woods, as far as you can see around you, are dead, stripped of the bark, their wintry-looking arms and bare trunks bleaching in the sun, and tumbling in ruins before every blast, presenting a frightful picture of desolation. And yet ignorance and prejudice stubbornly persist in directing their indignation against the bird now before us, the constant and mortal enemy of these very vermin, as if the hand that probed the wound to extract its cause, should be equally detested with that which inflicted it. Until some effectual preventive, or more complete mode of destruction can be devised against these insects and their larvæ, I would humbly suggest the propriety of protecting, and receiving with proper feelings of gratitude, the services of this and the whole tribe of Woodpeckers, letting the odium of guilt fall to its proper owners.

The Ivory-billed Woodpecker is not migratory; he is seldom found to the northward of Virginia; the Carolinas are his favourite states.

Downy Woodpecker. This is the smallest of our Woodpeckers, and is generally known by the appellation of the *Sap-Sucker.* The principal characteristics of this little bird are diligence, familiarity, perseverance, and a strength and energy in the head and muscles of the neck, which are truly astonishing. A serious charge has been brought against him by the naturalists of Europe, viz. that he is almost constantly boring and digging into apple trees; and that he is the most destructive to the orchards of his whole genus. The first part of this charge I shall not pretend to deny; how far the other is founded in truth will appear in the sequel. Of all our Woodpeckers none rids the apple trees of so many vermin as this, digging off the moss which the negligence of the proprietor has suffered to accumulate, and probing every crevice. In fact the orchard is his favourite resort in all seasons; and his industry is unequalled, and almost incessant, which is more than can be said of any other species we have. In the autumn he is particularly fond of boring the apple trees for insects, digging a circular hole through the bark just sufficient to admit his bill, after that second, third, &c. in pretty regular horizontal circles around the the body of the tree; these parallel circles of holes are often not more than an inch or an inch and a half apart and sometimes so close together, that I have covered eight or ten of them at once with a dollar. From nearly the surface of the ground up to the first fork, and sometimes far beyond it, the whole bark of many apple trees are perforated in this manner, so as to appear as if made by sucessive discharges of buck-shot; and our little Woodpecker is the principal perpetrator of this supposed mischief. I say *supposed*, for so far from these perforations of the bark being ruinous, they are not only harmless, but I have good reason to believe they are really beneficial to the health and fertility of the tree. In more than fifty orchards which I have myself carefully examined, those trees which were marked by the Woodpecker (for some trees they never touch, perhaps because not penetrated by insects) were uniformly the most thriving, and seemingly the most productive; many of these were upwards of sixty years old, their trunks completely covered with holes, while the branches were broad, luxuriant, and loaded with fruit. Of *decayed* trees more than three fourths were untouched by the Woodpecker. Several intelligent farmers, with whom I have conversed, candidly acknowledged the truth of these observations, and with justice look upon these birds as beneficial; but the most common opinion is that they bore the trees to suck the sap, and so destroy its vegetation; though pine and other resinous trees, on the juices of which it is not pretended they feed, are often found equally perforated. Were the *sap* of the tree their object, the saccharine juice of the birch, the sugar maple, and several others, would be much more inviting, because more sweet and nourishing than that of either the pear or apple tree; but I have not observed one mark on the former for ten thousand that may be seen on the latter; besides the early part of spring is the season when the sap flows most abundantly; whereas it is only during the months of September, October and November, that Woodpeckers are seen so indefatigably engaged in orchards, probing every crack and crevice, boring through the bark, and what is worth remarking, chiefly on the south and south west sides of the tree, for the eggs and larvæ deposited there by the countless swarms of summer insects. These if suffered to remain, would prey upon the very vitals, if I may so express it, of the tree, and in the succeeding summer give birth to myriads more of their race, equally destructive.

Here then is a whole species, I may say genus, of birds, which Providence seems to have formed for the protection of our fruit and forest trees from the ravages of vermin; which every day destroy millions of these noxious insects that would otherwise blast the hopes of the husbandman; and which even promote the fertility of the tree; and in return, are prescribed by those who ought to have been their protectors; and incitements and rewards held out for their destruction! Let us examine better into the operations of nature, and many of our mistaken opinions, and groundless prejudices, will be abandoned for more just, enlarged and humane modes of thinking.

The *Belted Kingfisher* is a general inhabitant of the banks and shores of all our fresh water rivers from Hudson's Bay to Mexico; and is the only species of its tribe found within the United States. This last circumstance, and its characteristic appearance, make it as universally known here, as its elegant little brother, the common Kingfisher of Europe, is in Britain. Like the love-lorn swains of whom poets tell us, he delights in murmuring streams and falling waters; not however merely that they may soothe his ear, but for a gratification somewhat more substantial. Amidst the roar of the cataract, or over the foam of a torrent, he sits perched upon an overhanging bough, glancing his piercing eye in every direction below for his scaly prey, which with a sudden circular plunge he sweeps from their native element, and swallows in an instant. His voice, which is not unlike the sound produced by the twirling of a watchman's rattle, is naturally loud, harsh and sudden; but it is softened by the sound of the brawling streams and cascades about which he generally rambles. Mill-dams are particularly visited by this feathered fisher; and the sound of his pipe is as well known to the miller as the rattling of his own hopper.

Marsh Wren. This little bird is remarkable for its notes, and curiously constructed nest. Standing on the reedy borders of the Schuylkill, or Delaware in the month of June, you hear a low crackling sound, something similar to that produced by air bubbles forcing their way through mud or boggy ground when trod upon: this is the *song* of the Marsh Wren. But as among the human race it is not given to one man to excel in every thing; and yet each, perhaps, has something peculiarly his own; so among birds we find a like distribution of talents and peculiarities. The bird now before us, if deficient and contemptible in singing, excels in the art of *design*, and constructs a nest, which, in durability, warmth and convenience, is scarcely inferior to one, and far superior to many, of its more musical brethren. This is formed outwardly of wet rushes mixed with mud, well intertwisted, and fashioned into the form of a cocoa nut. A small hole is left two-thirds up, for entrance, the upper edge of which projects like a pent-house over the lower, to prevent the admission of rain. The inside, is lined with fine soft grass, and sometimes feathers; and the outside, when hardened by the sun, resists every kind of weather. This nest is generally suspended among the reeds, above the reach of the highest tides, and is tied so fast in every part to the surrounding reeds, as to bid defiance to the winds and the waves. The eggs are usually six, of a dark fawn colour, and very small. The young leave the nest about the twentieth of June, and they generally have a second brood in the same season. They migrate to the southward in the month of August, and return to Pennsylvania in May.

Humming Bird. Though this interesting and beautiful genus of birds comprehends upwards of seventy species, all of which, with a very few exceptions, are natives of America and its adjacent islands, it is yet singular, that the species now before us, the *Trochilus colubris,* should be the only one of its tribe that ever visits the territory of the United States. According to the observations of Mr. John Abbot of Georgia, this species makes its first appearance at Savannah, from the south, about the twenty-third of March; two weeks earlier than it does in the county of Burke, sixty miles higher up the country towards the interior; and at least five weeks sooner than it reaches Philadelphia. As it passes on to the northward as far as the interior of Canada, where it is seen in great numbers, the wonder is excited how so feebly constructed and delicate a little creature can make its way over such extensive regions of lakes and forests, among so many enemies, all its superiors in strength and magnitude. But its very minuteness, the rapidity of its flight, which almost eludes the eye, and that admirable instinct, reason, or whatever else it may be called, and daring courage which Heaven has implanted in its bosom, are its guides and protectors. In these we may also perceive the reason, why an all-wise Providence has made this little hero an exception to a rule which prevails almost universally through nature, viz. that the smallest species of a tribe are the most prolific. The Eagle lays two, sometimes three, eggs; the Crow five; the Titmouse seven or eight; the small European Wren fifteen; the subject of this article two; and yet the last is abundantly more numerous than the European Wren.

The **Ruby-throated** Humming-bird is so well known, that a description of its splendid plumage and interesting habits is unnecessary. Its food is the honey of flowers and insects.

The *Red-winged Starling*, or Swamp Black-bird, as it is usually called, is scattered over the whole of the United States. About the twentieth of March, or earlier if the season be open, they begin to enter Pennsylvania in numerous, though small, parties. They continue to frequent the low borders of creeks, swamps and ponds, till about the middle of April, when they separate in pairs to breed. Towards the beginning or middle of August, the young birds begin to fly in flocks; and before the commencement of September these flocks have become numerous and formidable, and the young ears of Indian corn, being then in their soft, succulent, milky state, present a temptation that cannot be resisted. Reinforced by numerous and daily flocks from all parts of the interior, they pour down on the low countries in prodigious multitudes. Here they are seen, like vast clouds, wheeling and driving over the meadows and devoted corn fields, darkening the air with their numbers. It may be well supposed that the loss of the cultivator, by these rapacious visitors, is very great: whole fields have sometimes been laid waste in the space of a few days. Various modes have been put in practice to destroy the Blackbirds; and there are not a few who conceive that the extermination of the whole race would be a public benefit. To such we would observe that the Creator has made nothing in vain; and that however a *few* may suffer from the depredations of these birds, yet the good offices they confer upon the farmers *in general*, in ridding their fields of myriads of worms, insects and their larvæ, the silent but deadly enemies of all vegetation, whose secret attacks are more to be dreaded than the combined forces of the whole feathered tribes together, ought to awaken different feelings from those which would incite to utter extermination

Mocking-bird. This celebrated and extraordinary bird, in extent and variety of vocal powers, stands unrivalled by the whole feathered songsters of this or perhaps any other country. His plumage has nothing gaudy or brilliant in it; and, had he nothing else to recommend him, would scarcely entitle him to notice, but his figure is

well proportioned, and even handsome. The ease, elegance, and rapidity of his movements, the animation of his eye, and the intelligence
he displays in listening to, and laying up lessons from, almost every
species of the feathered creation within his hearing, are really surprising, and mark the peculiarity of his genius. To these qualities
we may add that of a voice full, strong and musical, and capable of
almost every modulation, from the clear mellow tones of the Wood
Thrush, to the savage scream of the Bald Eagle. In measure and
accent he faithfully follows his originals. In force and sweetness of
expression, he greatly improves upon them. In his native groves,
mounted on the top of a tall bush or half grown tree, in the dawn of
the morning, while the woods are already vocal with a multitude of
warblers, his admirable song rises pre-eminent over every competitor.
The ear can listen to *his* music alone, to which that of all the others
seems a mere accompaniment. Neither is this strain altogether
imitative. His own native notes, which are easily distinguishable
by such as are well acquainted with those of our various song birds,
are bold and full, and varied seemingly beyond all limits. They consist of short expressions of two, three, or at the most five or six
syllables; generally interspersed with imitations, and all of them
uttered with great emphasis and rapidity; and continued, with undi-
minished ardour, for half an hour, or an hour, at a time. His expanded wings and tail, glistening with white, and the buoyant gaiety
of his action, arresting the eye, as his song most irresistibly does the
ear.

The native notes of the Mocking-bird have considerable resemblance to those of the Brown Thrush or Thrasher, but may easily be
distinguished by their greater rapidity, sweetness, energy of expression and variety. Both, however, have in many parts of the United
States, particularly in those to the south, obtained the name of *Mocking-bird*. The Brown Thrush, from its inferiority of song, being called the French, and the other the English Mocking-bird. A mode
of expression probably originating in the predjudices of our forefathers,
with whom every thing *French* was inferior to every thing *English*.

Wood Thrush or *Wood Robin*. This sweet and solitary songster
inhabits the whole of North America from Hudson's Bay to the peninsula of Florida. He arrives in Pennsylvania about the twentieth of
April, and returns to the south about the beginning of October. As
soon as he arrives he announces his presence in the woods. With
the dawn of the succeeding morning, mounting to the top of some
tall tree that rises from a low thick-shaded part of the woods, he
pipes his few but clear and musical notes in a kind of ecstasy; the
prelude or symphony to which strongly resembles the double-tongue-
ing of a German flute, and sometimes the tinkling of a small bell.
The whole song consists of five or six parts, the last note of each of
which is in such a tone as to leave the conclusion evidently suspended; the finale is finely managed, and with such charming effect as to
sooth and tranquilize the mind, and to seem sweeter and mellower
at each successive repetition. Rival songsters, of the same species,
challenge each other from different parts of the woods, seeming to
vie for softer tones and more exquisite responses. During the burn-
ing heat of the day, they are comparatively mute; but in the evening the same melody is renewed, and continued long after sunset.
Even in dark wet and gloomy weather, when scarce a single chirp
is heard from any other bird, the clear notes of the Wood Thrush

thrill through the dropping woods, from morning to night; and it may truly be said that the sadder the day the sweeter is his song.

The favourite haunts of this species are low, thick-shaded hollows, through which a small brook or rill meanders, overhung with alder bushes that are mantled with vines. He delights to trace the irregular windings of the brook, where by the luxuriance of foliage the sun is completely shut out, or only plays in a few interrupted beams on the glittering surface of the water. Near such a scene he generally builds his nest, in a laurel, or alder bush; the eggs are from four to five, of an uniform light blue, without any spots.

The common *Robin* is one of our earliest songsters; even in March, while the snow yet dapples the fields, and flocks of them are dispersed about, some few will mount a post or stake of the fence, and make short and frequent attempts at their song. This song has some resemblance to the notes of the Thrasher or Ferruginous Thrush; but if deficient in point of execution, he possesses more simplicity, and makes up in zeal what he wants in talent. The notes of the Robin are the prelude to the grand general concert, that is about to burst upon us from the woods, fields and thickets, whitened with blossoms, and breathing fragrance.

The *Cat-bird* is one of our earliest morning songsters, beginning generally before break of day, and hovering from bush to bush with great sprightliness, when there is scarce light sufficient to distinguish him. His notes are more remarkable for singularity than for melody. They consist of short imitations of other birds, and other sounds; but his pipe being rather deficient in clearness and strength of tone, his imitations fail where these are requisite. Upon the whole, though we cannot arrange him with the grand leaders of our vernal choristers, yet he well merits a place among the most agreeable *general* performers. This bird has derived its name from the circumstance of its common note resembling the mewing of a cat.

Cardinal Grosbeak. This is one of our most common cage birds; and is very generally known, not only in North America, but even in Europe. The opinion which so generally prevails in England, that the music of the groves and woods of America, is far inferior to that of Europe, we cannot admit to be correct. We cannot with fairness draw a comparison between the depth of the forest in America, and the cultivated fields of England; because, it is a well known fact, that singing birds seldom frequent the former, in any country. But let the latter place be compared with the like situations in the United States, and the superiority of song would justly belong to the western continent. The few of our song birds that have visited Europe extort admiration from the best judges. "The notes of the Cardinal Grosbeak, says Latham, are almost equal to those of the Nightingale." Yet these notes, clear and excellent as they are, are far inferior to those of the Wood Robin; and even to those of the Brown Thrush. Our inimitable Mockingbird is also acknowledged, by the Europeans, to be fully equal to the song of the Nightingale "in its whole compass." Yet these are not one tenth of the number of our singing birds. Could these people be transported to the borders of our woods and settlements, in the month of May, about half an hour before sunrise, such a ravishing concert would greet their ears as they have no conception of.

Rice Bunting. This is the Boblink of the eastern and northern states, and the Rice and Reed-bird of Pennsylvania and the southern states. Though small in size, he is not so in consequence; his coming is hailed by the sportsman with pleasure; while the careful planter looks upon him as a devouring scourge, and worse than a plague of locusts. Three good qualities, however, entitle him to our notice, particularly as these three are rarely found in the same individual— his plumage is beautiful, his song highly musical, and his flesh excellent. In the Fall, the Reed-birds resort, in prodigious numbers, to the shores of our large rivers, where grow the *Zizania aquatica*, or Wild oats, on the seeds of which they feed, and soon become excessively fat. They are said to equal the far famed *Ortolan* of Europe.

Cow Bunting. The most remarkable trait in the character of this species, is the unaccountable practice it has of dropping its eggs into the nests of other birds, instead of building and hatching for itself; and thus entirely abandoning its progeny to the care and mercy of strangers. More than two thousand years ago it was well known that the Cuckoo of Europe never built herself a nest, but dropped her eggs in the nests of other birds; but among the thousands of different species that spread over that and other parts of the globe, no other instance of the same uniform habit has been found to exist, until discovered in the bird now before us. The Cow-bird generally lays but one egg in one place, though instances have been known of one nest containing two of her eggs.

The *Scarlet Tanager* is perhaps the most showy foreigner of all those that regularly visit us from the torrid regions of the south. He is drest in the richest scarlet with wings and tail of a deep black. On or about the first of May he makes his appearance in Pennsylvania. He rarely approaches the habitations of man, unless perhaps to the orchard, where he sometimes builds, or to the cherry trees in search of fruit. The depth of the woods is his favourite abode. This species builds its nest on the horizontal branch of a tree; the eggs are three in number, of a dull blue, spotted with brown or purple.

Among all the birds that inhabit our forests, there is none that strikes the eye of the stranger, or even a native, with so much brilliancy as this. Seen among the green leaves, with the light falling strongly on his plumage, he really appears beautiful. If he has little of melody in his notes to charm us, he has nothing in them to disgust. His manners are modest, easy and inoffensive. He commits no depredations on the property of the husbandman; but rather benefits him by the daily destruction of many noxious insects. He is a striking ornament to our rural scenery, and none of the the meanest of our rural songsters. Such being the true traits of his character, we shall always with pleasure welcome this beautiful, inoffensive stranger, to our orchards, groves and forests.

Pewee Flycatcher. This well-known bird is one of our earliest spring visitants, arriving in Pennsylvania about the first week in March, and continuing with us until October. It begins to build about the twentieth of March, on some projecting part under a bridge—in a cave—in an open well, five or six feet down—under a shed—in a spring house, and such like places: the eggs are five, pure white, with two or three dots of red near the great end. These birds sometimes rear three broods in one season.

The notes of the Pewee, like those of the Blue-bird, are pleasing, not for any melody they contain, but from the ideas of spring and returning verdure, with all the sweets of this lovely season, which are associated with his simple but lively ditty. Towards the middle

of June he becomes nearly silent; and late in the Fall he gives us a
few farewell and melancholy repetitions, that recall past imagery, and
make the decayed and withered face of nature appear still more
melancholy

Warbling Flycatcher. This sweet little warbler arrives in Pennsylvania about the middle of April, and inhabits the thick foliage of
orchards and high trees: its voice is soft, tender and soothing, and its
notes flow in an easy, continued strain that is extremely pleasing. It
is often heard among the weeping willows and lombardy poplars
of our cities; is rarely observed in the woods, but seems particularly
attached to the society of man.

Blue-bird. The pleasing manners and sociable disposition of this
little bird entitle him to particular notice. As one of the first mes-
sengers of spring, bringing the charming tidings to our very doors,
he bears his own recommendation always along with him,, and meets
with a hearty welcome from every body. The usual spring and summer song of the Blue-bird is a soft, agreeable and oft-repeated warble,
uttered with open, quivering wings, and is extremely pleasing. In
his motions and general character he has great resemblance to the
Robin Red-breast of Britain; and had he the brown olive of that
bird, instead of his own blue, he could scarcely be distinguishable from
him. Like him he is known to almost every child; and shews as
much confidence in man, by associating with him in summer, as the
other by his familiarity in winter. His society is courted by the
inhabitants of the city and country, and few neglect to provide for
him a snug little dwelling. For this favour he more than repays
them by the cheerfulness of his song, and the multitudes of injurious
insects which he daily destroys. In the month of October, his song
changes to a single plaintive note, as he passes over the many-
coloured woods; and its melancholy air recalls to our minds the
approaching decay of the face of nature. Even after the trees are
stript of their leaves, he still lingers over his native fields, as if loth
to leave them. About the middle or end of November, few or none of
these birds are seen; but with every return of mild and open weather,
we hear their plaintive note amidst the fields, or in the air, seeming
to deplore the devastations of Winter. Indeed the Blue-bird appears
scarcely ever totally to forsake us; but to follow fair weather through
all its journeyings till the return of spring.

House Wren. This well known and familiar bird arrives in Pennsylvania about the middle of April; and about the eighth of May it
begins to build its nest, sometimes in the wooden cornice under the
eaves, or in a hollow cherry tree; but most commonly in small boxes,
in or near the garden, to which it is extremely partial, for the great
number of caterpillars and other larvæ which are there found. The
immense number of insects which this social little bird removes from
the garden and fruit trees, ought to endear him to every cultivator,
even if he had nothing else to recommend him; but his notes, loud,
sprightly, tremulous, and repeated every few seconds with great
animation, are extremely agreeable. The eggs of this species are
from six to nine in number, of a red purplish flesh colour. They
generally raise two broods in a season: the first about the beginning
of June, the second in July.

Winter Wren. This species, in some respects, resembles the
foregoing, and is by the generality of common observers supposed to
be the same but it is quite a different bird. It visits us from the

north in the month of October, sometimes remaining with us all the
winter, and is always observed early in the spring, on the route back
to its breeding place. During his residence here he frequents the
projecting banks of creeks, old roots, decayed logs; he approaches
the farm house; rambles about the wood-pile, creeping among the
interstices like a mouse. He even ventures into our cities, and is
often observed in company with the Snow-birds and winter Sparrows
that frequent our gardens. It is not yet known whither this species
retires to breed.

The *Purple Martin* is a general inhabitant of the United States,
and a particular favourite wherever he takes up his abode. His
summer residence is universally among the habitations of man; who,
having no interest in his destruction, and deriving considerable advantage as well as amusement from his company, is generally his
friend and protector. Wherever he comes, he finds some hospitable
retreat fitted up for his accommodation and that of his young.

The Purple Martin, like the King-bird, is the terror of Crows,
Hawks and Eagles. These he attacks whenever they make their
appearance, and with such vigor and rapidity, that they instantly
have recourse to flight. Our farmers would do well to provide suitable boxes for this noble bird, who will keep at a respectful distance
all those winged plunderers who are unceasingly on the watch for an
opportunity to regale themselves upon the poultry. The Martins
have young but once in a season; and the male does not attain to his
perfect plumage until the third or fourth year.

Barn Swallow. There are but few persons in the United States
unacquainted with this gay, innocent and active little bird. Indeed
the whole tribe are so distinguished from the rest of small birds by
their sweeping rapidity of flight, their peculiar aerial evolutions of
wing, over our fields and rivers, and through our very streets, from
morning to night, that the light of heaven itself, the sky, the trees, or
any other common objects of nature, are not better known than the
Swallows. We welcome their first appearance with delight, as the
faithful harbingers and companions of flowery spring, and ruddy
summer; and when, after a long, frost-bound and boisterous Winter,
we hear it announced, that "*The Swallows are come!*" what a train
of charming ideas are associated with the simple tidings!

It has been long asserted, and the doctrine of torpidity has had many
supporters, that the Swallows winter in the mud, at the bottom of
lakes and mill-ponds. That the ignorant should believe in such
absurdities, is not surprising, but that men of intelligence and science
should for a moment indulge the preposterous idea, excites our
astonishment in no ordinary degree. The Geese, the Ducks, the Cat-
bird, and even the Wren which creeps about our outhouses in summer like a mouse, are all acknowledged to be migratory, and to pass
to southern regions at the approach of Winter:—the Swallows alone,
on whom Heaven has conferred superior powers of wing, must sink
in torpidity at the bottom of our rivers, or doze all winter in the
caverns of the earth! Is not this true, ye *wise* men of Europe and
America, who have published so many *credible* narratives on this
subject? Is the organization of a Swallow less delicate than that of
a man? Can a bird, whose vital functions are destroyed by a short
privation of pure air, and its usual food, sustain, for six months, a
situation where the most robust man would perish in a few hours or
moments? Away with such absurdities!—They are unworthy of a

serious refutation.—It has at length been ascertained that our Swallows pass the period of Winter at Honduras, myriads of them assembling together at their roosting places, which are usually amid the rushes of the watery savannas.*

Chimney Swallow. This species is peculiarly our own; and strongly distinguished from all the rest of our swallows by its figure, flight and manners. Like all the rest of its tribe in the United States, it is migratory, arriving in Pennsylvania late in April, or early in May, and dispersing themselves over the whole country wherever there are vacant chimneys sufficiently high and convenient for their accommodation. The nest of this bird is of singular construction, being formed of very small twigs, fastened together, not with the gum of trees as is generally supposed, but with a strong adhesive glue, which is secreted by two glands, one on each side of the hind head, and mixes with the saliva. With this glue, which becomes hard as the twigs themselves, the whole nest is thickly besmeared. The nest itself is small and shallow, and attached by one side or edge to the wall, and is totally destitute of the soft lining with which the nests of the other Swallows are so plentifully supplied. The eggs are generally four, and white. They commonly have two broods in the season.

Night-hawk. This bird in Virginia, and some of the southern districts, is called a Bat; the name Night-hawk is usually given it in the middle and northern states. On the last week in April, the Night-hawk commonly makes its appearance at Philadelphia. They soon after disperse generally over the country, from the sea shore to the mountains; and are seen towards evening, in pairs, playing about, high in air, pursuing their prey—wasps, flies, beetles, and various other winged insects of the larger sort. About the middle of May the female begins to lay; the eggs are placed on the bare ground, are commonly two, of a dirty bluish white, and marked with innumerable touches of dark olive brown.

The Night-hawk is a bird of strong and vigorous flight, and of large volume of wing. It often visits the city, darting and squeaking over the streets at a great height, and diving perpendicularly with a loud booming sound, very much resembling that produced by blowing strongly into the bunghole of an empty hogshead. This noise is caused by the sudden expansion of his capacious mouth, while he passes through the air. The female never precipitates herself in the manner of the male.

Whip-poor-will. This is a singular and very celebrated species, universally noted over the greater part of the United States for the loud reiterations of his favourite call in Spring; and yet personally he is but little known, most people being unable to distinguish this from the preceding species; and some insisting that they are the same. We must refer the reader to Mr. Wilson's history of this bird, wherein it appears that there has been strange confusion among naturalists with respect to our three species of the Caprimulgus genus, and in which it is satisfactorily shewn that this is a distinct species.

The *Chuck-will's-widow* is rarely found to the north of James River, in Virginia, on the sea-board, or of Nashville, in the state of Tennessee, in the interior. It arrives on the coast of Georgia about the middle of March, and in Virginia early in April. It commences its singular

*Henderson's Honduras, p. 119.

call generally in the evening, soon after sunset, and continues it, with short occasional interruptions, for several hours. Towards morning these repetitions are renewed, and continue until dawn has fairly appeared. During the day it is altogether silent. This call instantly attracts the attention of a stranger, and is strikingly different from that of the Whip-poor-will. In sound and articulation it seems plainly to express the words which have been applied to it, *Chuck-will's-widow*, pronouncing each syllable leisurely and distinctly, putting the principal emphasis on the last word. In a still evening this bird may be heard at the distance of nearly a mile, the tones of its voice being stronger and more full than those of the Whip-poor-will, who utters his with much greater rapidity.

This singular genus of birds, formed to subsist on the superabundance of nocturnal insects, are exactly and surprisingly fitted to their peculiar mode of life. Their flight is low, to accommodate itself to their prey; silent, that they may be the better concealed, and sweep upon it unawares; their sight most acute in the dusk, when such insects are abroad; their evolutions something like those of the Bat, quick and sudden; their mouths capable of prodigious expansion, to seize with more certainty, and furnished with long branching hairs or bristles, *serving as palisadoes to secure what comes between them. Reposing so much during the heats of day, they are much infested with vermin, particularly about the head, and and are provided with a comb on the inner edge of the middle claw, with which they are often employed in ridding themselves of these pests.

The *Passenger* or *Wild Pigeon* inhabits a wide and extensive region of North America, on this side of the Rocky Mountains, beyond which to the westward, we have not heard of their having been seen. They abound in the country round Hudson's Bay; spread over the whole of Canada; were seen by Lewis and Clark's party, near the Great Falls of the Missouri; were also met with in the interior of Louisiana by Pike; and extend their range as far south as the gulf of Mexico; occasionally visiting or breeding in almost every quarter of the United States.

But the most remarkable characteristic of these birds is their associating together, both in their migrations, and also during the period of incubation, in such prodigious numbers as almost to surpass belief; and which has no parallel among any other of the feathered tribes with which naturalists are acquainted.† I have witnessed these migrations in the Genesee country—often in Pennsylvania, and also in various parts of Virginia, with amazement; but all that I had then seen of them were mere straggling parties, when compared with the congregated millions which I have since beheld in our western forests, in the States of Ohio, Kentucky and the Indiana territory. These fertile and extensive regions abound with the nutritious beech nut which constitutes the chief food of the Wild Pigeon. In seasons when these nuts are abundant, corresponding multitudes of Pigeons may be confidently expected. It sometimes happens that having consumed the whole produce of the Beech trees in an extensive district, they discover another at the distance, perhaps, of sixty or eighty miles, to which they regularly repair every morning, and return as

*The Night-Hawk is an exception to some of these remarks, its flight being high, and its mouth destitute of the bristles.
†The reader will observe that Mr. Wilson is the narrator.

regularly in the course of the day, or in the evening, to their place of general rendezvous, or as it is usally called, the *roosting place*. These roosting places are always in the woods, and sometimes occupy a large extent of forest. When they have frequented one of these places for some time, the appearance it exhibits is surprising. The ground is covered to the depth of several inches with their dung; all the tender grass and underwood destroyed: the surface strewed with large limbs of trees broken down by the weight of the birds clustering one above another; and the trees themselves, for thousands of acres, killed as completely as if girdled with an axe. The marks of this desolation remain for many years on the spot: and numerous places could be pointed out where for several years after scarce a single vegetable made its appearance.

The *breeding place* differs from the roosting place in its greater extent. In the western countries above mentioned, these are generally in beech woods, and often extend in nearly a straight line across the country for a great way. Not far from Shelbyville, in the state of Kentucky, a few years ago, there was one of these breeding places, which stretched through the woods in nearly a north and south direction; was several miles in breadth, and said to be upwards of *forty* miles long. In this tract almost every tree was furnished with nests, wherever the branches could accommodate them. As soon as the young were fully grown, and before they left the nests, numerous parties of the inhabitants came with wagons, axes, beds, cooking utensils, and encamped for several days at this immense nursery. Several of them informed me, that the noise in the woods was so great as to terrify their horses, and that it was difficult for one person to hear another speak, without bawling in his ear. The ground was strewed with broken limbs of trees, eggs and squabs, which had been precipitated from above, and on which herds of hogs were fattening. Hawks, Vultures and Eagles were sailing about in great numbers, and seizing the squabs from their nests at pleasure; while from twenty feet upwards to the tops of the trees the view through the woods presented a perpetual tumult of crowding and fluttering multitudes of Pigeons, their wings roaring like thunder, mingled with the frequent crash of falling timber: for now the axemen were at work cutting down those trees that seemed to be most crowded with nests, and contrived to fell them in such a manner, that in their descent they might bring down several others; by which means the falling of one large tree sometimes produced two hundred squabs, little inferior in size to the old Pigeons, and almost one mass of fat. On some single trees upwards of one hundred nests were found, each containing one young only, a circumstance in the history of this bird not generally known to naturalists. It was dangerous to walk under these flying and fluttering millions, from the frequent fall of large branches, broken down by the weight of the multitudes above, and which in their descent often destroyed numbers of the birds themselves; while the clothes of those engaged in traversing the woods were completely covered with the excrements of the Pigeons.

I passed for several miles through this same breeding place, where every tree was spotted with nests, the remains of those above described. In many instances I counted upwards of ninety nests on a single tree; but the Pigeons had abandoned this place for another, sixty or eighty miles off toward Green river, where they were said at that time to be equally numerous.* From the great numbers that were constantly passing overhead to or from that quarter, I had no doubt of the truth of this statement. The mast had been chiefly consumed in Kentucky, and the Pigeons, every morning a little before sunrise, set out for Indiana territory, the nearest part of which was about sixty miles distant. Many of these returned before ten o'clock, and the great body generally appeared a little after noon. I had left the public road to visit the remains of the breeding place near Shelbyville, and was traversing the woods with my gun, on my way to Frankfort, when about one o'clock the Pigeons, which I had observed flying the greater part of the morning northerly, began to return in such immense numbers as I never before had witnessed. Coming to an opening by the side of a creek called the Benson, where I had a more uninterrupted view, I was astonished at their appearance. They were flying with great steadiness and rapidity, at a height beyond gunshot, in several strata deep, and very compact. From right to left, as far as the eye could reach, the breadth of this vast procession extended, seeming every where equally crowded. Curious to determine how long this appearance would continue, I took out my watch to note the time, and sat down to observe them. I continued there for more than an hour, but instead of a diminution of this prodigious procession, it seemed rather to increase both in numbers and rapidity; and anxious to reach Frankfort before night, I rose and went on. About four o'clock in the afternoon I crossed the Kentucky river, at the town of Frankfort, at which time the living torrent above my head seemed as numerous and as extensive as ever. Long after this I observed them in large bodies that continued to pass for six or eight minutes, and these again were followed by other detached bodies, all moving in the same south-east direction, till after six in the evening The great breadth of front which this mighty multitude preserved would seem to intimate a corresponding breadth of their breeding place, which by several gentlemen who had lately passed through part of it, was stated to me at several miles.

The vast quantity of mast which these multitudes consume, is a serious loss to the bears, pigs, squirrels and other dependants on the fruits of the forests. I have taken from the crop of a single Wild Pigeon, a good handful of the kernels of beech nuts, intermixed with acorns and chestnuts. To form a rough estimate of the daily consumption of one of these immense flocks, let us first attempt to calculate the numbers of that above mentioned as seen in passing between Frankfort and the Indiana territory. If we suppose this column to have been one mile in breadth, (and I believe it to have been much more) and that it moved at the rate of one mile in a minute, four hours, the time it continued passing, would make its whole length two hundred and forty miles. Again, supposing that each square yard of this moving body comprehended three Pigeons; the square yards in the whole space multiplied by three, would give *two thousand two hundred and thirty millions, two hundred and seventy-two thousand Pigeons.* An almost inconceivable multitude, and yet probably far below the actual amount. Computing each of these to consume half a pint of mast daily, the whole quantity at this rate would equal *seventeen millions, four hundred and twenty-four thousand*

*This was in the year 1810. Mr Wilson was then on his journey to New Orleans.

bushels per day. Heaven has wisely and graciously given to these birds rapidity of flight, and a disposition to range over vast uncultivated tracts of the earth; otherwise they must have perished in the districts where they resided, or devoured, the whole productions of agriculture, as well as those of the forests.

Every Spring, as well as Fall, more or less of these birds are seen in the neighborhood of Philadelphia, and particularly in New Jersey; but it is only once in several years that they appear in very great bodies; and this commonly when the snows are heavy to the north, the winter here more than usually mild, and forest nuts abundant.

Turtle Dove. This is a favourite bird with all those who love to wander among our woods in spring, and listen to their varied harmony. They will hear many a singular and sprightly performer, but none so mournful as this. The hopeless wo of confirmed sorrow swelling the heart of female innocence itself, could not assume tones more sad, more tender and affecting. Its notes are four: the first is somewhat the highest and preparatory, seeming to be uttered with an inspiration of the breadth, as if the afflicted creature were just recovering its voice for the last convulsive sobs of distress; this is followed by three long, deep and mournful moanings, that no person of sensibility can listen to without sympathy There is, however, nothing of real distress in all this: quite the reverse. The bird who utters it wantons by the side of his beloved partner, or invites her by his call to some favourite and shady retreat; it is the voice of love, of faithful connubial affection, for which the whole family of Doves are so celebrated. The flesh of this bird is considered superior to that of the Wild Pigeon: but its seeming confidence in man, the tenderness of its notes, and the innocency attached to its character, are with many its security and protection; with others, however, the tenderness of its *flesh*, and the sport of shooting, overcome all other considerations. The Turtle Dove lays two pure white eggs. The male and female unite in feeding the young, and they have rarely more than two broods in the same season.

The *Ground Dove* is a native of North and South Carolina, Georgia, Louisiana, Florida, Mexico, and the West Indies. In the last it is frequently kept in cages; is esteemed excellent for the table, and honoured by the French planters with the name of Ortolan. It is a bird of passage, retiring to the islands, and to the more southerly parts of the continent, on the approach of winter, and returning to its former haunts early in April. It is of a more slender and delicate form, and less able to bear the rigours of cold, than either of the two preceding species, both of which are found in the northern region of Canada as well as in the genial climate of Florida.

Wild Turkey. It was to America that the Europeans were indebted for the original stock of the domestic Turkey; a bird which has been spread over the greater part of the civilized world, and which contributes largely to the gratifications of life. Wild Turkies were formerly numerous in Pennsylvania; but population has driven to the westward these valuable birds; and at present what few remain are found chiefly in the Allegany ridge, and the unsettled parts to the west. In the states bordering on the Ohio and the Mississippi they are yet found in considerable numbers, though much decreased of late years, and ere long they will even there be very rare. In the Floridas and Louisiana they are numerous, particularly in the latter, but it does not appear that they extend much farther than the Big-bend of the Missouri. The Indians who accompanied Lewis and Clark's party on their return from the Pacific, knew nothing of this bird. The Turkey in its wild state becomes much larger, and its flesh is in greater esteem, than when it is domesticated. It is not unusual to kill them weighing upwards of thirty pounds.

Ruffed Grous. This is the *Partridge* of the eastern states, and the *Pheasant* of Pennsylvania and the southern districts. It is known in almost every quarter of the United States, and appears to inhabit a very extensive range of country. Its favourite places of resort are high mountains, covered with the Balsam pine, hemlock, and such like evergreens. Unlike the Pinnated Grous, it always prefers the woods: is seldom or never found in open plains; but loves the pine-sheltered declivities of mountains near streams of water. The manners of the Pheasant are solitary; they are seldom found in coveys of more than four or five together, and more usually in pairs or singly. The *drumming*, as it is usually called, is a singularity of this species. This is performed by the male alone. The bird standing on an old prostrate log, lowers his wings, erects his expanded tail, contracts his throat, elevates the two tufts of feathers on his neck, and inflates his whole body something in the manner of the Turkey-cock, strutting and wheeling about with great stateliness. After a few manoeuvres of this kind, he begins to strike his body with his stiffened wings in short and quick strokes: these are at first slow and distinct, but gradually increase in rapidity till they run into each other, resembling the rumbling sound of very distant thunder, dying away gradually on the ear. After a few minutes pause this is repeated: and in a calm day it may be heard nearly half a mile off. This drumming is most common in the spring, and is the call of the cock to his favourite female.

The Ruffed Grous hatches in May: the eggs are from nine to fifteen in number, of a brownish white, and nearly as large as those of a pullet. The young leave the nest as soon as hatched, and are directed by the cluck of the mother, very much in the manner of the common hen. These birds are very common in the Philadelphia markets and their flesh is much esteemed.

Pinnated Grous. This species in the middle states is simply termed Grous;* and the epithet *pinnated* has been applied to it by naturalists from the circumstance of the neck of the male being furnished with supplemental wings, each composed of eighteen feathers, which the bird can raise or depress at pleasure. He has another peculiarity which naturalists appear to have overlooked: This is two bags of yellow skin, one on each side of the neck, which, when the bird is at rest, hang in loose wrinkled folds; but when these bags are inflated, in breeding time, they are equal in size and very much resemble in color, a middle sized, fully ripe orange. By means of this curious apparatus, which is very observable several hundred yards off, he is enabled to produce the extraordinary sound, which is called *bumming*; this is uttered only in the season of love, and it is for the purpose of attracting the female.

This rare bird, though an inhabitant of different and very distant districts of North America, is extremely particular in selecting his place of residence: pitching only upon those tracts whose features and productions correspond with his modes of life; and avoiding immense

*In some places the common people call them Heath-hens.

intermediate regions that he never visits. Accordingly we find these
birds on the Grous plains of New Jersey, as well as on the Brushy
plains of Long Island—among the pines and shrub-oaks of Pocano,
in Northampton county, Pennsylvania—over the whole extent of the
Barrens of Kentucky; on the luxuriant plains and prairies of the
Indiana territory and Louisiana. In all these places preserving the
same singular habits. It is much to be regretted that attempts to
domesticate this exquisite bird have hitherto failed of success. There
can be little doubt that domestication may be affected if proper means
are employed; and we may add that the object is highly worthy of
further experiments.

The *Quail* or *Partridge* is a general inhabitant of North America,
from the northern parts of Canada and Nova Scotia, in which latter
place it is said to be migratory, to the extremity of the peninsula
of Florida. They are numerous in Louisiana; and Captain Henderson mentions them as being plenty near the Balize at the Bay of Honduras. Where they are not too much persecuted by the sportsmen,
they become almost half domesticated; approach the barn, particularly in winter, and sometimes mix with the poultry to glean up a
subsistence. The Partridge, like all the rest of the gallinaceous
order, flies with a loud whirring sound, occasioned by the shortness,
concavity and rapid motion of its wings, and the comparative weight
of its body. The flesh of this bird is peculiarly white, tender and
delicate; though it is dry, and not as much esteemed as that of the
Pheasant.

Roseate Spoonbill. This stately and elegant bird inhabits the sea
shores of America from Brazil to Georgia. It wades about in quest
of shell fish, marine insects, small crabs and fish. In pursuit of these
it occasionally swims and dives.

The *Whooping Crane* is the tallest and most stately species of all
the feathered tribes of the United States. It is the watchful inhabitant of extensive salt marshes, desolate swamps, and open morasses,
in the neighborhood of the sea. Its migrations are regular and of
the most extensive kind, reaching from the shores and inundated
tracts of South America to the arctic circle. In these immense periodical journeys they pass at such a prodigious height in the air as
to be seldom observed. They have, however, their resting stages
on the route to and from their usual breeding places, the regions of
the north. A few sometimes make their appearance in the marshes
of Cape May, in December, and on Egg island in the Delaware Bay,
where they are known by the name of *Storks.* Some linger in these
marshes the whole winter, setting out for the north about the breaking up of the ice. During their stay they wander along the marsh
and muddy flats of the shore in search of marine worms, moving occasionally from place to place, with a low and heavy flight, a little
above the surface; and have at such times a very formidable appearance. Now and then they utter a loud, clear and piercing cry, which
may be heard at the distance of two miles. They have also various
modulations of this singular note, from the peculiarity of which they
derive their name.

Least Bittern. This is the smallest known species of the whole
tribe of Herons. It is commonly found in fresh water meadows, and
rarely visits the salt marshes. When alarmed it seldom flies far, but
takes shelter among the reeds or long grass. In the autumn this

bird becomes very fat, and is then excellent eating, little inferior to a Snipe or Rail.

The *Long-billed Curlew* appears in the salt marshes of New Jersey about the middle of May, on its way to the north; and in September, on its return from its breeding place. Their food consists chiefly of small crabs, which they are very dexterous at probing for, and pulling out of the holes, with their long bills: they also feed on those small sea snails so abundant in the marshes, and on various worms and insects. They are likewise fond of bramble berries, frequenting the fields and uplands in search of this fruit, on which they get very fat, and are then tender and good eating, altogether free from the sedgy taste with which their flesh is usually tainted while they feed in the salt marshes.

The *Esquimaux Curlew*, or as it is called by our gunners on the coast, the *Short-billed Curlew*, arrives in large flocks on the coast of New Jersey early in May from the south; frequents the salt marshes, muddy shores and inlets, feeding on small worms and minute shell fish. They fly high and with great rapidity. In the month of June, while the dewberries are ripe, these birds sometimes frequent the fields in company with the Long-billed kind, where brambles abound, soon get very fat, and are at that time excellent eating. In the early part of spring, and indeed during the whole time that they frequent the marshes, they are much less esteemed for the table. They retire to the north to breed.

Red-breasted Snipe. This bird has a considerable resemblance to the common or *English Snipe*, not only in its general form, size and colours, but likewise in the excellence of its flesh, which is in high estimation. It differs, however, greatly from the common Snipe in its manners, and in many other peculiarities. It arrives on the coast of New Jersey early in April, is seldom or never seen inland; early in May it proceeds to the north to breed, and returns by the latter part of July. During its stay here it flies in flocks, sometimes very high, and has then a loud and shrill whistle, making many evolutions over the marshes; forming, dividing and reuniting. They sometimes settle in such numbers, and so close together, that upwards of eighty have been shot at one discharge of a musquet.

Semipalmated Snipe. This is one of the most noisy and noted birds that inhabit our salt marshes in summer. Its common name is the *Willet*, by which appellation it is universally known along the shores of New York, New Jersey, Delaware and Maryland, in all of which places it breeds in great numbers. The Willet is peculiar to America. It arrives from the south, on the shores of the middle states, about the twentieth of April; and from that time to the last of July its loud and shrill reiterations of *Pill-will-willet*, resound, almost incessantly, along the marshes; and may be distinctly heard at the distance of more than a half a mile. About the twentieth of May the Willets begin to lay; the eggs are usually four in number, very thick at the great end, and tapering to a narrower point at the other than those of the common hen; they are excellent eating. Towards the fall, when these birds associate in large flocks, they become extremely fat, and are then accounted a great delicacy.

Common Snipe. This bird is well known to our sportsmen; and, if not the same, has a very near resemblance to the common Snipe of Britain. It is usually known by the name of the *English Snipe*, to

distinguish it from the Woodcock, and others of the same genus. It
arrives in Pennsylvania about the tenth of March, and remains in the
low grounds for several weeks; the greater part then move off to the
north, and to the higher inland districts, to breed. A few are occasionally found, and consequently breed, in our low marshes during
the summer. When they first arrive they are usually lean; but when
in good order they are excellent eating. These birds are not found in
the salt marshes of the coast, except on their borders, where there
happen to be fresh water springs; consequently their flesh is never
sedgy. In places where they are not sought after by epicures and
sportsmen, they become tame, excessively fat, and are then an exquisite morsel.

Woodcock. This bird, like the preceding, is universally known to
our sportsmen. It arrives in Pennsylvania early in March, sometimes
sooner. During the day they keep to the woods and thickets, and at
the approach of evening seek the springs, and open watery places to
feed in. They soon disperse themselves over the country to breed.
About the beginning of July, particularly in long continued hot weather, they descend to the marshy shores of our large rivers, their
favourite springs and watery recesses inland being chiefly dried up.

To the former of these retreats they are pursued by the merciless
sportsman, flushed by dogs, and shot down in considerable numbers.
This species of amusement, when eagerly followed, is still more
labourious and fatiguing than that of Snipe-shooting; and from the
nature of the ground, or cripple as it is usually called, viz. deep mire,
intersected with old logs which are covered and hid from sight by
high reeds, weeds and alder bushes, the best dogs are soon tired
out. The Woodcock usually begins to lay in April. The nest is
placed on the ground, in a retired part of a field, or the woods, frequently at the root of an old stump, and generally near a cripple. The
female lays four, sometimes five, eggs, of a dun clay colour, thickly
marked with spots of brown, and interspersed with others of a very
pale purple. In a moderate season the Woodcock has been known to
lay in February.

This bird, in its general figure and manner, greatly resembles the
Woodcock of Europe, but it is considerably less, is differently marked below, and is a distinct species. Its food consists of various larvæ
and other aquatic worms, for which during the evening it is almost
continually turning over the leaves with its bill, or searching in the
bogs. Its flesh is highly prized. The flight of the Woodcock is slow,
and he is easily shot. The notion that there are two species of Woodcock in this country probably originated from the great difference of
size between the male and female, the latter being considerably the
larger.

Red-breasted Sandpiper. Birds of the *Sandpiper* genus are not distinguished, by common observers, from the *Snipes,* so nearly do they
resemble each other. Naturalists, however, have given us the characteristic designations of each, which convince us of the importance
of system in our inquiries into the operations of Nature. Yet it must
be confessed that we sometimes meet with species, the generic characters of which are so equivocal, that we are not a little confounded
in our endeavours to class them. Hence the necessity of studying
living nature in order to determine in a case ivnolving doubt or uncer-
tainty. The bird before us from its general appearance would be

called a Snipe, but when we take into view its habits, and the length of its bill, we are at no loss to discover its relationship to the family of the *Tringæ* or Sandpipers.

The common name of this species, on our coast, is the *Gray-back*; and among the gunners it is a particular favourite, being generally a plump, tender and excellent bird for the table; and, consequently, bringing a good price in market. The Gray-backs do not breed on the shores of the middle states. Their first appearance is early in May. They remain a few weeks, and disappear until October. They usually keep in small flocks, and alight in a close body together on the sand flats, where they search for the small bivalve shells. They do not run about in the water as much as some others, nor with the same rapidity, but appear more tranquil and deliberate. In the month of November they retire to the south.

Spotted Sandpiper. This very common species arrives in Pennsylvania about the twentieth of April, tracing the courses of our creeks and streams towards the interior. It is remarkable for perpetually wagging the tail; for whether running on the ground, or on the fences, along the rails, or in the water, this motion seems continual. About the middle of May they resort to the adjoining corn fields to breed; the eggs are four, and large in proportion to the size of the bird. The young run as soon as freed from the shell. The flight of the Spotted Sandpiper is usually low. It skims along the surface of the water, while it utters its rapid notes of *weet weet weet*, seldom steering in a direct line up or down the river, but making a long circuitous sweep, stretching a great way out, and gradually bending in again to the shore.

The *Purre* is one of the most numerous of our *Strand-birds*, or *Sand Snipes*, as they are usually called, that frequent the sandy beach, on the frontiers of the ocean. They trace the flowing and recession of the waves with great nimbleness, wading and searching among the loosened particles for their favourite food, which is a small thin oval bivalve shell-fish, of a white or pearl colour, and not larger than the seed of an apple. During the latter part of summer and autumn, these minute shell-fish constitute the food of almost all those busy flocks that run with such activity along the sands, among the flowing and retreating waves. It is amusing to observe with what adroitness they follow and elude the tumbling surf, while at the same time they seem wholly intent on collecting their food. These birds, in conjunction with several others, sometimes collect together in such numbers, as to seem, at a distance, a cloud of thick smoke, varying in form and appearance every instant, while it performs its evolutions in air. As this cloud descends and courses along the shores of the ocean, with great rapidity, in a kind of serpentine flight, alternately throwing its dark and white colours to the eye, it forms a very grand and interesting appearance. At such times the gunners make prodigious slaughter among them; while, as the showers of their companions fall, the whole body often alight, or descend to the surface with them, till the sportsman is completely satiated with destruction. All the Strand-birds become very fat, and are good eating.

Black-bellied Plover. This bird is known in some parts of the country by the name of the large *Whistling Field Plover*. It generally makes its first appearance in Pennsylvania late in April; frequents the countries towards the mountains; seems particularly attached to newly ploughed fields, where it forms its nests of a few slight materials; lays four eggs, and has frequently two broods in the same season. They feed on worms, grubs, winged insects, and various kinds of berries, particularly dewberries, and are considered excellent eating. About the beginning of September they abound on the plains of Long Island, and afford considerable amusement to the *cockney* sportsmen, who generally make their approaches to the birds by means of *wagons*. They have a loud whistling note; often fly at a great height; and are called by many gunners along the coast the Black-bellied Kildeer.

Golden Plover. This beautiful species visits the coast of New York and New Jersey in spring and autumn; but does not, as far as has been discovered, breed in any part of the United States. Although they are occasionally found along our coast from Georgia to Maine, yet they are no where numerous; and we have never met with them in the interior.

Kildeer Plover. This restless and noisy bird is known to almost every inhabitant of the United States, being a common and pretty constant resident. During the severity of winter, when snow covers the ground, it retreats to the seashore, where it is found at all seasons: but no sooner has the ice of the rivers broken up, than its shrill notes are again heard, either roaming about high in air, tracing the shore of the river, or running amidst the watery flats and meadows. Nothing can exceed the alarm and anxiety of these birds during the breeding season. Their cries of *kildeer, kildeer,* as they winnow the air over head, dive and course around you, or run along the ground counterfeiting lameness, are shrill and incessant. They lay usually four eggs, of a yellowish clay colour, thickly marked with blotches of black.

Pied Oyster-catcher. This singular species, although no where numerous, inhabits almost every sea shore, both on the new and the old continent, but is never found inland. It is the only one of its genus hitherto discovered. It frequents the sandy sea beach of New Jersey, and other parts of our Atlantic coast, in summer, in small parties of two or three pairs together. They are extremely shy, and except about the season of breeding, will seldom permit a person to approach within gunshot. They walk along the shore in a watchful stately manner, at times probing it with their long wedge-like bills in search of small shell-fish. The small crabs called *Fiddlers,* that burrow in the mud at the bottom of inlets, are frequently the prey of the Oyster-catcher; as are muscles, spout-fish, and a variety of other shell-fish and sea insects with which those shores abound. The principal food, however, of this bird, according to European writers, and that from which it derives its name, is the *Oyster,* which it is said to watch for, and snatch suddenly from the shells, whenever it surprises them sufficiently open. For this purpose the form of its bill seems very fitly calculated. Yet the truth of these accounts is doubted by the inhabitants of Egg-harbour, and other parts of our coast, who positively assert that it never frequents oyster-beds, but confines itself almost solely to the sands; and this opinion I am inclined to believe correct, having myself uniformly found these birds on the smooth beach bordering the ocean, and on the higher dry and level sands, just beyond the reach of the summer tides. On this last situation, where the dry flats are thickly interspersed with drifted shells, they lay three eggs in a slight hollow; the young are hatched about the twenty-fifth of May. This bird is the *Sea-pie* of navigators.

Clapper Rail. This is a very numerous and well known species, inhabiting our whole Atlantic coast from New England to Florida. It is designated by different names, such as the Mud-hen, Meadow-clapper, Big Rail, &c. Though occasionally found along the swampy shores and tide waters of our large rivers, yet its principal residence is in the salt marshes. It is a bird of passage, arriving on the coast of New Jersey about the twentieth of April, and retiring again late in September. The shores of New Jersey, within the beach, seem to be the favourite breeding places of these birds, as they are there acknowledged to be more than double the number of all other marsh fowl. These shores consist of an immense extent of flat marsh, covered with a coarse reedy grass, and occasionally overflowed by the sea, by which it is cut up into innumerable islands. The Mud-hen soon announces its arrival in the marshes, by its loud, harsh and incessant cackling, which very much resembles that of a Guinea-hen. This noise is more general during the night; and is said to be always greatest before a storm. About the twentieth of May they generally commence laying and building at the same time: the first egg being usually dropt in a slight cavity, lined with a little dry grass, which as the number of the eggs increases to their usual complement *ten*, is gradually added to, until the nest rises to the height of twelve inches or more. Over this the long salt grass is artfully arched and knit at the top, to conceal it from the view above. The eggs are excellent eating, surpassing those of the domestic hen. The height of laying is about the first of June, when the people of the neighbourhood go off to the marshes *an egging*, as it is called. So abundant are the nests of this species, and so dexterous are some persons at finding them, that one hundred dozen of eggs have been collected by one man in a day. The food of the Clapper Rail consists of small shell-fish, particularly those of the snail form, so abundant in the marshes; they also eat small crabs. Their flesh is dry, tastes sedgy, and will bear no comparison with that of the common Rail.

Common Rail or *Sora.* The natural history of the *Rail*, or as it is called in Virginia the *Sora*, and in South Carolina the *Coot*, is to the most of our sportsmen involved in profound and inexplicable mystery. It comes, they know not whence; and goes, they know not whither. No one can detect their first moment of arrival; yet all at once the reedy shores and grassy marshes of our large rivers swarm with them, thousands being sometimes found within the space of a few acres. These, when they do venture on wing, seem to fly so feebly, and in such short fluttering flights among the reeds, as to render it highly improbable to most people that they could possibly make their way over an extensive tract of country. Yet, on the first smart frost that occurs, the great body suddenly disappear.

The Rail or Sora belongs to a genus of birds of which about thirty different species are enumerated by naturalists; and these are distributed over almost every region of the habitable parts of the earth. Their general character is everywhere the same. They run swiftly, fly slowly, and usually with the legs hanging down; become extremely fat; are fond of concealment; and, wherever it is practicable, prefer running to flying.   Early in August, when the reeds along the shores of the Delaware have attained their full growth, the Rail resort to them in great numbers, to feed on the seeds of this plant, of which they, as well as the Reed-birds and several others, are immoderately fond.   On their first arrival they are generally lean, and unfit for the table; but as the seeds ripen they rapidly fatten, and from the early part of September to the last of October they are excellent, and eagerly sought after.   The usual method of shooting them in Pennsylvania, is as follows: The sportsman furnishes himself with a light bateau, and an experienced boatman, with a pole of twelve or fifteen feet long.   About an hour or two before high water they enter the reeds, and each takes his post, the sportsman standing in the bow ready for action, the pole-man on the stern seat pushing the boat steadily through the reeds.   The Rail generally spring singly, as the boat advances, at a short distance ahead, and are instantly shot down, while the boatman, keeping his eye on the spot where the bird fell, directs the bateau forward and picks up the game as the gunner is loading.   The sport continues till an hour or two after high water. Several boats are sometimes within a short distance of each other, and a perpetual cracking of musquetry prevails along the whole reedy shores of the river and islands.   In these excursions it is not uncommon for an active and expert marksman to kill from six to ten dozen Rail in a tide.   These birds, in common with many others, always migrate in the night   and hence the reason why many are at a loss to ascertain what becomes of them, when it is discovered that they have disappeared: as these observers cannot have *ocular* evidence of the migration, they still remain incredulous as to the fact. The first north-easter which takes place in the latter part of October, or beginning of November, the great body of the Rail depart: and it is then that these birds are found to be most abundant in Virginia and elsewhere to the south.   The Rail, though considered a great delicacy by many, is yet far inferior to the Snipe.

The *Purple Gallinule* is found in the southern parts of our continent.   In the state of Georgia it frequents the rice fields and marshes; it is rare, and extremely shy.   In respect to its manners, it is said to be a docile bird when tamed; to feed with the poultry, and scratch the ground with its feet like the cock and hen.   It will feed on many things, such as fruits, roots of plant and grain: will frequently stand on one leg, and lift the food to its mouth with the other, like a Parrot. The flesh is said to be exquisite in taste.

This is a most splendid bird: the head, part of the neck, throat and breast, are of a rich violet purple; the back and scapulars brownish green; the sides of the neck ultramarine; wings the same, tinged with green; the belly of a purplish black; the vent pure white; the naked crown, legs and feet are red; the bill of the same colour, tipt with yellow.

The *Coot* makes its appearance in Pennsylvania about the first of October.   Among the muddy flats and islands of the river Delaware, which are periodically overflowed and which are overgrown with the the reed or wild oats and rushes, the Coots are found.   They are not numerous, and are seldom seen, except their places of resort are covered with water: in that case they are generally found sitting on the fallen reeds, waiting for the ebbing of the tide.   Their food consists of various aquatic plants, seeds, insects and small fish.   The

Coot swims remarkably well, and, when wounded, will dive like a Duck. It is known in Pennsylvania by the name of the Mud-hen.

American Avoset. This species arrives on the coast of Cape May late in April; rears its young, and departs to the south early in October. It almost constantly frequents the shallow pools in the salt marshes; wading about, often to the belly, in search of marine worms, snails, and various insects that abound among the soft muddy bottoms of the pools. It is a shy and noisy bird; and from its perpetual clamour it is called by the inhabitants of Cape May, the *Lawyer.* The nest of this species is generally fixed in a tuft of grass, at a short distance from one of the above mentioned pools: the eggs are four in number, of a dull olive colour, marked with large irregular blotches of black.

The *Long-legged Avoset* arrives on the coast of New Jersey about the same time as the foregoing: and frequents the like situations, in the salt marshes. But they are considerably more numerous than the American Avoset. They breed in small communities: the nests of six or eight pair being generally found in the vicinity of one of the pools. The eggs are also four in number, of a dark yellowish clay colour, thickly marked with large blotches of black. These nests are often placed within fifteen or twenty yards of each other; but the greatest harmony seems to prevail among the proprietors. While the females are sitting, the males are either wading through the ponds, or roaming over the adjoining marshes; but should a person make his appearance, the whole collect together in the air, flying with their long legs extended behind them, keeping up a continual yelping of *click, click, click.* Their flight is steady and not in short sudden jerks like that of the Plover. The names by which this species is known on the coast, are Stilt or Tilt, and Long-shanks.

Red Flamingo. This is a very singular bird; and is occasionally seen on the southern frontiers of the United States; but it is more common on the peninsula of East Florida. Its flesh is esteemed pretty good meat; and the young thought by some equal to a Partridge; but the greatest dainty is the tongue, which was esteemed by the ancients an exquisite morsel.

The *Great Northern Diver* or *Loon* is migratory in Pennsylvania. It is found along the coast as well as in the interior. They are commonly seen in pairs; and procure their food, which is fish, in the deepest water of our rivers, diving after it, and continuing under for a length of time. Being a wary bird, it is seldom they are killed, eluding their pursuers by their astonishing faculty of diving. They seem averse from flying, and are but seldom seen on the wing. The Loon is said to be restless before a storm; and an experienced master of a coasting vessel informed me that he always knew when a tempest was approaching by the cry of this bird, which is very shrill, and may be heard at the distance of a mile or more.

Black Skimmer or *Sheerwater.* This truly singular fowl is the only species of its tribe hitherto discovered. Like many others, it is a bird of passage in the United States; and makes its appearance on the shores of New Jersey early in May. Its favourite haunts are low sand bars, raised above the reach of the summer tides. On such places it usually breeds; the eggs, three in number, being placed in a hollow formed in the sand, without any materials. The Sheerwaters form themselves into small societies in the breeding season, which commences early in June; and it is not unusual to find the nests of fifteen or twenty pair within the compass of half an acre. The females sit on them only during the night, or in wet and stormy weather.

The singular conformation of the bill of this bird has excited much surprise; and some writers, measuring the divine proportions of nature by their own contracted standards of conception, in the plenitude of their vanity have pronounced it to be "a lame and defective weapon." Such ignorant presumption, or rather impiety, ought to hide its head in the dust on a calm display of the peculiar construction of this singular bird, and the wisdom by which it is so admirably adapted to the purposes or mode of existence for which it was intended. The Sheerwater is formed for skimming, while on wing, the surface of the water for its food, which consists of small fish, shrimps, young fry,&c. whose usual haunts are near the shore, and towards the surface. That the lower mandible,* when dipt into and cleaving the water, might not retard the bird's way, it is thinned and sharpened like the blade of a knife; the upper mandible being at such times elevated above water, is curtailed in its length, as being less necessary, but tapering gradually to a point, that, in shutting, it may offer less opposition. To prevent inconvenience from the rushing of the water, the mouth is confined to the mere opening of the gullet, which indeed prevents mastication taking place there; but the stomach or gizzard, to which this business is solely allotted, is of uncommon hardness, strength and muscularity, far surpassing in these respects that of any other water bird with which we are acquainted. To all these is added a vast expansion of wing, to enable the bird to sail with sufficient celerity while dipping in the water. The general proportion of the length of our swiftest Hawks and Swallows, to their breadth, is as one to two; but in the present case, as there is not only the resistance of the air to overcome, but also that of the water, a still greater volume of wing is given: the Sheerwater measuring nineteen inches in length, and upwards of fourty-four in breadth. In short, whoever has attentively examined this curious apparatus, and observed the possessor with his ample wings, long bending neck, and lower mandible occasionally dipt into and ploughing the surface, and the facility with which he procures his food, cannot but consider this exercise mere playful amusement when compared with the dashing immersions of the Tern, the Gull, or the Fish Hawk, who, to the superficial observer, appear so superiorly accommodated.

Goosander. This large and handsomely marked bird belongs to a genus different from that of the *Duck*, on account of the particular form and serratures of the bill. Naturalists have denominated it *Merganser.* In this country, the birds composing this genus are generally known by the name of Fishermen, or Fisher Ducks. The Goosander is called by many the Sheldrake. This bird is a winter inhabitant of our coast and rivers. They usually associate in small parties of six or eight, and are almost continually diving in search of food. From their common habit of feeding almost entirely on fin and shell-fish, their flesh is held in little estimation, both smelling and tasting strongly of fish. Four species of the genus *Mergus* are known to inhabit the United States, of which the Goosander is the

---

* The bill of a bird is composed of two parts, termed *mandibles.*

largest and most beautiful. All these birds live chiefly on fish, and consequently are unfit for the table.

The *Widgeon* is a prettily marked and sprightly species, very common in winter along our whole coast, from Florida to Rhode Island; but most abundant in Carolina, where it frequents the rice plantations. It is the constant attendant of the *Canvass-back Duck*, by the aid of whose labour it has ingenuity enough to contrive to make a good subsistence. The Widgeon is extremely fond of the tender roots of that particular species of aquatic plant on which the Canvass-back feeds, and for which that Duck is in the constant habit of diving. The Wigeon, who never dives for food, watches the moment of the Canvass-back's rising, and before the latter has the water well off his eyes, the former snatches the delicious morsel from his mouth and makes off. On this account the Canvass-backs and Widgeons, or as they are generally called, *Bald-pates*, live in a state of perpetual contention. The flesh of this species is excellent.

Red-headed Duck. This is another common associate of the Canvass-back, frequenting the same places, and feeding on the *stems* of the same grass, the latter eating only the *roots*. Its flesh is little inferior to that of the Canvass-back; and it is often sold in our market for this last mentioned bird. The Red-headed Duck is supposed to be the *Pochard* of Europe.

Summer Duck. This most beautiful of all our Ducks has probably no superior among its whole tribe for richness and variety of colours. It is called the *Wood Duck*, from the circumstance of its breeding in hollow trees; and the *Summer Duck*, from its remaining with us during the summer. It rarely visits the sea shore, or salt marshes; its favourite haunts being the solitary, deep and muddy creeks, and mill-ponds of the interior. In Pennsylvania the female usually begins to lay late in April or early in May. Instances have been known wherein the nest was constructed of a few sticks laid in the fork of a tree; usually, however, the inside of a hollow tree that overhangs the water is selected for this purpose. The writer of this article visited an old truncated white oak, having a wide hollow six feet deep, which was tenanted by a pair of these Ducks. The eggs, thirteen in number, were the colour of old polished ivory, and lay on the rotten wood, in a slight cavity, and covered with down. When the young are hatched, the mother carries them in her bill, one by one, to the margin of the water she intends to rear them in; and when the whole are collected she launches into the element, followed by her lively and delighted little brood. This beautiful species is easily domesticated; but its flesh is not in great esteem.

Eider Duck. This species has been long celebrated in Europe for the abundance and excellence of its *down*, which for softness, warmth, lightness and elasticity, surpasses that of all other Ducks. The quantity found in one nest more than filled the crown of a hat, yet weighed no more than three quarters of an ounce; and it is asserted that three pounds of this down may be compressed into a space scarcely bigger than a man's fist, yet it is afterwards so dilatable as to fill a quilt five feet square. These birds associate in flocks, generally in deep water, diving for shell-fish, which constitute their principal food. They are numerous on the coast of Labrador, and are occasionally seen in winter as far south as the capes of the Delaware.

Dusky Duck. This species is generally known by the name of the

Black Duck, being the most common, and most numerous of all those of its tribe that frequent the salt marshes. Their principal food, on the coast, consists of those minute snail shells, so abundant in the marshes. In our fresh water marshes, where they likewise abound, they feed upon the roots and seeds of the aquatic plants and insects. The Black Ducks of the coast are generally fatter than those which frequent our fresh water rivers: but the flesh of the latter is in greater esteem, in consequence of its being free from that sedgy taste which is so remarkable in the former. Their voice resembles that of the Mallard: but their meat is greatly inferior.

Mallard. This is the original stock of the common domesticated Duck, reclaimed immemorially from a state of nature, and now become so serviceable to man. It is found in every fresh water lake and river of the United States in winter: but seldom frequents the sea shores or salt marshes. The Mallard is an excellent bird.

Muscovy Duck. It was to America that the Europeans were indebted for this noble Duck, which is in such great esteem for the table. Its domesticated descendants are scattered over those parts of the world where good eating is appreciated; and the original stock is found in the southern part of the continent of North America, and in Brazil.

Scaup Duck. This is a common Duck in our markets, and is generally known by the name of the *Blue-bill*. It is sometimes called the *Broad-bill*, and along the waters of the Chesapeake the *Black-head*. It is a great diver, and commonly feeds on the snails which abound in our fresh and salt marshes. When fat, its flesh is of tolerable flavour. The Blue-bills of the Chesapeake and its waters are infinitely preferable to those of the Delaware or the coast. This species is the last that leaves us in the spring for the purpose of breeding, numbers being annually seen as late as the middle of May

Shoveller. If we except the singularly formed and disproportionate size of the bill, there are few Ducks more beautiful, or more elegantly marked than this. The excellence of its flesh, which is juicy, tender, and well tasted, is another recommendation to which it is equally entitled. It occasionly visits the coast: but is more commonly found on our lakes and rivers. It is one of our winter birds; and is not known to breed in any part of the United States.

Buffel-headed Duck. This pretty little species, usually known by the name of the *Butter-box* or *Butter-ball*, from the circumstance of its becoming exceedingly fat, is common to the sea shores, rivers and lakes of the United States, in every quarter of the country, during autumn and winter. They feed much on shell-fish, shrimps,&c. The male exceeds the female in size, and greatly in beauty of plumage. They are dexterous divers, and fly with great velocity. Their flesh is good.

The *Blue-winged Teal* is the first of its tribe that returns to us in the autumn from its breeding place in the north. They are usually seen in September, along the shores of the Delaware, where they sit on the mud, close to the edge of the water, so crowded together that the gunners often kill great numbers at a single discharge. They fly rapidly; and when they alight they drop down suddenly, like the Snipe or Woodcock, among the reeds or on the mud. They feed eagerly on the seeds of the reed or wild oats, and become very fat. They are considered a great delicacy, and command a high price in our markets.

Green-winged Teal. This, like the preceding, is a fresh water Duck, common in our markets in autumn and winter. It frequents ponds, marshes, and the reedy shores of creeks and rivers. Is very abundant among the rice plantations of the southern states; flies in small parties, and feeds at night. It associates often with the Mallard, feeding on the seeds of various kinds of grapes and water plants, and also on the tender leaves of vegetables. Like the foregoing its flesh is excellent.

Canvass-back Duck. This celebrated American species, as far as can be judged from the best figures and descriptions of foreign birds, is altogether unknown in Europe. It approaches nearest to the *Pochard* of Britain; but differs from that bird in being superior in size and weight, in the greater magnitude of its bill, and the general whiteness of its plumage. The Canvass-back arrives in the United States from the north about the middle of October; numbers descend to the Hudson and Delaware, but the great body of these birds resort to the numerous rivers belonging to, and in the neighbourhood of, the Chesapeake Bay, particularly the Susquehannah, the Patapsco, Potowmac, and James' rivers, which appear to be their general winter rendezvous. At the Susquehannah they are called *Canvass-backs,* on the Potowmac, *White-backs,* and on James' river *Sheldrakes.* They are seldom found at a great distance up any of these rivers, or even in the salt water bay; but in that particular part of tide water where a certain grass-like plant grows, on the roots of which they feed. This plant, which is said to be a species of *Valisineria,* grows on fresh water shoals of from seven to nine feet water, but never where these are occasionally dry, in long narrow grass-like blades of four or five feet in length; the root is white, and has some resemblance to small celery. This grass is in many places so thick that a boat can with difficulty be rowed through it, it so impedes the oars. Wherever this plant grows in abundance, the Canvass-backs may be expected in corresponding numbers. It occurs in some parts of the Hudson; in the Delaware near Gloucester, and in the vicinity of Petty's island, both places within sight of Philadelphia; and in most of the rivers that fall into the Chesapeake, to each of which particular places these Ducks resort; while in waters unprovided with this nutritive plant they are altogether unknown, or are only occasionally seen when on their migrations.

On the first arrival of these birds they are generally lean, but towards the beginning of November they are in pretty good order, and about the last of the month they are in perfection. They are excellent divers, and swim with great speed and agility. They sometimes assemble in such multitudes as to cover several acres of the river, and when they rise suddenly, produce a noise resembling distant thunder. They float about the shoals, diving and tearing up the grass by the roots, which is the only part they eat. They are extremely shy, and can rarely be approached unless by stratagem. When slightly wounded in the wing, they dive to such prodigious distances, and with such rapidity, continuing it so perseveringly, and with such cunning and active vigor, as almost always to render the pursuit hopeless. The Canvass-back, in the rich juicy tenderness of its flesh, and its delicacy of flavour, stands unrivalled by the whole feathered creation. It becomes so exceedingly fat, that when shot from a tolerable height it will often burst with the fall. Those killed in the waters of the Chesapeake are generally esteemed superior to all others; but the compiler of this article has shot them of equal fatness and flavour in the Delaware, although many will not admit that our Canvass-backs at all resemble those of the boasted Chesapeake. The inhabitants of New York have but lately discovered that *they* too have the legitimate Canvass-backs on their Hudson; though ignorance and prejudice from the south will doubtless stigmatize them as a spurious race, unworthy of the name. Yet it is true that in all these places this exquisite bird is found, and will continue to be found there, so long as its favourite food abounds. Would it not be worth the experiment to transplant this celebrated grass in other similar waters, in the hope of drawing thither the delicious Canvass-back? It has been ascertained that wheat will attract them. Some years since, a vessel, loaded with this grain, was wrecked at the entrance of Great Egg-harbour, in the autumn, and went to pieces. The Canvass-backs, before unknown to the people of Egg-harbour, at that time on their way from the north, collected in immense numbers, and fed upon the wheat, remaining as long as it lasted. At our public dinners, hotels, and particular entertainments, the Canvass-backs are universal favourites. They not only grace but dignify the table; and their very name conveys to the imagination of the eager epicure the most comfortable and exhilerating ideas. Hence on such occasions it has not been uncommon to pay from two to three dollars a pair for these Ducks; and, indeed, at such times, if they can they must be had, whatever may be the price.

The *Pintail Duck*, or as it is generally called, the *Sprigtail*, is a common Duck in our markets, but not in much esteem; it being seldom fat, although its flesh is generally tender. It is a shy and cautious bird; feeds on the mud flats, and in shallow fresh water marshes; but rarely visits the coast. Like the Mallard and Black Duck it does not dive for its food; though it is tolerably expert in diving when wounded. The Sprigtail has a kind of whistling or chattering note, and is very noisy. It is vigilant in giving the alarm on the approach of the gunner, who often curses the watchfulness of this bird.

The *Brant*, or as it is usually written, *Brent*, is a bird well known on both continents; and was celebrated in former times throughout Europe for the singularity of its origin; and the strange transformations it was supposed to undergo previous to its complete organization. Its first appearance was said to be in the form of a *Barnacle shell*, adhering to old water-soaked logs, trees, or other pieces of wood taken from the sea. Of this *Goose-bearing tree*, Gerard, in his Herbal, published in 1597, has given a formal account. Ridiculous and chimerical as this notion was, it had many advocates, and was at that time as generally believed, and with about as much reason too, as the present opinion of the annual immersion of *Swallows*, so tenaciously insisted on by *some* of our philosophers, and which, like the former absurdity, will in its turn disappear before the penetrating radiance and calm investigation of truth.

The Brant is expected at Egg-harbour, on the coast of New Jersey, about the first of October, and has been sometimes seen as early as the twentieth of September. In their migrations they uniformly travel over the sea, parallel with the coast; their line of march very much resembles that of the Canada Geese, with this exception, that frequently three or four are crowded together in the front, as if striving for precedency. During their stay on the coast, they feed on the bars of the sound, or bays, at low water, never in the marshes; their principal food being a remarkably long and broad-leaved marine plant, of a bright green colour, which adheres to stones, and is called by the country people Sea-Cabbage; they also eat small shell-fish. During the time of high water they float in the bay, in long lines, particularly in calm weather. Their voice is hoarse and honking, and when some hundreds are screaming together, it reminds one of a pack of hounds in full cry. When they change their feeding grounds, or are aroused on wing, they will always endeavor to avoid crossing the land. Hence, according as the wind blows the gunners conceal themselves on certain points or tongues of land which project into the bay; and if a gale should impel the birds to leeward, they will earnestly labour to gain the windward point, flying a few feet above the surface of the water; but when they reach the extremity of the land, in endeavouring to double it they are frequently driven over the spots where the gunners lie on their backs, who instantly spring up with loud shouts: the Brant become alarmed, cluster confusedly together, and, instead of pushing straight forward, turn to avoid the danger; this is the critical moment for the gunners, who pouring into the panic-struck flock their well-directed fire, bring many of them to the ground. About the twentieth of May the Brant pass the coast of New Jersey on their route to the north, but seldom stop, unless driven in by tempestuous weather. Should a south east gale occur at that time, they soon become fatigued, and fly slowly over the surf of the sea beach, frequently affording the gunners rare sport. At this season they are very fat, and of a fine flavour. In the month of November they are likewise excellent; though after their favourite sea-cabbage becomes scarce their flesh tastes somewhat sedgy. When the winter sets in with severity the Brant principally move off to the south.

Snow Goose. This species, called on the coast the *Red Goose*, and by others the *Pied Goose* and *White Brant*, arrives in the river Delaware from the north early in November, sometimes in considerable flocks, and is extremely noisy, their notes being shriller and more squeaking than those of the Canada or common Wild Goose. On their first arrival they make but a short stay, proceeding, as winter approaches, farther to the south; but from the middle of February until the breaking up of the ice in March, they are frequently numerous along both shores of the Delaware, about and below Reedy Island, particularly near Old Duck Creek, in the state of Delaware. They feed on the roots of the reeds, tearing them up from the marshes like hogs. Their flesh, like that of most others of their tribe that feed on vegetables, is excellent.

Gray Goose. This is said to be the original stock of the common domesticated Goose, and is called by the naturalists of Britain the *Gray-lag Goose.* It is found in various parts of the old and new continents; but seldom appears within the limits of the United States. At Hudson's Bay this species arrives early in May, as soon as the ice disappears; they collect in flocks of twenty or thirty, stay about three weeks, then separate in pairs, and take off to breed. In July they moult, at which time the Indians destroy many of them. About the middle of August they return to the marshes, with their young, and continue there till September.* The Gray Goose was observed by Lewis and Clarke on the waters of the Columbia.

*Pennant, Arct. Zool. vol. 2, p. 268.

Canada Goose. This is the common Wild Goose of the United States, universally known over the country; whose regular periodical migrations are the sure signals of returning spring, or approaching winter. The tracts of their vast migratory journies are not confined to the coast or its vicinity. In their voyages to and from the north, these winged pilgrims pass over the interior on both sides of the mountains. Their first arrival on the coast of New Jersey is early in October; and their first numerous appearance is the sure prognostic of severe weather. Those which continue all winter frequent the shallow bays and marsh islands; their principal food being the sea-cabbage, and the roots of the sedge. Every few days they make an excursion to the inlets on the beach for gravel. They cross, indiscriminately, over land or water, generally taking the nearest course to their object; differing in this respect from the Brant, who will often go a great way round by water rather than cross over the land. Wounded Geese have, in numerous instances, been completely domesticated, and readily pair with the domestic Geese. The offspring are said to be incapable of propagation; they are larger than either of the parents: but the characteristic marks of the Wild Goose still predominate. The Canada Goose is now domesticated in numerous quarters of the country, and is remarked for being extremely watchful, and more sensible of approaching changes in the atmosphere than the common Gray Goose. In England, France and Germany, they have also been long domesticated. Thus has America already added to the stock of domestic fowls three species, the Turkey, the Muscovy Duck, and the Canada Goose, inferior to none in usefulness; for it is acknowledged by an English naturalist of good observation, the ingenious Bewick, that this last species ‘‘is as familiar, breeds as freely, and is in every respect as valuable as the common Goose.’’

The *Wild Swan* breeds in the northern parts of North America, multitudes of them having been seen, with their young, by both Hearne and Mackenzie, in their journies to the northern ocean. When these birds are moulting or changing their feathers, the Indians, taking advantage of their inability to fly, pursue them and kill numbers; their eggs and young are likewise sought after with avidity. In the Chesapeake bay these noble birds appear every autumn; often associating with the Canada Geese, but generally feeding by themselves in shallow water, where they can reach the bottom with their bills. They are a wary bird, and can seldom be approached within gunshot. Seen at a distance, in strings of one hundred or more, gracefully floating on the smooth expanse, they give great interest to the watery landscape; their snow-white plumage, contrasted with the russet hue of the adjacent shores, producing a fine effect, while they arouse in the mind of the classic voyager some of the most amiable and affecting fables of antiquity. The old Swans, as an article of food, are in no esteem, being tough, insipid, and far inferior to the Geese; but the cygnets or young Swans are considered good eating.

The *Snake-bird* is an inhabitant of the Carolinas, Georgia and the Floridas. It seems to have derived its name from the singular form of its head and neck, which at a distance very much resemble some species of serpents. In those countries where noxious animals abound, we may readily conceive that the appearance of this bird, extending its long neck through the foliage of a tree, would tend to startle the wary traveller, whose imagination had portrayed objects of danger lurking in every thicket. These birds frequent the ponds, rivers and creeks, during the summer; build in the trees of the swamps, and those of the islands in the ponds; they construct their nests of sticks; the eggs are of a sky blue colour, and from six to eight in number.

ZOOLOGY OF THE UNITED STATES.

CLASS *AMPHIBIA.*

ORDER *REPTILES.*

GENUS *TESTUDO.*

Speckled land Tortoise	*Testudo Carolina.*
Close shelled T.	*T. clausa.*
Pennsylvania T.	*T. Pennsylvanica.*
Mud T.	*T. denticulata.*
Soft-shelled T.	*T. cartilaginea.*
Great land T.	*T. terrestris.*
Tarrapin	*T. ————*

GENUS *RANA.*

Horned Toad	*Rana cornuta.*
Virginia Frog	*R. Virginica.*
Tree F.	*R. abore.*
Common Toad	*R. bufo.*
Pond Frog	*R. ocellata.*
Bull F.	*R. boans.*
Clamorous F.	*R. pipiens.*
Green Fountain F.	*R. esculenta.*
Common F.	*R. temporaria.*
White-spotted F.	*R. leucophylla*

GENUS *LACERTA.*

Alligator	*Lacerta alligator.*
Pennsylvania Lizard	*L. bimaculata.*
Orbicular L.	*L. orbicularis.*
Chameleon	*L. chameleon.*
Six-lined Lizard	*L. sexlineata.*
Five-lined L.	*L. quinquelineata.*
Blue-tailed L.	*L. fasciata.*
Four lined L.	*L. quadrolineata.*
Brown L.	*L. punctata.*
Lumbriciform L.	*L. lumbricoides.*
Copper-coloured L.	*L. dracana ?*
Blue-bellied L.	*L. ————*
Green Carolina L.	*L. bullaris.*

GENUS *SIREN.*

Carolina Siren	*Siren lacertina.*

ORDER *SERPENTS.*

GENUS *CROTALUS.*

Ground Rattle Snake	*Crotalus miliarius.*
Great R. S.	*C. horridus.*
Yellow R. S.	*C. dryinus.*

Bastard R. S.	*C. durissus.*

GENUS *BOA.*

Indian Boa	*Boa constrictor.*

GENUS *COLUBER.*

Canada Viper	*Coluber teberis.*
Spotted Moccasin Snake	*C. simus.*
Small Brown Adder	*C. striolatus.*
Mexican Viper	*C. Nova Hispania.*
Crowned Viper	*C. coronatus.*
Water V.*	*C. aquaticus.*
Wampum Snake	*C. fasciatus.*
Barred S.	*C. doliatus.*
Truncheon S.	*C. tisiphone.*
Florida Viper	*C. cocrineus.*
House Snake	*C. homasus.*
Brown Snake	*C. sipedon.*
Corn Snake	*C. fulvius.*
Pearl S.	*C. pantatus.*
Brown Viper	*C. sirtalis.*
Dark Blue Snake	*C. getulus.*
Black Snake	*C. constrictor.*
Dotted S.	*C. cariaatus.*
Virginian V.	*C. Virginicus.*
Bluish Green V.	*C. aestivus.*
Black V.	*C. cacodaemon.*
White Snake	*C. atropos.*
Green-striped S.	*C. sipsas.*
Green Snake	*C. mycterizans.*
Little Brown Bead S.	*C. maculatus.*
Couch Whip S.	*C. flagellum.*
Copper-Bellied S.	*C. erythrogaster.*
Ribbon S.	*C. saurita.*
Small Black and Red S.	*C. torquatus.*
Garter S.	*C. ————*
Moccasin S.	*C. ————*

GENUS *ANGUIS.*

Glass Snake	*Anguis ventralis.*
Brownish spotted S.	*A. reticulatus.*
Yellowish White S.	*A. lumbricalis.*
Striped S.	*A. eryx ?*
Chicken S.	*A. maculatus ?*

GENUS *AMPHISBAENA.*

Ring Snake	*Amphisbaena.*
Joint or Hoop S.	*A. fuliginosa ?*

The *Soft-shelled Tortoise* is the largest of the Testudo genus found in North America. When full grown it weighs upwards of 40 pounds. Its flesh is very delicate. It is fierce, and when attacked defends itself by biting. They are found in Florida, and are common in many parts of South America. Of the Tortoise, commonly known by the name of *Tarrapins*, there appears to be several species. Those brought from the Susquehannah are the largest, being from a foot to 18 inches in length. The head, claws and sides, are black, with bright yellow lines; shell, gibbous, oval, and of a dusky brown colour. Those which are found near Egg Harbour, and on the eastern

---

*Frequently called the *horn snake*, from a blunt horny point, half an inch in length, which terminates the tail. This appearance has misled some writers to class it among the *crotali* under the name of the *water rattle snake*. It is very venomous.

shore of Maryland, are entirely black. The shell is nearly round and convex. They seldom exceed a foot in length. These animals are brought in great numbers to the Philadelphia market, where they form one of the greatest delicacies of the table.

The Alligator is an animal very much resembling the Crocodile of the Nile. Their common length is about 12 feet; but they have been seen as long as 23 feet. They are strong, fierce and formidable. They move through the water with great velocity. They are covered with scales which are impenetrable to the ball of the rifle. They are however, vulnerable about the head and belly, and so many of them have been destroyed by the inhabitants for their skins, that their number has considerably diminished. They inhabit the waters of the Mississippi, the streams of Florida and Mexico, and the Atlantic coasts of Carolina and Georgia. The *Chameleon* is found in Mexico. The *Green Carolina Lizzard* has sometimes been called the Chameleon from the different shades of colour it assumes. The Chameleon is however much larger, and its usual colour is grayish.

The *Rattle-Snake* is the most venomous of serpents. He is, however, never known to attack man unless he has been touched or affrighted. We may pass very near him without disturbing him, or his shewing the least disposition to bite. The rattles make no noise, as commonly supposed, when the snake creeps: but when they are affrighted, they coil upon themselves, remain motionless, and are ready to dart forward. Then only, they move with an inconceivable velocity the rattles which advise us of their vicinity. In time of danger, the young snakes take refuge in the maw of the old one. It is commonly supposed that the number of rattles is proportioned to the age of the animal, and that it acquires one rattle every year: this however is a mistake; they have been found to acquire two or three bells in one year. The venom of the rattle-snake is of a clear transparent yellow colour. It is contained in a bladder beneath each fang, and towards the middle of the lower jaw, communicating with the root of the teeth, which, are pierced at their bases, and this opening communicates with the bladder containing the poison. The effects of this venom are very various, not only in different species of animals, but even in different individuals of the same species. It sometimes induces most violent pain, which, if we may judge from the cries of the bitten animal, continuing nearly to the close of its life. At other times, it induces death without creating any, or but very little pain. Warm blooded animals sometimes struggle through the danger and recover.* The *crotalus horridus* somtimes grow to the length of eight feet, and weigh between eight and nine pounds. The other species, though smaller, do not appear to be less venomous.

The *Boa* was first ascertained to be a native of the United States by Dr. Mitchell of New York. The individual he saw was on Long Island. It was seven feet four inches in length and thick in proportion. Its back was covered with black or dark brown spots. The Boa has no fangs or biting teeth, and is of course not venomous. It lives upon squirrels, rabbits, small birds, &c. This animal is known in the southern states by the name of the pine or bull snake. In India it grows to the length of forty feet, and not unfrequently attacks tygers, horses, &c.

*Mease's United States, p. 389.

The *Barred Snake* is a very beautiful little animal. Its general colour is milk-white, marked throughout with large, oval, jet-black rings. It inhabits the Carolinas. The *House Snake* is a native of New Spain, where it is said frequently to be domesticated. The *Pearl Snake* is also found in Mexico. Its body is of a beautiful pearl colour; its head and tail are sea-green, the former marked by a red spot. It is about two feet and a half long.

The *Black Snake* is one of the most common snakes of the United States. It is very large, sometimes attaining to the length of six feet. They are entirely of a shining black colour. They feed upon rats, mice, moles, &c. and are very useful in destroying these vermin. They move along the grass, or dry leaves, with great rapidity; are noted for robbing birds nests; and many strange stories are told of their powers of fascination over squirrels, small birds, &c. which it is said they can attract from the tops of the tallest trees. The mode pursued by the *Crotalus Horridus*, and *Black Snake*, in fighting, is curious. Each one entwines his tail around a shrub, and both rising, they dart at each other, endeavouring to throw their heads round the neck of their antagonist; the one that succeeds pulls with great violence, and endeavours to drag the other down to the ground. In this struggle they frequently lose their holds, which they again resume and proceed as before. A person who was an eye-witness to such a combat, saw the Rattle Snake completely conquered and dragged into the water.

The *Black Viper* is one of the most venomous of the small *coluber* genus. It is very thick in proportion to its length, which is about eighteen inches. It is slow in its motions, and, when irritated, dilates its naturally large head to a surprising width; threatening at the same time with a horrid hiss, whence it has been peculiarly denominated the *hissing snake*. Its fangs are large, and it is said to be as dangerous as the rattle-snake. The *Green Snake* is common in many parts of North America. It is of a beautiful grass-green colour, with a bright yellow line extending on each side from head to tail. It is generally found on trees, is very active, and feeds on insects.

The *Coach-whip Snake* is very long and slender; its length being from four to seven feet. Its colour is a chocolate-brown, varied with black and white. It is very active in its motions, and perfectly innocent. The Indians believe it can cut a man in two with a jerk of its tail. The *Ribbon Snake* resembles the *Green Snake* in its manners. It is smaller. Its general colour is brown above, with three longitudinal bluish-green stripes. The *Black and Red Snake* is the smallest of the serpent kind. It is not larger than an earth worm. The head and back are of a glossy jet black, with a white collar around the neck. The head is rather large, and covered with scales; belly red, eyes flame coloured. It is a rare species, a native of Pennsylvania, where it inhabits crevices of rocks, old walls, &c. and feeds on insects. The *Moccasin Snake* inhabits the swamps and low grounds of the southern states. It grows to the length of five feet, and is said to be very venomous.

"The *Glass Snake* has a very small head; the upper part of its body is of a colour blended brown and green, most regularly and elegantly spotted with yellow. Its skin is very smooth and shiny, with small scales, more closely connected than those of other serpents, and of a different structure. A small blow with a stick will separate the body, not only at the place struck, but at two or three other places, the muscles being articulated in a singular manner, quite through to the vertebra. They are numerous in the sandy woods of the Carolinas and Georgia." * They are also found in the middle states.

"The *Joint Snake* has a skin as hard as parchment, and as smooth as glass. It is beautifully streaked with black and white. It is so stiff, and has so few joints, and those so unyielding, that it can hardly bend itself into the form of a hoop." †

Thus far we have given as complete a list as could be procured of the animals of the United States according to the Linnean arrangement. A long catalogue might also be given of the fish, and a list of the insects would fill a volume. The latter is of course impossible, and a list of the fish would not be sufficiently interesting to compensate for the room it would occupy. We shall therefore confine ourselves to a few of the most interesting species of these two classes.

Fish. The *Sturgeon* is the largest fresh water fish of the United States. It is found in almost all the considerable rivers of the Union. The *Blue-bream* of the southern states is a beautiful and delicious fish. The body is dark blue, powdered with sky-blue, gold and red specks. *Herrings* appear off the coast about the latter end of March, and by the middle of April are caught in immense quantities. *Shad* of a superior quality, pay a regular annual visit to the Atlantic coasts, a short time after the herrings. *Perch*, *Rock*, *Old Wives*, *Catfish*, *Salmon*, *Black-fish*, *Mackarel*, and many others, abound in the rivers. Excellent *Trout* are found in the cold water creeks. The *Lamprey* abounds in the rivers of New-England. *Pike* are found in all the states, and sometimes are caught very large. *Cuttle-fish*, *Sharks*, *Sword-fish*, *Dolphins*, and other sea fish, are found off the coast of the United States. *Cod-fish* abound along the shores of New-England.

Insects. One of the most distinguished of the American insects, from the destruction which it occasionally commits, is the locust, *cicada septendecim*. This insect is found in all the quarters of the world, in almost all the parts of the torrid and temperate zones. The singularity of their periodical visits, and their immense numbers at those seasons, make them too well known to need much description. Their visits to the United States are not regular, varying from eight to fourteen years, nor do they appear in all parts of the country in the same season. The *Hessian Fly* is an insect which annually commits great ravages among the wheat. Common opinion has ascribed its introduction to the troops from Hesse Castle which served in the British army during the revolution. This opinion has however been questioned by many, and some authors assert that the insect is not known in Germany. Promising harvests of wheat are frequently totally destroyed by this insect. There is also a species of Bug which does considerable mischief to the wheat, maize, and other grain. The maize also suffers in various stages of its growth by the *Bud-worm*. Different grasses, maize, &c. are often destroyed by the *Grass-caterpillar*. There are two species of *Pea-bugs* found in the southern states, which occasionally commit dreadful havoc among the peas. Among the other insects which injure the vegetables and fruit are the *May-bug*, *Rose-bug*, *Cucumber-fly*, *Potatoe-fly*, different species of weavels, moths, &c.

* Morse.   † idem.

The beautiful appearance produced by the *Fire-fly* has excited the admiration of all the travellers in America. On a summer's evening they are seen in myriads along the meadows and woods. The light they produce is very brilliant, varying in magnitude according to the state of the atmosphere. It is produced and vanishes suddenly like the flash of a pistol. *Glow-worms* are also very numerous in the summer and autumn.

One of the most troublesome of the American insects is the *Mosquito*; they are very numerous in swamps, on the low banks of creeks and rivers, and on the seashore. From these places however they make excursions into all parts of the country, and are frequently very troublesome in the cities. On the Mississippi they are innumerable.

Their bite is very irritating, and is followed by inflammation and swelling. Many species of flies, spiders, beetles, grasshoppers, crickets, butterflies, wasps, hornets, bees, ants, &c. abound in the United States.

APPENDIX.

In the preparation of this Appendix it was found necessary to examine somewhat exhaustively the literature relative to that part of Ord's Zoology included in his tabulated lists. In this labor I have been exceptionally favored by free access to the unexcelled scientific library of the Academy of Natural Sciences of Philadelphia. The results of this study, especially with respect to the Mammals, seem to show that the nomenclature of Mammalogy yet affords a wide field for critical investigation, ere we shall be able to give due credit to the work of pioneers in this branch of natural history.

The labors of American Ornithologists during the past twenty years have left comparatively little to be done in our scientific ornithology. The appended notes on Ord's catalogue of Birds were mainly compiled by my friend, Mr. Witmer Stone, of the Academy of Natural Sciences. To Dr. Elliott Coues I am much indebted for his critical inspection of the manuscript of this Appendix and for valuable suggestions regarding the bibliographic and historical questions involved. I am also indebted to Prof. E. D. Cope for a similar service in respect to the table of "Amphibia." The names of those species to which Ord gave new binomial names are printed in heavy faced type. A summary of the changes in nomenclature proposed may be found at the end of this Appendix.

TITLE PAGE.

As noticed in the Introduction, the Title Page of the only copy of the Second American Edition of Guthrie's Geography seen by Dr. Coues was defective, (Birds of the Colorado Valley, 1878, Bibliographical Appendix, P. 603.). The titles of the first and third American editions of Johnson and Warner (afterwards Benjamin Warner) are as follows:

The title page of the first (1809) edition is identical in word and spacing with the second edition to and including the words "To which are added:" under the table of contents; from this it reads— ‖ A geographical index with the names of places alphabetically ar: ‖ ranged. 2. A table of the coins of all nations. 3. A chro- ‖ nological table of remarkable events, from the ‖ creation to the present time. ‖ By William Guthrie, Esq. ‖ The astronomical part by James Ferguson, F. R. S. ‖ To which have been added, ‖ the late discoveries of Dr.

Herschel and other eminent astronomers. ‖ Illustrated with twenty-five correct maps. ‖ The first American edition improved. ‖ In two volumes . . . . . Vol. I. ‖ Published by Johnson and Warner, and for sale at their book stores in ‖ Philadelphia; Richmond Virginia; and Lexington, Kentucky ‖ . . . . ‖ 1809. ‖ This quarto edition has no scientific value except in its historic connection with that of 1815.

The title of the third American Edition differs materially from those of its predecessors; it reads, ‖ A ‖ Universal Geography; ‖ or ‖ a view of the present state of ‖ the known world. ‖ containing ‖ [here follows double column table of contents, same as in second edition with item number twelve omitted] to which are added, ‖ 1. a geographical index with the names of places alphabetically ‖ arranged. 2. A chronological table of remarkable events, from the creation to the present time. 3. A list ‖ of men of learning and science ‖ originally compiled by William Guthrie, Esq. ‖ The astronomical part by James Ferguson, F. R. S. ‖ to which have been added ‖ the late discoveries of Dr. Herschel and other ‖ eminent astronomers ‖ accompanied with twenty-one correct maps. ‖ third American edition, ‖ with extensive alterations and additions, by several American editors. ‖ In two volumes vol. II. [I] ‖ = ‖ Philadelphia: ‖ published by Benjamin Warner, No. 171 High Street ‖ also for sale at his store in Richmond, (Va.) and by Wm. P. Bason, ‖ Charleston, (S. C.) ‖ == ‖ 1820. ‖   Pp. 9 to 640. I. Vol. of Maps.

Page ~~299~~ *290.*

Upon whose authority Ord makes the statement that America contains one half of the Quadrupeds of the known world, I do not discover. At the present day the list of strictly North American species of mammals found North of Mexico numbers nearly *four hundred.* In Ord's list one hundred of these species are enumerated; of those remaining in the list, fifteen are undeterminable, twenty-four are Mexican and South American species, eighteen are synonyms of other names in the list and ten are old world forms having no close specific affinities with those of America.

From this it is evident that Ord's acquaintance with the mammalogy of America was chiefly that of a compiler from the works of foreign authors and that the new matter in his Zoology is almost exclusively based on the researches of those intrepid explorers, Lewis and Clark, who had just returned from the new West and the account of whose travels had been made public the previous year.* Viewed from the present standards of research in North American Mammalogy, the list of George Ord forms a striking commentary on past and present methods in zoological science.

That Ord did much toward reformation is well proven; in view of which we may charitably forget that he included in his "Zoology of North America," not only forms exclusively South American, but several species which neither the "ingenious Mr. Pennant," nor the

---

* February 20th, 1814, was absolute date of publication.

versatile Dr. Turton had ever assigned to the fauna of the New World.

The edition of Linnæus, by Dr. Turton, alluded to by Ord, was in all probability that of 1806, from which Prof. Baird and Dr. Coues make their references. The earlier edition of 1802, I presume has been overlooked by these writers, a fact to be regretted, as the original names and descriptions of all the mammals ascribed by them to Turton's edition of 1806 were published prior to that date.

Page 291.

GENUS *VESPERTILIO*.

"New York Bat *Vespertilio noveboracensis.*" The synonymy of this species is essentially as follows

New York Bat ; Pennant, Syn. Quad., 1771, 367.

Vespertilio borealis P. L. S. Müller, (Der Neujorker), Natursys. Suppl., 1776, (No. 21), 21.

Vespertilio noveboracensis Erxleben, Syst. Regn. Anim., 1777, (No. 14), 155.

Atalapha americana Rafinesque, Precis des descouvertes, 1814, 12.

Atalapha noveboracensis Peters, M. B. Akad. Berl., 1870, 908.

Atalapha borealis (Müll), (vid. infra.).

Priority for the naming of the New York or Red Bat has been long accorded to Erxleben, as cited above. I am unable find any reason for discarding the name *"borealis"* given this species by Müller in the Supplement to his edition of the Systema Naturæ. This earlier name is cited by Erxleben as a synonym ; but why he gave the New York Bat of Pennant another name does not appear.

Müller's name preoccupies the *Vespertilio borealis* of Nillson (Illum Fig. Scand. Faun. haft., 19; pl. 36-1838). Nillson's animal will have to stand as *Vesperugo ~~nillsoni~~* Keys. & Blas., Wiegm. Archiv., 1839, 315.

"**BLACK BAT *VESPERTILIO AMERICANUS.*"** Ord probably refers to the Silver Black Bat of Leconte, *Lasionycteris noctivagans* (Cuv. An. King., McMurtrie ed. 1831, Vol. I., App., 431). The absence of any reference to indicate this makes it questionable. In any event Ord's binomial is antedated by the *Vespertilio americanus* of Turton (Syst. Nat., 1802, 27), who gives it no English name. His characters for it are utterly worthless, viz.: "Very large, with long straggling hairs, *ears* large." No habitat is given. Ord certainly did not mean to refer to this as his Black Bat, nor can the latter term apply to the *Noctilio americanus* (*N. leporinus*) of the tenth and twelfth editions of Linnæus.

. "Brown Bat *Vespertilio fuscus.*" Palis. de Beauv., Cat. Peale's Mus., Phila., 1796, 14.=*Vesperugo serotinus fuscus* Dobs., Cat. Chir., 1878, 192.= *Adelonycteris fuscus* H. Allen, Proc. Acad. Nat. Sci., Phila., 1892.

"Hang-lip Bat *Vespertilio labialis.*" Turton in his first (1802) edition of Linnæus separates this as a species from the *Vespertilio (Noctilio)*

lepornius Linn, evidently basing his diagnosis on Pennant's description (Syn. Quad., 365, B.) of a small specimen given him by John Ellis, Esq. Pennant's intention was to class it as a probable variety of the Peruvian Bat, No. 279, the *N. leporinus*=*N. americanus* of Linnæus. It is quite probable that this small specimen described by Pennant, and which he states, "differed from the former" (*N. leporinus*) "in size, being less, in all other respects agreed," is the same as the *N. albiventer* of Spix (Sim. et Vesp. Brasil, 1823, 58.,) which Dobson (Cat. Chir. B. Mus., 1878, 398.) affirms "resembles *N. leporinus* very closely," and that "externally the only character by which this species may be at once distinguished is found in the conspicuously shorter foot."

There is reason for considering Turton's *labialis* entitled to supersede the later name of Spix. Turton's description of *labialis* states the color of belly is "ash," and the extent of wings 20 inches, which I find to agree with three spirit specimens of "*albiventer*" from Surinam in the collection of the Philadelphia Academy of Natural Sciences, but not agreeing with three alcoholic Trinidad specimens. The latter, however, agree perfectly with Dobson's diagnosis of *leporinus* (Cat. Chir, p. 394) in an extent of 26 inches (see also Pennant, sup. cit., B.) and in the fur of the lower parts being very slightly paler than that of the back.

The small size of the foot in the Surinam specimens is also noticeable. This feature is not mentioned by Pennant for the obvious reason that he considered it due to the smaller size of the animal, and not diagnostic in a comparison with young *leporinus* of same size. Turton gives "Peru and the shores of the Mosquito" as the habitat of *labialis*.

"**RED BAT *VESPERTILIO RUBRA.*"**=*Atalapha borealis* (Müll.). *Supra cit.*

Page 291.

GENUS *MYRMECOPHAGA.*

"**Least Ant-eater *Myrmecophaga didactyla.*"**=*Cycloturus didactylus* (Linn.) Gray.

"**Striped Ant-eater *Myrmecophaga pentadactyla.*"** Taken from Turton, who describes it as a species with five toes on the fore feet, but gives no habitat. I cannot find the name in synonymy and suppose it is original with Turton.

It is possible that Ord may have known the source of Turton's description and that it was taken from an American species. It has nothing to do with *Manis*, but appears to be a genuine Ant-eater.

Page 291.

GENUS *DASYPUS.*

"**Three-banded Armadillo *Dayspus tricinctus.*"**=*Tolypeutes tricinctus* (Linn.) Illiger.

"**Eight-banded Armadillo *Dasypus octocinctus,*"** and "**Nine-banded Armadillo *Dasypus novemcinctus.*"**=*Tatusia novemcincta* (Linn.) Lesson. *Tatu-*

sia peba Desmarest, a name by which this species has very generally
gone, is an imposition on the good sense not only of Linnæus, but of those
who have perpetuated its use.

"Arctic Walrus or Morse *Trichechus rosmarus."=Rosmarus trichechus*
Scopoli+Lamont, Seas. with S. Horses, 1661, 141 : Gill, Johnson's Univ.
Cyclop., 1877, 633.=*Rosmarus rosmarus*, A. O. U. Code.

"Manati *Trichechus australis."*=West Indian Manatee, *Trichechus manatus,* (vid infra).

The *Trichechus manatus* of Linnæus' tenth edition of the Systema
Naturæ is the only species enumerated for the genus in that edition.

The subsequent arrangement in the twelfth edition, by which the
Walrus was given place and precedence in the genus *Trichechus*, led to its
early adoption for the Walrus, the generic name *Manatus* of Tilesius
(1802) being substituted for it in the case of the Manatee. This arrangement, due to the rejection of the tenth edition of Linnæus by earlier
systematists, is not now sanctioned, *Trichechus* in the generic sense,
being solely applicable to the Manatees.

Linnæus gives the habitat of the Manatee described in his tenth edition,
as, "Habitat in mari Americano," referring in his synonymy to the
"*Manatus*" of Rondelet, Gesner and Hernandez. The page reference
to Gesner appears to be incorrect, nor can I find any unmistakable allusion
by that fanciful author to such an animal. Both Rondelet and Hernandez give the West Indies as the habitat of the "Manati," the latter
author stating this was the name applied to it by the Haitians. The
West Indian Manatee should therefore stand as the type of the family
and genus, *Trichechidæ et Trichechus*, under Linnæus' original name,
Trichechus manatus. Its more important synonyms are :—

Trichechus manatus a *australis* Gmel., Syst. Nat., 1788, 60. (in part.)

Manatus australis Tiles., Jahrb. f. Naturg., "1802," 1. 23.

Manatus americanus Desm., Nouv. Dict. Hist. Nat., 1817, xvii, 262.

Manatus latirostris Harlan, Jour. Acad. Nat. Sci., Phila., 1823, iii, 94.

The *Manatus inunguis* Natterer, "Cat. msc. 1830," (quoted from Hartlaub) is considered to be another good American species, and
Manatus senegalensis Desm. (Nouv. Dict. Hist. Nat., 1817, 262.) is
the name of the Old World form, both of course bearing the generic
title of *Trichechus*, as now understood. For a comprehensive list of the
synonymy of the family, with voluminous commentary and history, the
student is referred to Dr. C. Hartlaub's paper in Zoologische Jahrbücher
i, 1886, pp. 1-112.

Trichechus being inapplicable to it, the Walrus has been placed by
some modern writers in the genus *Odobænus*, attributed to Linnæus
(Syst. Nat., 1735, 39) and adopted by Brisson, (Regne Anim., 1756, 48),
who applied it to both the Walrus and Manatee This name is not only
objectionable in part for the same reasons as those given for *Trichechus*,

but also antedates the recognized birthday of our biomial system.
The next available generic name for the Walrus is apparently that of
Rosmarus, given that rank by Klein in 1751 (Quad. Disp. Brev. Hist.
Nat., 40 & 92,) and so adopted by Scopoli in 1777 (Introd. Hist. Nat.,
p. 490,) and by Prof. Gill in 1866, (Proc. Essex Inst., V, 7.).

Dr. J. A. Allen, after considering the question at great length. (N.
Amer. Pinnipeds, 1880, 12-26) assigns the name *Odobænus rosmarus*,
Malmgren, Ofver. Vet. Akad. Forh., 1863, (1864,) to the Walrus, admitting, however, that the question of "choice evenly lies between *Odobænus* and *Rosmarus*." The fact that Klein did not use *Rosmarus* in the
"binomial" sense, whereas Linnæus did use *Odobænus* in that sense
is a point in favor of the adoption of Klein's name, though the Linnæan
name has 16 years priority

"Siren or Sea Ape *Trichechus siren.*" Based on the "Sea Ape," of
Pennant (Hist. Quad., 1781, ii, 544); quoted from Steller, to whose
work I am unable to refer. Dr. J. A. Allen, whose researches in this
class of Mammals are exhaustive, informs me (in epist.) that this
species "is not entitled to serious consideration," because of its unrecognizable description. It probably had reference to the Northern
Fur-Seal, *Callorhinus ursinus* (Linn.).

Turton's binomial name is evidently original, but has not found its
way into synonymy.

Page 291.

"GENUS *PHOCA.*"

"Maned Seal *Phoca jubata.*"=*Otaria jubata* ("Forster") Blainville ;
vid. J. A. Allen., N. Amer. Pinnip., 1880, 208. etc. Not North American
in the restricted sense.

"Sea Calf *Phoca vitulina.*"=*Phoca vitulina* Linn., Syst. Nat., 1758, i, 38.

"Harp Seal *Phoca Grœnlandica.*"=*Phoca* (*Pagophilus*) **grœnlandica**
Fabricius, Müller's Zool. Dan. Prod., 1776, viii.

"Rough Seal *Phoca hispida.*"=*Phoca hispida* Schreber, Saugt., iii,
1778, 312.=*Phoca fœtida* Fabricius, Müll. Zool. Dan. Prod., 1776, viii.

"Crested Seal *Phoca cristata.*"=*Phoca cristata* Erxl., Syst. Reg. Anim.,
1777, 590.=*Cystophora cristata* Nillson, "K. Vet. Akad. Hand. Stockh.,
1837." *Nilsson,*

"Hooded Seal *Phoca monachus.*"=*Phoca monachus* Hermann, Besc. de
Berl. Ges. Nat. Freunde, iv, 1779, 456.=*Monachus albiventer* (Boddaert)
Gray. Vid. J. A. Allen, N. A. Pinn. p. 465. etc., also *Monachus tropicalis*
Gray, (ibid, p. 708), not then (1815) recognized. Turton gives the
Hooded Seal as a resident of Dalmatia. Ord has included it on some
other authority, perhaps.

Page 291.

GENUS *CANIS*.

"**Indian Dog** *Canis Americanus.*"=*Canis americanus*, Gmel., Syst. Nat., 1788, 69. See Hernandez, Hist. Mex., 1651, 466, "*Canis mexicana,*"—also (infra) note to page 294.

"**Common Wolf** *Canis lupus.*"=*Canis occidentalis* Auct. recent. This name of course applies to the northern American Wolf as not distinct from the European species, a question yet unsettled in the opinion of many.

"**Black Wolf** *Canis niger.*" The name *niger*, here used by Ord, does not appear to have been previously used, binomially. Turton refers to it in the vernacular, as a Canadian variety under *C. lupus.*

"**Mexican Wolf** *Canis Mexicanus.*"="Xoloitzcuintli *Lupus mexicanus,*" Hernandez., Hist. Mex., 1651, 479.=*Canis mexicanus* Linn., Syst. Nat., 1766, 60. 71.=*Canis occidentalis* var *mexicanus*, Baird., Mam. N. A., 1857. 113; Mex. B. Surv., 1859, 14. If the Mexican or Lobo Wolf of Hernandez, above quoted, on which this binomial is based, is, as supposed, not separable in a specific sense from the Gray or Timber Wolf of northern N. America, the name "*mexicanus*" should stand first, on the ground of priority, above that of *occidentalis.* Some modern zoologists are of the opinion that the American and European Gray Wolves are not only specifically distinct but that the Canadian and Mexican representatives of the former species are at least sub-specifically separable. Granting this, the correct arrangement would be ;—1. Mexican Gray Wolf, *Canis mexicanus* Linn., Syst., Nat., 1759, 60. 2. Northern Gray Wolf, *Canis mexicanus occidentalis* (Richardson), Fau. Bor. Amer., 1829, 66.

Continuing the use of these names, if the European and American Gray Wolves are not distinct species, they would stand—1. *Canis lupus* Linn. 2. *Canis lupus mexicanus* (Linn.). 3. *Canis lupus occidentalis* Rich. Dr. J. A. Allen[*] designates the northern Gray Wolf by the name *Canis lupus griseo-albus* taken by Baird from Sabine's Appendix to Franklin's Narrative (1823, pp. 654, 655,) and compounded as a variety of *occidentalis !* Such a manipulation of names seems to me unjustifiable. Sabine's name *Canis lupus griseus* (sup. cit.) has priority over *C. l. occidentalis* Rich., but it is preoccupied by *Canis griseus* Bodd., Elench., Anim., 1784, 97, given the Gray Fox.

A review of whole matter favors the opinion that these American and European Wolves are specifically inseparable, as follows :—

1. *Canis lupus* Linn. (Europe).
2. " " *mexicanus* (Linn.), (Mexico).
3. " " *occidentalis* (Rich.), (Northern N. America).

[*] Bull. Amer. Mus. N. H., 1894, 94.

"Large Prairie Wolf *Canis————.*"=*Canis mexicanus occidentalis* (Rich.), supra cit.=? *Lupus gigas* Townsend, Jour. A. N. S., Phila., 1850, 75.="Large wolf of the plains," Lewis & Clark, Hist. Exp., 1814, 167.

"Small Prairie Wolf *Canis————.*"=*Canis latrans* Say, Long's Exp. R. Mts., I, 1823, 168.="Small wolf of the plains," Lewis & Clark, Hist. Exp., 1814, 167.

"Large Red Fox *Canis————.*"=*Vulpes macrourus* Baird, Mam. N. Amer., 1857, 130.="Large red fox of the plains," Lewis & Clark, Hist. Exp., 1814, 168.

"Small Red Fox *Canis————.*"=*Canis velox* Say, Long's Exp. R. Mts., 1823, 487.="Kit fox, or small fox of the plains," Lewis & Clark, Hist. Exp., 1814, 168.

"Varied Fox *Canis alopex?*" This is Linnæus' name for the European Red Fox, *Vulpes vulpes* (Linn.), with black-tipped tail.
The presence of a similar variety in America has induced Ord to include it in the list as a questionable species.

"Silvery Fox *Canis cinereo-argenteus?*" Müller, (Natursys. Suppl., 1776, 29), has priority over Erxleben for the use of this name in the binomial sense. Erxleben, (Syst. Reg. Anim., 1777, 567), quotes Müller as above in his synonymy. He gives to his *"cinereo-argenteus"* the habitat, "in America boreali," and, as generally construed, describes the "Silvery" form or variety of the Red Fox, *Vulpes fulvus* of authors.
Müller's *"Canis cinereo argenteus"* (sup. cit.) is founded on the "Canis ex cinereo argenteus Bris., Lawson's Carolina," as cited by Pennant (Syn. Quad., 1771, 157) which is the Gray Fox, *Urocyon virginianus* (Erxleben), (Syst. Reg. Anim., 1777, 567), of modern authors. Müller's name, therefore, not only has priority but it is the first one correctly applied to the Gray Fox of Lawson. As such it will stand as *Urocyon cinereo-argenteus* (Müll.). See Coues & Yarrow, Wheeler Rep., 1875, v., 56.

"Black Fox *Canis lycaon.*"=*Canis lycaon* of Müller (1776), Erxleben (1777), and Schreber (1778). This is the "Black Fox" of Pennant. Mivart (Mon. Canidæ, 1890, 4) makes *C. lycaon* one of the synonyms of the *C. lupus*, and Schreber's figure of it (Saugt. iii, pl. 7, lxxxix.) represents a wolf-like animal. His page reference to a *Vulpes nigra* of Gesner is wrong, nor can I find any index reference to this name in Gesner's work. Schreber's next reference is to the "Loup noir. Buff. 9, p. 362. tab. 41 a.," from whose plate Schreber's wolf-like animal is reproduced. Erxleben and others have added to the confusion by confounding this with the black wolf, giving in some cases the habitat of the fox, a-la-Pennant, with a description both fox-like and wolfish in character. It appears most likely that it originally was the first distinctive name applied to the black variety of the Red American Fox (vid. infra) but owing to its subsequent treatment it is now worse than useless.

"**Gray Fox** *Canis Virginianus.*"=*Canis virginianus* Erxleben.=*Urocyon cinereo-argenteus* (Müll.), (supra, q. v.).

"**Common Red Fox** *Canis vulpes.*" Ord considered our Red Fox distinct from his black "*lycaon*" and the "*crucigera*" mentioned later, and questionably distinct from "*alopex*" and "*cinereo-argenteus.*" The Red Fox of America, if specifically distinct from the European Red Fox, should go by the name "*C. V. var. Pensylvanicus,*" of Boddaert, (Elench. Anim., 1784, 97), founded on the Brant Fox of Pennant (Hist. Quad. 1781, 235.). This name is revived by J. E. Gray, (Cat. B. M., Carniv., (etc.) 1869, 205).* As above stated, the "Black Fox," (*V. lycaon*), though named earlier, has no valid claim to recognition in this connexion. Boddaert's name, modernized to *Vulpes pensylvanicus* (Bodd), is tenable enough, and has long priority over *Vulpes fulvus* (Desmarest), (Mamm., 1820, 203.), in common use.

"**Cross Fox** *Canis crucigera.*" This name was first technically applied as a varietal name of the Cross Fox of Asia, Europe and America by Erxleben (Syst. Reg. Anim. 1777. 520.).
It cannot apply, for similar reasons to those given under "Black Fox" (sup. cit.), to the American Red Fox more than to any other going under that surname.

"**Corsak Fox** *Canis corsac.*" That Mr. Ord could have intentionally confounded this Asiatic species with any American form seems doubtful. None of his predecessors seem to have done so.

Page 291.

GENUS *FELIS*.

"**American Panther** *Felis couguar.*"

"**Brown Tiger** *Felis concolor.*"

As Ord surmises (see foot note), these are the same.
Turton is apparently responsible for the synonym "*couguar.*" Should the North and South American Panthers ever prove separable, Turton's name may yet apply to the northern form.
The name "Brown Tiger," here used by Ord, is taken from Pennant (Syn. Quad., 179). It originated probably with Barrere, who calls it "Tigris fulvus, Tigre rouge," (France Aequin., 166). "Couguar" or Cougouar was Buffon's spelling of the "Cugacuarana" of Marcgrave (Brasil, 1658, 235.). Puma is the Mexican "Puma seu Leo," of Hernandez (Mexico, 1651, 518.).

"**Black Tiger** *Felis discolor.*" Pennant mentions a "Black Tiger," based in part on the "Jaguarete, Marcgrave, Brasil, 235." Elliot in his Monograph of the Felidæ makes the Black Tiger of Schreber (Saugt. 1778, 394.) a synonym of *Felis concolor* Linn., and from the appearance

* See Coues & Yarrow, Wheeler Rep., 1875, v. 52.

of Schreber's plate (q. v.) this seems a fair inference. Schreber, however, quotes Pennant, as above. Marcgrave's description reads:—"It
has short glossy hair, black, mixed with brown and its coat is variegated
with black spots, with various figures as in the other," i. e., the Jaguar,
first described. Marcgrave's figure (not lettered or numbered) opposite
the above quotation is evidently intended for his "Cuguacuarana,"
(*F. concolor* Linn.) next described on the same page. How Pennant
confounded his "Black Tiger," with the Jaguarete of Marcgrave is a
problem.

Schreber correctly puts the Jaguarete as a questionable synonym of
the Black Tiger (*F discolor* Schreb.) of Pennant. These names, as
originally used by Marcgrave and Pennant, refer to different species, the
first to a spotted cat resembling the Jaguar, the latter to a *Felis* resembling the Puma.

The present confusion was probably due to Pennant supposing Marcgrave's figure of the "Cuguacuarana" to apply to his description of the
"Jaguarete," which the printer has incorrectly placed opposite the
former species.

The same confusion has resulted in the use of the name *Felis nigra*
(Erxl., Syst. Reg. Anim., 1777, 512.) which may apply to both the Puma
and the black variety of the Jaguar. There is some probabilty that the
spotted young of the Puma has had something to do with the confusion
in this case.

"**Brasilian Tiger** *Felis onca.*"=Jaguar, *Felis onca* Linn. The term
Brasilian Tiger is original with Pennant.

"**Mountain Lynx** *Felis montana.*," is based on the "Mountain Cat" of
Pennant, (Syn. Quad. 1771, 185) and is apparently the same as his "Bay
Cat," (ibid. p. 188, pl. xix, 1), which is the *Felis ruffa* Guldenstaedt,
(Nov. Com. Petr., 1776, 499.). "*Montana*" was first legitimately applied
to it by Turton. (Syst. Nat. 1802, 50.) not by "Desmarest, 1820" as given
by Elliot. LeConte (Proc. Acad. N. Sci., Phila., 1854, 9.) thinks Pen-
nat's "Bay Cat" is not *Lynx rufus* (Guld.) but a "lost" species, and
that the name of Ray, (Syn. Meth. Anim., "1713" p. 169), *Catus montanus*, should stand; an arrangement, of course, not to be thought of.

"**Common Lynx** *Felis lynx.*"=European Red Lynx, *Felis lynx* Linn.
Turton includes America in the habitat of this species. Ord's reference,
of course, is to the Canada Lynx, *Lynx canadensis* (Desm.) Raf.

"**Mexican Cat** *Felis pardalis.*"=Ocelot, of same name.=*Felis pardalis*
Linn., Syst. Nat., 1758, 42.

"**Mexican Tiger Cat** *Felis Mexicana.*" Copied from Turton. Whence
the latter takes it, or to what species it applies is difficult to determine,
but the brief description seems only applicable to one of the color
variations of *pardalis*. The name appears original with Turton and
precedes the *F mexicana* of Desmarest, Saussere, etc.

Page 291.

GENUS *VIVERRA*.

"**Vulpecula** Weasel or Squash *Viverra vulpecula.*" Founded on the "Yzquiepatl" of Hernandez (N. Hist. Mex. 1651, 332.) and, as Ord uses it, was so named first by Erxleben (Reg. Anim., 1777, 490.) who quotes Schreber. The plates of Hernandez and Schreber (after Buffon) indicate a brown, Mink-like animal. The same animal (after Hernandez) was made by Linnæus the original of his *Viverra memphitis*, (Syst. Nat., 1758, 44), though his description tallies imperfectly with that of Hernandez. There is little doubt that both described from hearsay of different species, combining interchangeably the habits of a Skunk with the colors of no known member of the *Mephitide*. The *V. vulpecula* of Erxleben and Schreber is, in part, a synonym of the *V memphitis* of Linnæus. Squash is derived from *Quasie*, an Indian name applied to the Coati, *Nausa rufa*, on which in part, the *V. vulpecula* of Schreber is founded. The Quasje was said to have a fetid odor, hence, *memphitis* Linn. (?). See however, (infra) that the Mexican weasel was also called Squash.

"**Mexican Weasel** *Viverra prehensilis.*" I find this nowhere mentioned save by Turton, whose description is lengthy. It is almost certainly the *ly 1* Kinkajou, *Cercoleptes caudivolvulus* (Pallas) Tomes, (1777).

"**Striated** Weasel or Skunk *Viverra putorius.*"=*V. putorius* Linn. (Syst. Nat., 1758, 44). Ord must have thought this name applicable to the common Skunk of northern N. America, but, as well is well established, the Linnæan name was chiefly based on the little Striped Skunk of the Carolinas, *Spilogale putorius* (Linn.) Gray.

"**WHITE WEASEL** *VIVERRA ALBUS.*" From Ord's reference to Lewis and Clark under this heading I am able to find mention of such an animal in only one place (page 191, Coues' 1893 edition) where a Weasel was procured from an Indian, November, 1804, near Bismarck, N. Dakota, "perfectly white except the extremity of the tail, which was black." If this is the specimen examined by Ord at Peale's Museum, *Viverra albus* Ord, antedates *Putorius longicauda* Bonap.

But Ord says this specimen had "dusky" feet. On this account, a very peculiar feature in the genus, it is as probable the specimen was *P. nigripes* (Aud. & Bach., Quad. N. A., II, 1851, 297.) as *P. longicauda*, the habitat of both species being in the region where the Indian procured the weasel mentioned by Lewis & Clark. The fact that Ord puts *V. albus* in *Viverra* and not in *Mustela*, in which he puts the Ermine and American Sable, seems to confirm this supposition. As we are not sure, however, that the specimens mentioned respectively by Lewis and Clark and Ord were identical, (Ord making no book reference to L. & C. as in other instances), the *Viverra albus* Ord must stand as a *nomen nudum*. See Ord, Jour. de Phys., 1818, 152.

Page 291.

GENUS *MUSTELA*.

"**Sea Otter** *Mustela lutris.*"=*Enhydris lutris* (Linn.) Fleming.

"**Common Otter** *Mustela lutra.*"=*Lutra vulgaris* (Erxl.).

"**Canada Otter** *Mustela Canadensis.*"=*Lutra canadensis* (Schreb.) Turton. Turton included America in the habitat of the European Otter, *L. vulgaris*, but alludes to another species (Syst. Nat., 1802, 57.) as "Black; fur smooth; tail long, taper," applying to it the name "Canadensis," with "North America" for its habitat. Dr. Coues, (Fur B. Anim., 1877, 295.) gives this of Turton priority over any other name applicable to the American Otter, expressly stating in parentheses to reference that the "*Mustela canadensis*" of Turton is not the *M. canadensis* of Schreber. While this is *literally* true, there is a "*Mustela lutra canadensis*" described, indexed and figured by Schreber (Saugt. iii, 1778, 458 and 588; Pl, cxxvi, B.) which undoubtedly refers to the animal in question. Though put in trinomial form, and as a variety only, of the European animal, there are good reasons why this name of Schreber should be first accredited to him and not to Turton. The "*Mustela canadensis*" of Schreber (1778) is the same animal as "*M pennantii* of Erxleben (1777). Erxleben's *M. canadensis* is the Mink, *Lutreola vison*. Owing to its page sequence in the Saugthiere the name "*canadensis*" is applicable to only one member of the genus *Mustela* as Schreber defines it, and that (if recognized as a tenable form) is the trinomial "*M. Lutra canadensis.*" The other, in such an event, is a synonym.

For discussion of synonymy of *Enhydris lutris*, see Coues (sup. cit.), for that of "*Mustela canadensis*," (sic), see Baird, Mam. N. Amer., 1857, 141.

"**Minx** *Mustela minx.*"
"**Tawny Weasel** *Mustela vison.*" } = *Lutreola vison.* American Mink, Schreb., Saug., iii, 1778, 463; Pl. 127 B.

"**Fisher Weasel** *Mustela nigra.*" This name is original with Turton. In the 1802 edition of his System it follows his "*M. Canadensis*, Pekan," of which it is a synonym. Turton evidently based *nigra* on the Fisher Weasel of Pennant, (Syn. Quad., 1771, 223).

"**Common Weasel** *Mustela vulgaris.*"=*Putorius vulgaris* (Erxl.). Ord agrees with Turton that this species is cosmopolitan, as also the Ermine *P. erminea* (Linn.). See Coues, (Fur B. An., 1877, 136), on this subject.

"**PEKAN** *MUSTELA HUDSONIUS.*" Ord is certainly responsible for this name of the *Mustela pennantii* of Erxleben. He has justly discarded Turton's name *canadensis* as a synonym, because of its use under this genus on a previous page, for the Otter, (vid. sup. cit.).

"**American Sable** *Mustela Americanus.*" Turton's claim to precedence in thus naming the American, as distinct from the European, Marten, is well established.

Page 261.

GENUS *URSUS*.

"**GRIZZLY BEAR** *URSUS HORRIBILIS.*" This of Ord's, is the first tenable name for the West American form, which many eminent naturalists consider too intimately related to *Urus arctos* to form a distinct species. For further discussion of it see notes on page 299. See also, Ord., Jour. de Phys., 1818, 152.

"**American Bear** *Ursus Americanus.*" The term, American Bear, first used by Turton and copied by Ord, is a better name for our animal than "Black Bear," by which it is so generally called. Black bears are to be found among several so-called species, and not infrequently our "Black Bear," is brown. Custom, however, will probably retain the name in spite of any effort to establish the more distinctive title.

"**Badger** *Ursus meles.*" ·

"**American Badger** *Ursus Labradorius.*" The critical reader is referred to Dr. Coues' history of the American Badger (Fur. B. Anim. 1877, 261-292,) for discussion of the points of synonymy, etc., involved in its separation from the European Badger. Dr. Coues makes his first reference in the synonymatic list to the "*Ursus taxus,*" of Schreber (Saugt. iii, 1778, 520, Pl. 142 B.). This reference was not verified by Dr. Coues, as he states on page 276, adding that Schreber "is cited for a name, "*Ursus taxus*" as applicable to the American Badger though quoted as considering our species as distinct from the European." It is unfortunate Dr. Coues did not make this reference, as he evidently thinks the name "*Taxus,*" first used for a Badger by Aldrovanus (?) and in a specific sense by Schreber, as above quoted, was originally intended (as now universally and erroneously applied) for the European species.

That this view is erroneous the description of Schreber, (sup. cit.) and his plate plainly show. In these he has almost as explicitly shown the external differences between his American Badger, *U taxus*, and his European Badger, *U. meles*, as has Dr. Coues, and often in equivalent terms.

Taxidea taxus (Schreber, 1778) should therefore stand as the proper name of the American Badger. The later use of the name "*taxus*" by Boddaert, (Elench. Anim., 1784), after the specific name "*Meles,*" of Linnæus was made generic, for the European form, is inadmissible. This, as well as his "var. *americanus,*" are synonyms of *taxus.*

Blumenbach, (Hand. Natur., 1799, 96), misquoted by Gray (B. M. Cat. Carniv., (etc.) 1869, 124), gives to the European Badger the name "*taxus*", quoting Schreber (sup. cit.), having mistaken the *taxus* of that author for the European animal and ignoring his "*Ursus meles*" entirely. Blumenbach's description refers solev to the European form.

The proper name for the European Badger is *Meles meles*(Linn.).

"Wolverene *Ursus luscus.*"
"Glutton *Urus gulo.*" } =*Gulo luscus* (Linn.) J. Sabine. As hinted by
Ord in the foot note, these refer to one species, of Arctogæan distribution.

GENUS *DIDELPHIS.*

"Virginian Opossum *Didelphis opossum.*" Turton, followed by Ord, first gives (?) the name *opossum* to the Virginian species, the *Didelphys virginiana* of Kerr, (1798) and Shaw (1800).

Dobson, (perhaps on rather scanty material, viz, rather less than fifty skins, stands, skulls and skeletons from northern N. America, (vid. B. Mus. Cat., Marsup. & Monot., 1888, 327-329.)), includes *D. virginiana, cancrivora, aurita, californica* and *breviceps,* (with *azaræ* as a subspecies), under the Linnæan *D. marsupialis.* The *D. opossum* of Linnæus, (*D. quica* of Temminck), Dobson considers plainly applicable to a small Neotropical species belonging to another subgenus. It is likely that the *D. virginiana* of Kerr, wrongly accredited to Shaw, is as entitled to subspecific rank as *azaræ.* That it is a distinct species from typical *marsupialis,* as defined by Dobson, (sup. cit.), seems doubtful.

"Mexican Opossum *Didelphis cayopollin*"=*Didelphys murina* Linn., Syst. Nat., 1758, 55. See Dobson, (sup. cit.), p. 343.

GENUS *TALPA.*

"Long-tailed Mole *Talpa longicaudata.*" A synonym of Erxleben's (Syst. Reg. An., 1777, 118.) for the Star nosed Mole *Condylura cristata* (Linn.), based on Pennant's "Long-tailed Mole"; the same as the "Radiated Mole" of Pennant.

"Red Mole *Talpa rubra.*" Originating in the "*Talpa americana*" of Seba (Thes. I, 51; T. 32, fig. 2.) and based on a specimen said to have three toes on the fore feet; in other respects similar to *Talpa europæa* and of a brownish red. A remote suggestion can be conceived in the description to a *Geomys*; and Schreber in his synonymy of it tentatively included "Le Tucan" of Buffon. It is unidentifiable, though Pennant, Müller and Erxleben give it a place in their Systems.

GENUS *SOREX.*

"Crested Shrew *Sorex cristatus.*"=*Condylura cristata* (Linn.). See note (supra) on *Talpa longicaudata.*

"Aquatic Shrew or Common Mole *Sorex aquaticus.*"=*Scalops aquaticus* (Linn).

"Fetid Shrew *Sorex araneus.*" Ord includes this European species on authority of Turton, who refers to a form; "2. Head, upper parts dusky; sides brownish rusty. Inhabits Hudson's Bay and Labradore."

"**Black Shrew,** *Sorex niger.*" Not mentioned in Turton nor in Pennant, nor elsewhere that I can find, unless it refers to the "*Talpa Virginianus niger supinus*" of Seba (Thes., II, p. 51.) quoted in the synonymy of *Scalops* ("*Sorex*") *aquaticus* of earlier authors, and which originated, perhaps, in a specimen of *Condylura cristata.*

"**Mexican Shrew** *Sorex Mexicanus.*" Ord bases this on the *S. mexicanus* of Turton, Turton on Pennant's name and description, and Pennant on the "De Tucan, seu Talparum Indicarum quodam genere, Cap. XXIV," of Fernandez, (Hist. Quad. Nov. Hisp., 1651, 7.). Erxleben confounds it (De Tucan) with the "Talpa rubra Americana" of Seba (vid. sup. cit.) questioning, however, if the latter be the same as the Mexican Shrew of Pennant. Fernandez's description is that of a "tawny" *Geomys* with "short tail and legs, sharp nose, small rounded ears, long incurved claws and living in burrows with numerous passages, which are a nuisance to travelers."

Pennant translates, "two long fore-teeth above and below . . . length from nose to tail nine inches," and adds "M. de Buffon thinks it a mole, but by the ears it should be classed here," (viz. as a shrew). Turton makes the same diagnosis, prefacing it, however, with, "fore-feet, 3-toed, hind-feet 4." evidently taken (after Erxleben) from Seba's erroneous description of the aforesaid "Talpa rubra americana." Fernandez's meaning in that passage, translated by Pennant, "two long fore-teeth above and below," is very difficult to make out and may have reference to the grooved incisors. In this case the animal was a true *Geomys,* (not *Thomomys*); *Thomomys,* however, has not been reported from southern Mexico. Fernandez's "Tucan" was evidently either *Geomys hispidus,* Leconte, or the *G. mexicanus* (Licht.), (Abhand. K. Acad. Wiss. Berl, 1827, 113), of late authors. The probability is strongly in favor of this assumption, and, judging by the abundance of the animal described by Fernandez as compared with what we know of the comparative abundance and scarcity, respectively, of *G. mexicanus* and *G. hispidus* there is small doubt that Fernandez's "Tucan" was the same as Liechenstein's animal.

Fortunately for synonymy, Lichtenstein selected the same specific name for the Tucan that had been applied to it 25 years previously by Turton. Briefly summarized, the synonymy of the Tucan should be—

Tucan, Fernandez, Hist. Quad. N. Hisp., 1651, 7.

Mexican Shrew, Pennant, Syn. Quad., 1771 (No. 240), 309.

Sorex mexicanus, Turton, Syst. Nat., 1802, 72.

"   "   Ord, Guth. Geog., 1815, 291.

Ascomys mexicanus Licht., Abhan. K. Akad. Wiss. Berl., 1827, 113.

Geomys mexicanus Rich., Rep. Brit. Assn. Ad. Sci., 1836 & '37, 150.

"   "   Baird, Mam. N. Am., 1857, 387.

Page 291.

GENUS *HYSTRIX*.

"Brazilian Porcupine *Hystrix prehensilis.*" ⎫
"Mexican Porcupine *Hystrix Mexicana.*" ⎬ =*Synetheres prehensilis*
(Linn.) Cuv.

"Canada Porcupine *Hystrix dorsata.*"=*Erethizon dorsatus* (Linn.) Cuv.

Page 292.

GENUS *MUS*.

"American Rat *Mus Americanus.*" This is undoubtedly the "American" Rat" of Turton, whose description is a virtual quotation of the diagnosis of the "American Rat" of Pennant, (No. 229., Hist. Quad. 1781, 441.), who quotes Bartram, referring to Kalm's Travels (ii, 48).

Bartram's references, as quoted, apply to the Cave Rat of the Alleghany Mountains, the extinct (?) *Neotoma magister* of Baird, (Mam. N. Am., 1857, 498, (in text)), which, as *N. pennsylvanica*, Stone, (Proc. Acad. Nat. Sci., Phila., (1893, 16,) has been described as a recent species. This animal, which is distinct from *N. floridana* Ord, would be entitled to the name *americanus* imposed by Turton (q. v.) were not that name preoccupied by the "*Mus americanus*" of Kerr (Syst. Nat., 1792, 231.) which is now accepted as the first tenable name of the eastern White-footed Mouse, *Sitomys americanus*. Some earlier authors have confounded the two in their synonymy.

"Water Rat *Mus amphibius.*" The *Arvicola pennsylvanica* (Ord) (vid infra) was identified by Turton and his predecessors with the large Water Vole of Europe. See Lawson's History of Carolina, page 122.

"SAND OR EARTH RAT *MUS TUZA.*" Prof. Baird's quotation of this name is incorrectly spelled *tuzu* in his work on N. American Mammals. Dr. Coues has rightly insisted on the adoption of Ord's specific name for the Georgian Hamster or Salamander of the Gulf States, which has generally gone under the name *Geomys pinetis* of Rafinesque, (Amer. Month. Mag., 1817, 45.). Both names are probably based on the same descriptions, notably those of Mitchill, (N. York Med. Repos., 1802,) 89— Ib., Bewick's Quad., 1st. Amer. ed., 1804, 525).

"Louisiana Earth Rat or Gopher *Mus Ludovicianus.*" Ord's foot-note reference to this animal leaves us in doubt whether he referred to the common Pocket Gopher, *Geomys bursarius* (Shaw), (Linn. Trans., v., 1800, 237) or not. It is probable that he did. Shaw's name in any case, has priority.

"ASH-COLOURED RAT *MUS CINEREUS.*"=*Neotoma (cinerea.)* Say & Ord, Jour. A. N. Sci., Phila., 1825, 346. Another of Ord's species, for the honor of naming which he acknowledges his indebtedness to the painstaking narrative of Lewis and Clark. The *N. drummondii* (Rich.)

(Zool. Jour., 1828. 517.), and the *N. occidentalis* "Cooper, Mss." (Baird, Proc. A. N. Sci., Phila., 1855, 335) were applied to the same species. These have been revived as subspecies of *N. cinerea*, the first by Dr. Merriam (Proc. Biol. Soc. Washn., 1892, 25.) as inhabiting the Rocky Mountains of British Columbia, the second by Dr. J. A. Allen, (Bull. Amer. Mus. N. Hist., 1891, 287.), with habitat in "Idaho and Shoalwater Bay, Washington." The habitat of *N. cinerea* (typical) is the east slope of the Rockies near Great Falls, Montana. See Coues' Lewis & Clark, 1893, pp. 400, 863. It probably extends much farther north, into Alberta, B. America.

"**Rustic** Mouse *Mus agrarius*." Turton, under this name, includes a "No. 2." equivalent to the "No. 230 a" or American **Rat** of Pennant (Syn., Quad., 1771, 303.) which (sup. **cit.**) is the White-footed Mouse, *Mus agrarius* var *americanus=Sitomys americanus* (Kerr). It is probable that Ord intentionally applied this name, (*Mus agrarius*), to the Pennsylvania W. F. Mouse, not considering it separable from the European animal. His "*Mus Americanus*", the American Rat, No. 299 of Pennant's History of Quadrupeds, is, as we have seen, (sup. cit.), widely different.

"**Mexican Mouse** *Mus Mexicanus*." Turton's brief description, "A large reddish brown spot each side the belly. Inhabits Mexico, whitish mixed with red," is from Pennant, (Hist. Quad., 1781, 446), who quotes Seba (Thes. Mus., 1734, 74, Tab. xlv, fig. 5.). Seba's figure looks like that of a House Mouse or a species of *Reithrodontomys*. The peculiar color-pattern, if diagnostic of an indigenous species, should make its recognition an easy task. It is probably a partial albino.

"**Virginian Mouse** *Mus Virginianus*," is another production of the indefatigable Seba, which Pennant recognizes in his History of Quadrupeds. The type of this creation was probably the result of albinism and outrageous stuffing, being described as a white "Rat" (mouse ?) with base of tail very thick. It may have been a mole.

"**Hudson's Mouse** *Mus Hudsonius*." This is an Arvicoline animal described under the same name by Pallas (Nov. Sp. Glires, 1778, 208.) who quotes Foster. It is not a *Zapus*, as its specific name would suggest, but (see Coues, Mon. N. Am. Rod., 1877, 249) a synonym of *Mus torquatus* Pallas (sup. cit., pp. 77 & 206). Should it be proven that the American and Asiatic animals are separable, (Dr. Coues considered them identical), the *Mus hudsonius* of Pallas will still apply to the former as *Cuniculus hudsonius* (Pallas), (Coues, Mss.).

"**AMERICAN WANDERING MOUSE** *MUS CANADENSIS*." By the reference of Dr. Coues, (Mon. Am. N. Rod., 1877, 50) it appears the vernacular part of this name was applied originally by Barton ("Med. & Surg. Jour., 1805, 31") to the White-footed Mouse *Sitomys americanus* (Kerr). I am unable to find the Journal referred to. If certainly identifiable as such, the subspecific name "*canadensis*," applied by Mr. G. S. Miller Jr.

(Proc. Biol. Soc. Washn., viii, 1893. 55) to the form of White-footed Mouse inhabiting northern New York and New England, would appear to be preoccupied by the "*canadensis*" of Ord.

"Meadow Mouse *Mus arvalis*." Turton erroneously includes Newfoundland in the habitat of this Old World species, and Ord follows suit.

"PENNSYLVANIA MEADOW **MOUSE** *MUS PENNSYLVANICA.*" While admitting that this name in strictness is justly applicable to Wilson's "Meadow Mouse", Dr. Coues prefers to use Ord's later name of "*riparius*", stating (Mon. Rodentia, p. 156, foot note) that "the name (*pennsylvanica*) is simply based, without sufficient description, upon a scarcely recognizable figure incidentally introduced in an ornithological work." As will be seen, Ord's reference is not made to the figure at all, but to Wilson's description. (Amer. Orn., vi, 59.), which fact Dr. Coues appears to have overlooked. This desciption is a full one and unmistakably applies to the same animal subsequently described by Ord (Jour. Acad. Nat. Sci., Phila., 1825, 305.) with the name *riparius*. Wilson' figure, good or bad, (and it is poor enough), is of secondary importance.

Rafinesque's *Mynomes pratensis* (Amer. Mon. Mag., ii, 1817, 45) also makes it imperative that Ord's earlier name should stand, if Ord is to get the credit due him. Baird incorrectly quotes Ord's *pennsylvanica*, in his synonomic list, under *Arvicola* instead of *Mus*, and he seems to have been imitated by subsequent writers.

Page 292.

GENUS ARCTOMYS.

"Maryland Marmot or Ground Hog *Arctomys* **monax.**" } These names apply
"Canadian Marmot *Arctomys empetra.*" to the same species. The *Arctomys empetra* of Pallas was originally imposed by him on Parry's Spermophile of Richardson. In Pallas' references, however, he cites the Quebec Marmot of Pennant and Foster as synonyms of the Spermophile. This originated much confusion among later authors, in which Ord has followed Turton. Dr. Allen (Mon. N. Am. Rod., pp. 915-917.) fully discusses these perplexing questions.

"**Hoary Marmot** *Arctomys pruinosa.*"=*A. priunosus* Gmelin.

"Tailless Marmot *Arctomys Hudsonius.*" Founded on "No. 265, Tailless M." of Pennant (Hist. Quad., 1781, 405) whom Turton copies and imposes the binomial. I find no subsequent reference to it in literature. It seems unidentifiable, being described as having two upper and four lower cutting teeth and no tail: "inhabits Hudson's Bay. In the Leverian Museum." It is not impossible that it was a *Lagomys* from the Hudson's Bay Territory.

"**Earless Marmot** *Arctomys citillus.*" Ord has made a pencil foot note, "not in America," under this species.

"**LOUISIANA MARMOT OR PRAIRIE DOG** *ARCTOMYS LUDOVICIANA.*"= *Cynomys ludovicianus* (Ord) Rafinesque. See below, note for page 302.

"**COLUMBIA MARMOT** *ARCTOMYS COLUMBIANUS.*"=*Spermophilus columbianus* (Ord) Merr. See Merriam, N. Am. Fauna No. 5, 1891, 39; also Coues, Lewis & Clark, 1893, iii, 856 (foot note); also my notes, below, for page 303. Type locality, Camp Chopunnish on the Kooskooskee (Clear-water) River, near town of Kamai, Idaho.

Page 292.
GENUS *SCIURUS.*

"**Large Black Squirrel** *Sciurus niger.*"=*Sciurus niger* of the tenth edition of Linnæus, now understood in the restricted sense to apply to the Fox Squirrel of the southeastern United States.

"**SMALL BLACK SQUIRREL** *SCIURUS PENNSYLVANICA.*" Dr. J. A. Allen, after discussing (Mon. N. Am. Rod., 1877, 709) the synonymy of the eastern Gray Squirrel, *Sciurus carolinensis* of Gmelin, (Syst. Nat., i, 1788, 148), prefers to retain the varietal name *leucotis* of Gapper (Zool. Jour., v, 1830, 206) for the northern form in preference to the above name of Ord, applied to it fifteen years earlier. Dr. Allen, not having access to Ord's work, objected to the validity of *pennsylvanica* on the plea that it was based on specimens from the Middle States, an intermediate locality between those of the southern and northern forms and so not typical of either. This objection is fully met by Ord's foot note, which gives the habitat of the Small Black Squirrel as "those parts of Pennsylvania which lie to the westward of the Allegany ridge." The region thus designated is assigned by Dr. Allen (Bul. Am. Mus. N. Hist., iv, pl. viii.) almost wholly to the Alleghanian and Canadian faunæ, and it is well known that the "Black Squirrel" is very rarely met with in Pennsylvania east of the Susquehanna River, and rarely west of it, except in the *northwestern* parts of the state, in a region typically Canadian in its faunal characters. There seem therefore, no valid objections to allowing *Sciurus carolinensis pennsylvanicus* (Ord) to stand as the name of the northern Gray Squirrel.

"**Cat or Fox Squirrel** *Sciurus vulpinus.*" This is Gmelin's name for the *Sciurus niger* of Catesby and Linnæus.

"**Gray Squirrel** *Sciurus cinereus.*" Ord probably applied this name to the normal gray phase (sup. cit.) of his "Small Black Squirrel," *S. carolinensis pennsyvlanicus.* The name *S. cinereus* Linn. (Syst. Nat., 1758, 64)is considered to properly belong to the northern race of *Sciurus niger*, the "Cat Squirrel" of Bachman, and should read *Sciurus niger cinereus* (Linn.) J. A. Allen.

"**Louisiana Gray Squirrel** *Sciurus Ludovicianus.*" This species is not given in either edition of Turton. It was so named by Custis in Barton's Medical and Physical Journal (vol. ii., 1806, p. 43) from which Ord must

have **taken it. Dr.** Allen makes it stand (Mon. N. Am. Rod.) for the
western **race** of *S. niger* Linn. **as** *S. n. ludovicianus* (Custis).

"Virginian Squirrel *Sciurus Virginianus."* Turton is responsible for this
name, which appears, from the description, to be a synonym of one of
the *S. niger* group.

"NEW JERSEY SQUIRREL *SCIURUS HIEMALIS."* Undoubtedly named
in **good** faith, but, as the description implies, based on such fanciful
characters as any individual of the *S. carolinensis* group may assume **at**
some period of its existence. *S. hiemalis* is a synonym of *S. c. pennsylvanicus,*(Ord), (sup. cit.).

"Varied Squirrel *Sciurus variegatus."=S. variegatus* Erxleben, which
is based on two or more Mexican species.*=S. boothiæ* Gray (List Mam.
B. Mus., 1843, 149). **For** discussion of its synonymy, **see** Allen, Mon.
N. Am. Rod., 1877, **741.**

"Mexican Squirrel *Sciurus Mexicanus."* This is possibly *Spermophilus
mexicanus,* (Licht.) Wagner. Turton's description indicates this genus,
or *Tamias,* certainly not *Sciurus.*

"Hudson's Bay Squirrel *Sciurus Hudsonius."* This is Pallas' name **for**
the typical **northern** Red Squirrel or Chickaree. See Pallas, Nov. sp.
Glir., 1778, **376.** It is strictly a synonym of Erxleben's *S. hudsonicus,*
(Syst. Anim., 1777, 414), a synonym, however, which later authors have
allowed **to** stand because Erxleben clasified it **as a** variety of *Sciurus
vulgaris* Linn.

Usage may permit, but good rules **will not sanction such an interpre-**
tation. *S. hudsonicus* is Erxleben's **name, but hitherto** Pallas got the
credit of it.

"CAROLINA OR CHICKAREE SQUIRREL *SCIURUS CAROLINENSIS."* A syn-
onym of *Sciurus hudsonicus* Erxleben. The **name** is also preoccupied by
the *S. carolinensis* Linn. (sup. cit.), and **by one of** Gmelin's synonyms.

"Fair Squirrel *Sciurus flavus."* This is one of Linnæus' original species.
Its habitat is given as "Carthagena America." Pennant (Syn. Quad.,
285.) says "it inhabits the woods near Amadabad the capital of Guzarat,"
and then quotes Linnæus as above. It is an unidentifiable species.

"Flying Squirrel *Sciurus volucella."=Sciuropterus volucella* (Pallas)
Geoff.

"HUDSON'S BAY FLYING SQUIRREL *SCIURUS LABRADORIUS."* The
Flying Squirrel of northeastern N. America, the species here designated,
has, either as a species or variety, gone under the names *hudsonius* of
Gmelin (Syst. Nat., i, 1788, 153) and *sabrinus* of Shaw (Gen. Zool.,
ii, 1801, 157). Contrary to the arguments of Dr. Allen (Mon. N. Am.
Rod., 1877, 660), Shaw's name must hold for the Hudson's Bay race,
because Gmelin's *Sciurus hudsonius* (p. 153, sup. cit.) is only applicable to the Chickaree, *S. hudsonicus* Erxl. (sup. cit.), to which Gmelin
applies it on **a** previous page **(p.** 147) of the same book.

Ord's name *Labradorius* for this animal is apparently his own. Turton does not use it, nor, so far as I can search, does anyone else.

"COLUMBIA GRAY SQUIRREL *SCIURUS————.*" A brief of the synonymy of this Squirrel is as follows :—

"The large gray squirrel," Lewis & Clark, Hist. Exp., ii, 1814, 172.
"*S. griseus*", Ord, Guth. Geog., 1815, 292, (Mss. annot. in author's copy: no date of entry).
"Columbian Gray Squirrel *sciurus griseus;*" Ord, Jour. de Phys., lxxxvii, 1818, 150.*

Sciurus fossor Peale, Mam. & B'ds., U. S. Expl. Exp., 1848, 55.

A consultation of the above references shows unmistakably Ord's priority in giving the Gray Squirrel of the Pacific slope a permanent name. It is to be hoped the title "Columbian Gray Squirrel," will be hereafter adhered to by all patriotic Americans. It is geographically correct, this Squirrel having been taken not only on the Oregon side of the Columbia River, but as far north in Washington as Puget Sound. I have examined specimens taken in the vicinity of Olympia, now in the collection of Edwards Bros., Tacoma, Washington.

"RED-BREASTED SQUIRREL *SCIURUS————.*" The synonymy of this species, is in part, as follows :—

"The small brown squirrel", Lewis & Clark, Hist. Exp., ii, 1814, 174.
"*S. rubricatus*" Ord, Guth. Geog., 1815, 292, (Mss. annot. in author's copy: no date of entry).
"Red-breasted Squirrel *S. rubricatus;*" Ord, Jour. de Phys., lxxxvii, 1818, 150.

Sciurus douglassi Bachman, Proc. Zool. Soc., Lon., 1838, 99.

As in the case above cited, *Sciurus rubricatus* Ord, legitimately antedates Bachman's name for the Red Squirrel of the West Cascade region of Oregon and Washington. The citations from Lewis and Clark made by Ord in Guthrie's Geography, and the consensus of opinion as to the identity of their "small brown squirrel" with *Sciurus douglassi* Bach., make it almost as plain a case as that of the Columbia Gray Squirrel.

Sciurus rubricatus should not, in my opinion, be made subspecific of *S. hudsonius*.

"ROCKY MOUNTAIN GROUND SQUIRREL *SCIURUS————.*" Its earlier synonymy now stands:—

"The ground squirrel," Lewis & Clark, Hist. Exp., 1814, 175.
"*S. troglodytus*" Ord, Guth. Geog., 1815, 292, (Mss. annot. in authors' copy: no date of entry).
"Rocky Mountain Ground Squirrel *S. troglodytus;*" Ord, Jour. de Phys., lxxxvii, 1818, 150.

*This and the two succeeding citations occur in the following passage :

"My friend Lesueur has figured for me the greater part of the quadrupeds brought back by Lewis (and Clark), or at least those whose skins were in a perfect state of preservation, the common Badger, *Ursus labradoricus* of Linnæus; the Marmot of Louisiana, *Arctomys Ludoviciana*; the *Viverra alba*; the Columbia grey Squirrel; *sciurus griseus*; the Red breasted Squirrel, *S. rubricatus*; the Rocky mountain ground Squirrel, *S. troglodytus*, the Great Grizzly Bear, *Ursus horribilis*; I have of this last, two figures from two fine individuals in the Museum."

Sciurus quadrivitattus Say, Long's Exp. R. Mts., ii, 1823, 45. + *Tamias townsendi* Bachman, Jour. Acad. N. Sci., Phila., viii, 1839, 68, and varieties.

The **Ground** Squirrel of **Lewis** and Clark above cited, and to which Ord's *Sciurus troglodytus* was applied, included at least two or three species or subspecies and is of too composite a character to make the name of any fixed value.

"Brown Squirrel *Sciurus————*." Ord in the foot note reference surmises the other Brown Squirrel of Lewis and Clark to be *Sciurus hudsonius* and there is no doubt that by this term, which is rather vaguely and loosely applied by Lewis and Clark, they meant to designate the . forms of *hudsonius* found east of the Cascade Mountains, now going under the names, *S. hudsonius richardsoni* (Bach.) and *S. hudsonius fremonti* (Aud. & Bach.).

Page 292.

· GENUS *DIPUS*.

"**Labrador** Jerboa *Dipus Labradorius*," Turton, Syst. Nat , 1802, 99.

"**Canada** Jerboa *Dipus Canadensis*", Davies, Trans. Lin. Soc., 1798, 157.

"**American** Jerboa *Dipus Americanus*", Barton, Amer. Philos. Trans., 1798, 115.

This trio of names apply, so far as can be ascertained, to one species, the *Zapus hudsonius* (Zimmerman) Coues (Mon. N. Am. Rod., 1877, 461-479.). They may apply in part to the *Zapus insignis* Miller, (Amer. Nat., 1891, 472, and Proc. Biol. Soc. Washn., 1893, 1.), a very distinct species, confined to the more boreal parts of the eastern habitat of *hudsonius*.

Page 292.

GENUS *LEPUS*.

"Common Hare *Lepus* **timidus**."=*Lepus timidus arcticus* (Leach), Ross' Voy., ii, 1819, app. iv, 170.

"Varying Hare **Lepus** **varibialis**."=*Lepus americanus* Erxleben, Syst. Reg. Anim., 1777, 330.

"American Hare or Rabbit *Lepus* **Americanus**."=*Lepus sylvaticus* Bachman, Jour. Acad. N. Sci., 1837, 403.

For discussion of the perplexing synonymy of the N. American Hares, see Allen, Mon. N. Am. Rod., 1877, 288-343.

Page 292.

GENUS *CERVUS*.

"Greater Stag or Elk *Cervus* **major**."=*Cervus canadensis* Erxleben, Syst. Reg. Anim., 1777, 305. Ord's name *major* is the second pure synonym of Erxleben's, the first being the *C. wapiti* of Barton, (Amer. Phil. Trans., vi, 1809. 79.)* Turton makes the Elk an American representative of *Cervus elaphus* Linn.

"**Mexican Deer** *Cervus Mexicanus.*" Gmelin (Syst. Nat., 1788, 179) is apparently the first to use this name in the binomial sense. His description has been considered by Baird and others to apply to the Mexican form of *Cariacus virginianus* and by some authorities it has been considered a distinct species. Gmelin's first citation of authority for his *C. mexicanus* is the Mexican Deer, No. 52, of Pennant (Hist. Quad., 1781, 110), his third citation is "Teutlal macame. Hernandez an. mexic. 324." Pennant's first citation is the same as Gmelin's, viz: "Teutlamacame, Hernandez An. Mexic. 324." The Teutlamacame is therefore the basis of the Mexican Deer of Pennant, Gmelin and later authors. But it has been asserted on the authority of the Berlandier Manuscripts (Baird, Main. N. Am., 1857, 666., Alston, Biol. Cent. Am., 1879—'82, 113) that the Teutlamacame or Berrendo of the Spanish Mexicaus is the Pronghorn Antelope, *Antilocapra americana* Ord, (infra). If this can be proven, Ord's name would have to go, and the Mexican *Cariacus* receive a new name. Reference to Hernandez' description of the Teutlamacame shows quite conclusively that, whatever the Mexicans considered a "Berrendo" in Berlandier's day, this name was understood by Hernandez to apply to a gray deer about the size of a goat with ample branching horns. This is confirmed by Pennant's description and figure which unmistakably relates to a *Cariacus*. Hernandez' description, which is not on page 324, but near the middle of 325, is as follows:—"moreover concerning the Teutlalmacame which is a little larger than a medium sized goat. Covered with gray hair, easily pulled out, and yellowish ("fulvoq."); but with sides and belly hoary white, hence the Spanish natives are accustomed to call them Berrendos.(†) They wear ample (wide) evenly branching horns, (but in some they are small), long tapering sharp pointed, divided into branches and reaching beyond (or below) the eyes, of which (viz: the animal) we show a figure." This figure, from the context, is the one on page 324. The figure on page 325 is of the Temamacame next described, which Hernandez likens to the "Fallow Deer, with the shortest and sharpest of horns color fulvous, brown, and beneath, white." The *figure* shows a spike-horned animal, which Mr. Alston (Biol. Cent. Am., p. 119) considers to be *Cariacus rufinus* (Bourcier & Pucheran). The figure of the Teuhtlalmacame is the real cause of the confusion of authors, owing to the resemblance of its horns to those of the Antelope, *Antilocapra americana* Ord. It is not impossible that this figure was based on the Antelope, but as it differs in many other respects from that animal, and the most liberal translation of

*I find in the Journal de Physique, 1818, p. that Ord gets his name *C. major* from Artorby, who, he affirms, gave the Wapiti this name long before that of Gmelin, viz. *C. canadensis* Erxl. Artorby seems to be so obscure an individual as not to merit citation in any of the scientific literature at my command. It is probable that Artorby gave it this name before the binomial system was recognized as authoritative.

†Spanish, *Berrendo*—tinged with two colors.

Hernandez' *description* cannot be made to fit it, we must base conclusions on the text. As has been stated, Pennant's interpretation, on which Gmelin's description of *C. mexicanus* is based, makes the case decisive in favor of regarding the "Teuhtlalmacame" as the oldest literary reference to *Cariacus virginianus mexicanus* (Gmel.).

"**Spring-back Deer** *Cervus*———." I fail to find any reference to such a name in literature.

"**Mule Deer** *Cervus* ————"="The mule deer" Lewis & Clark, Exped., 1814, 167, No. 3.=*Cervus macrotis* Say, Long's Exped., ii, 1823, 88.=*Cariacus macrotis* (Say) Gray, Knows. Menag., 1850, 67.

"**Long-tailed Fallow Deer** *Cervus*———"="The common red deer" (tail 17 in. long), Lewis & Clark, ibid, p. 166, No. 1.=*Cervus virginianus* Boddaert, Elench. Anim., I, 1784, 136,=*Cariacus virginianus macrurus* (Rafinesque), Amer. Mon. Mag., 1817, 436.

"**Black-tailed Fallow Deer** *Cervus*———"="The black-tailed fallow deer" Lewis & Clark, ibid, p. 166, No. 2.=*Cervus macrotis, var columbianus* Richardson, F. B. Amer., I, 1829, 255. See foot notes, Dr. Coues' 1893 edition Lewis & Clark, pp. 843—845.

We are here again confronted with the question why Ord refrained from giving specific names to animals so fully described in the History of the Lewis and Clark Expedition. It is evident however that unless a species had been noticed by other writers, or was minutely described, as in the case of the "Columbia Marmot," or unmistakably distinct from any other then known form, as the "Ash-coloured Rat," Ord did not impose a technical name. See also in this connexion note on page 307 and foot note page 292, Columbia Gray Squirrel, etc.

Page 292.
GENUS *ANTILOPE.*

"**AMERICAN OR PRONG-HORNED ANTELOPE** *ANTILOPE AMERICANUS.*" =*Antilocapra americana* Ord, Jour. de Phys., 1818, 149. The above name, with Ord's quotations and remarks on page 308, constitute the original description of this remarkable species. In the later reference Ord established for it a new genus which has since been made the type of the family *Antilocapridæ*. See my notes (infra) to page 308 ; also Dr. Coues' Lewis & Clark, 1893 ed., p. 849.

"**Barbarian Antelope** *Antilope dorcas.*" Henderson's book, on which this so called antelope is based is unobtainable in Philadelphia. It may have been the Wood Brocket. See note (infra) on Big-horned Sheep.

Page 292.
GENUS *OVIS.*

"**Big-horned Sheep or Argali** *Ovis ammon.*" Considered inseparable by many earlier authors, from the Siberian Argali, *Ovis argali.* Cuvier,

(Reg. An., i, 1817, 267) was the first to recognize the Rocky Mountain
Sheep as distinct from the Asiatic Argali, but he gave it the same
binomial as that previously given by Ord (vid. infra) to the Rocky Mountain Goat ("Sheep") *Mazama montana* (Ord) Rafinesque.

Shaw, (Nat. Misc., xv., t. 610) figured and described this species under
the name *Ovis canadensis*, but this work, being without any date whatever,
the name is unavailable, though it probably has priority over any other.
Ovis cervina Desmarest (Nouv. Dict. Hist. Nat., 1818, 551) is the next
available name.*

Desmarest (sup. cit.) quotes Geoffroy for "*Ovis montana*" but his reference, "Ann. Mus., 2, pl. 40," shows he did not consult it, as the plate is
numbered "58" and named "Berlier de Montagne." In Geoffroy's description (pp. 360—363) the plate is numbered "Pl. LX"! Nowhere is a
binomial Greek or Latin name applied to the animal. Gray (Cat. B.
Mus., i, 1850, 177) wrongly makes the same reference to Geoffroy in the
synonymy of this species and even attributes the same name to Richardson, who never used it!

"ROCKY MOUNTAIN SHEEP *OVIS MONTANUS*."= Rocky Mountain Goat,
Mazama montana (Ord) Rafinesque. The context, (pp. 309, 310)
shows that Ord intended this name for what is now known as the Goat.
For discussion of the confusion of the Rocky Mountain Goat and Sheep
by earlier authors, see my notes for pages 308, 309 & 310, also Dr. Coues,
Lewis & Clark, ed. 1893, pp. 850, 851. Prof. Baird (Mam. N. Am., 1857,
665) rejects the generic name *Mazama* Rafinesque (Amer. Month. Mag.,
i, 1817, 44) because of its heterogeneous character. In this view he is
supported by Mr. Alston (sup. cit. p. 113). Rafinesque certainly intended to represent by this genus a class of animals "with solid, simple,
straight, round and permanent horns." The Temamazame (sup. cit.) is
the first of the three given under this genus with the name *Mazama tema*
but it has been since identified as a *Cervus*, *C. rufinus* (B. & P. sup. cit.)
and hence cannot stand as the type of *Mazama*. The next two, *M. dorsata* and *M. sericea* refer unmistakably to the Rocky Mountain Goat,
Rafinesque quoting Ord's *Ovis montana* for the first and Blainville's *Antilope (Rupicapra) Americana* (Bull. des Sci. Philom., 1816, 80) for the
second.

Contrary to the assertions of some earlier writers, *Mazama*, as defined
by Rafinesque, has not the remotest reference to *Antilocapra americana*
Ord. If Mr. Alston's assertion, that the Temamacame of Hernandez is
the Black-faced Brocket, *Cariacus rufinus* (B. & P.), (sup. cit.), be true,
it should stand as *Cariacus tema* (Raf.).

The general acceptation of certain other genera of Rafinesque's, of
doubtful status, makes it quite consistent that *Mazama* should be retained, but the law of priority in sequence of enumeration of species
under a newly proposed genus, if strictly adhered to, makes *C. tema* the
type ; and the genus *Mazama* by such an interpretation is worthless.

*Since this was written I find that Mr. Alston (Biol. Cent. Amer., p. 111 (foot note) comes to the
same conclusion.

Page 292.

GENUS *BOS.*

"Bison **or American Ox** *Bos Americanus.*"=*Bos bison* Linn., Syst. Nat. 1758, 72.=*Bos americanus* Gmelin, Syst. Nat., 1788, 204.=*Bison americanus* H. Smith, Griff. Cuv., v, 1827, 374.=*Bison bison* (Linn.) H. Smith, **A. O. U. Code.**

Page 292.

GENUS *TAPIR.*

"**Long-nosed Tapir** *Tapir Americanus.*"=*Tapirus terrestris* (Linn.) Cuv. of South America. The N. American, (Mexican and Central American) forms, *Tapirus bairdi* and *T. dowi* were both described under his genus *Elasmognathus* by Prof. Gill, the former in the Proc. Acad. N. Sci., Phila., 1865, 183, the latter in the Amer. Jour. Sci., 1870, 142. *Elasmognathus* is considered by the best American authorities as a strongly characterized genus.

Page. 292.

GENUS *SUS.*

"**Mexican Hog or Peccary** *Sus tajassu.*"=*Sus tajacu* Linn., Syst. Nat., 1766, 103. The *Dicotyles torquatus* Cuv. is a synonym. Ord's spelling, "*tajassu,*" is original, perhaps unintentional. See Alston (Biol. Cent. Amer., 1879—'82, 107) for discussion of this subject. *Dicotyles angulatus* Cope (Amer., Nat., 1889, 147) is the Texan representative of this genus.

"**Darien Hog or Warree** *Sus———*" This is another instance where Ord's apparent hesitation to impose a possible synonym deprives him of the honor of naming an anonymous species. Cuvier, in 1817, gave this animal the name *Dicotyles labiatus.* See my note (infra) for page 312.

Page 292.

GENERA *MONODON, PHYSETER, DELPHINUS.*

Owing to the involved condition of the classification and synonymy of the *Cetaceæ,* any attempt on the part of the author to unravel the mysteries of this section of Ord's list would involve useless expenditure of time and space.

Page 293.

"Arctic Walrus."

The first paragraph relating to this animal is nearly a literal translation of Molineux Shuldham's account, published in 1775 in the Philosophical Transactions (vol. **xlv, p.** 249). Before Ord's day the Walrus had been exterminated in the St. Lawrence region. A live specimen was taken in the Straits of Belle Isle in 1869. See J. A. Allen, N. Am. Pinn., 1880, 67—69.

Page 294.
"Wolf."

Nearly eighty years have elapsed since Ord prophesied the early extinction of the Wolf in Pennsylvania. One of these animals was killed in Potter Co., Pennsylvania in 1891. They have been reported since that time from Monroe County, and it is the concurrent testimony of reliable hunters in the western parts of the state that several Wolves continue to exist in the Alleghany wilderness. Since my note on the Mexican Wolf, page 7 of this Appendix was printed I find that the name *Canis occidentalis* Richardson, is antedated by *Canis nubilus* Say (Long's Exp. R. Mts., i, 1823, 168, (foot note)). The Gray Wolf of northern N. America should stand *Canis lupus nubilus* (Say).

Pages 294, 295.
"Indian Dog."

The problem of the relationships between wild and domestic Dogs and Wolves is not much nearer solution than in 1815. The reader may get a fair summary of what we know on this question in Mivart's Monograph of the Canidæ. The final conclusion of Darwin, that domestic Dogs had a multiple origin, arising from several races of Wolves and Jackals and at least one South American species, is indorsed by Mr. E. Harting and not denied by Prof. Mivart.

It is not improbable that the Indian Dog traces its decent from Old-World forms introduced to America in prehistoric times. Its consanguinity with the Coyote, *Canis latrans*, is well proven. As we go north beyond the habitat of the Coyote this admixture decreases and, in the Esquimaux Dog, the salient characters closely approach those of the Gray Wolf. Mr. Bartlett asserts that the Esquimaux Dog is nothing more than a domesticated Wolf.

Page 296.
"Couguar or Panther."

Ord evidently had no personal knowledge of the Panther, and from what follows it seems likely he was not sure of its presence in Pennsylvania, where they still exist and are occasionly taken by the hunters.

Page 296.
"Lynx."

The confusion of names and identities, existing in Ord's day on account of the use of the name "Catamount," has been perpetuated. It is still applied by hunters to the Lynx, *Lynx canadensis*, the Wild Cat, *L. rufus* and the Panther, *Felis concolor*.

The promiscuous use of these names resulted also in the multiplication of binomial names to match, in which Rafinesque, as usual, caps the climax in the American Monthly Magazine (1817, p. 46).

The Catamount of Morse's Geography, referred to, was, no doubt, a Panther. The Brown Tiger of Pike was a large, dark-colored specimen of the same, such as are often encountered in the well-watered regions of the far west.

Page 297.
"Striated Weasel."

As already implied in a previous note, it is here evident that Ord mistook Pennant's description of the Striated Weasel to apply to the common Skunk. It is not likely that the Little Striped Skunk of the Gulf States had ever come under Ord's notice.

Page 299.
"Grizzly Bear."

Because of the endless controversy among zoologists respecting the status of the black, brown and grizzly Bears of America and their affinities with *Ursus arctos*, this original description and naming of *Ursus horribilis* has done more than anything else to keep the name of Ord prominently in scientific notice. This interest has been increased by the absolute lack of other references to Ord's description than the synonymatic ones made to it by Say, Godman and Baird.

Owing to the disappearance of the only known copy of Guthrie from which Baird took his references, it has been impossible to improve upon them until now. It may be disappointing to many, who now for the first time scan the description, to find that Ord in this, as in similar cases, makes no personal deductions or diagnosis of the case, as presented by Brackenridge, which might absolutely fix the type and type locality of this form as contrasted with others in the United States nearly related to it. Ord's quotations being wholly taken from Brackenridge's account, (in which are included the Lewis and Clark quotations made by Ord, their sequence only being changed), we may justly define the typical habitat of *horribilis* to be western North Dakota, eastern Montana and north-eastern Wyoming. Brackenridge's description, apart from its Lewis and Clark quotations, is unquestionably taken from hearsay rather than personal experience and we must therefore base conclusions mainly on Lewis and Clark's narrative of the Bears in this region. The type specimen of *horribilis* is the "brown bear" (Coues' 1893 ed. L. & C., pp. 297, 298.) whose measurements Brackenridge and Ord copied from Lewis & Clark. This specimen is described as the largest they had seen up to that time; it was killed May 5, 1805, near old Fort Charles at the mouth of Little Dry or Lackwater Creek, flowing into the Missouri, in Dawson County, north-eastern Montana.

In a recent paper "On the Character and Relationships of *Ursus cinna-*

momeus Aud. & Bach."* Mr. Arthur Erwin Brown gives a resume of
the relationships of the North American Bears to each other and to those
of Europe, deciding finally that *Ursus arctos* should stand as the type,
isabellinus, syriacus, horribilis, cinnamomeus and *americanus* being only
subspecifically distinct therefrom. A strong consensus of opinion to-day
is largely in agreement with this view. Nevertheless it is a patent fact
that a trustworthy, representative series of skins, with accompanying
skulls and full data, of these bears does not exist in all the museums of
of the world, nor is it likely that they will be secured for many years to
come. Until such a collection shall have been made, the verdict cannot
be final, though it is likely that it will closely approximate the conclusions of Mr. Brown.

The case of the American and European Wolves is a parallel one, and
we must confess that the affinities between many New and Old World
forms of the North Temperate Carnivora indicate a specialization so perfectly fitted for resisting the normal influence of environment, and at
the same time permit a range of local and individual variation so great,
that the common rules of classification fail to assign them a permanent
place in nomenclature.

It should be stated that the type specimen and given habitat of the
cinnamomum of Audubon and Bachman indicate, with considerable
certainty, that it is identical with Ord's *horribilis* as now defined, and
that Mr. Brown's brown and yellow Bears are nothing more nor less than
the "brown" and "white"† Bears which continually harassed the westward march of Lewis and Clark from the Mandan villages to the eastern
slopes of the Rocky Mountains This is corroborated by the description
of a skull of a "brown bear" killed on the Missouri (sup. cit. p. 307) which
mentions the "sharp projection of the centre of the frontal bone" and
the great thickness of the skull, as defined by Mr. Brown for his *cinnamomeus*. The evidence, so far as I can sum it, makes *cinnamomum*
a pure synonym of *horribilis*.

The Californian Grizzly is thought by some to represent a type sub-
specifically distinct from that of the Missouri Valley. Should this be
agreed to, the only applicable *existing* name is *horriaus*, applied by Baird
(Mex. Bdry. Surv., 1859, 24) to a small Sonoran form which he thought
differed from the Grizzly of northern California. If possible, this name
should be retained in preference to giving a new one.

The *Ursus luteolus*, Griffith, revived by Dr. Merriam (Proc. **Biol. Soc.
Wash.**, 1893, 147) seems not identical with the yellow Bears of Mr.
Brown's paper; its affinities seem to be closer to *americanus* than to
horribilis, forming, indeed, another link in the mysterious chain which
makes our most honest attempts to classify these Bears appear more
hopeless than ever.‡

---

* Proc. Acad. Nat. Sci., Phila., 1894, 119.   † "brown gray" Gass' Jour.
‡ I consider *Ursus americanus* a good species in any case.

Pages 302, 303.

"Columbia Marmot."

For an amusing and trustworthy interpretation of the affiliation of Snakes Lizards, Owls and Prairie Dogs, consult Dr. Coues' Birds of the Northwest, 1874, p. 324. Rafinesque named this animal *Cynomys socialis* in 1817.

Pages 303, 304.

"Louisiana Marmot."

It seems evident, from the context, that Ord never saw a specimen of this Spermophile but was induced, by the minute description, to risk naming it.

Dr. Merriam's identification of it has, we trust, settled forever one of the strangest cases of mistaken identity that has arisen in American Zoology.

Page 304.

Squirrels Discovered by Lewis and Clark.

This paragraph is important, and to be better understood may be amended as follows :—"Our Catalogue, it will be perceived, is enriched with the [vernacular and generic] names of those animals of this genus which were discovered [and described] by Lewis and Clark, the stuffed skins of which have been deposited in Peale's Museum. The history of their [Lewis and Clark's] journey gives an account of some others [squirrels, chipmunks and spermophiles] but as this notice [Lewis & Clark's account] is a mere record of their existence [the existence of these animals] we are not enabled [in the absence of specimens] to determine whether or no they are nondescripts." It is evident therefore, and the paragraph quoted (supra) from the Journal de Physique confirms it, that Ord did not refrain from imposing specific names on these Squirrels because they were not represented by specimens, but that he was content to defer the final naming of them until he could bring out his illustrated work on the zoology of Lewis and Clark's Journey, spoken of in his letter to Blainville.

Page 307.

Lewis and Clark Deer.

We have no account that any specimens of these deer were brought to Philadelphia. If there had been, Ord would undoubtedly have given them specific names in his catalogue.

Page 308.

Prong-horned Antelope.

Though the Antelope had been vaguely and imperfectly characterized by former travelers, Ord rightly credits Lewis and **Clark** with the **first** detailed account of this interesting animal.

Pages 309, 310.
"Another Animal of the Ovis Genus."

Though given under **the** name of Sheep, Lewis and Clark's **description** of the Mountain Goat is unmistakable. Many years, however, **elapsed** ere the true affinities of this animal, in contradistinction with **those of the** Mountain Sheep, **were** made known. The name "White **Buffaloe"** is peculiarly applicable **to** this species, from the striking **resemblance of** the configuration of the neck and shoulders to that of **the Bison. As** Prof. Dyche (Camp Fires of a Naturalist, Edwords) has shown, **this** character is due to the great length and fixity of the spinous processes of the interscapular vertebræ and the low poise of the neck, which combine to prevent the animal from raising its nose much above a horizontal position even when **on** the alert.

Pages 313, 314.
"Ornithology."

Ord **may be said to stand** among his cotemporaries as preeminently **the Patriot** Naturalist, **and his** frequent allusions **to the** injustice done American Zoology **by** the dogmatic ignorance of such "foreigners" as Buffon **show the** amount **of** prejudice and misrepresentation which he felt it his **peculiar** mission **to** withstand and refute. Natural Science in America **to-day,** notably in the realm of Ornithology, has splendidly vindicated **the** cause in which Wilson was the inspired pioneer. From him Ord probably drew the original inspiration, adding thereto a strong loyalty to his native America which it was impossible for Wilson to feel. It was this impulse more than any other which induced the modest patron and biographer of Alexander Wilson to risk an irksome notoriety by editing and completing the American Ornithology.

The beautiful tribute paid by Ord in this and succeeding pages of **the** Zoology to the genius of a Scottish emigrant shows his patriotism to have been thoroughly republican, free of self-interest or jealousy, and that the attainment of truth was its highest ambition.

Page 315.
CLASS *AVES*.

As in his list of the Mammalia, Ord's table of North American Birds is evidently copied in the main from Turton's Linnæus, edition of 1806. All the species there accredited to North America (inclusive of Mexico) are entered in the list and to these the author has added the new species described by Wilson, eliminating some however, which he was convinced were synonyms of names already on his list. In addition to this are **a** few new species proposed by Mr Ord himself, and with two exceptions, based upon the descriptions in Lewis and Clark's narrative. As may be supposed, many of the birds which were entered on the authority of Turton (or Gmelin) were wrongly attributed to North America, some being European and some South American. Quite a number of other names, originally proposed by Gmelin, are entirely unrecognizable.

Gmelin's edition of the Systema Naturæ of Linnæus is the one most frequently referred to in the following notes. Ord's references to Lewis and Clark are to be found in the edition of Nicohlas Biddle published in Philadelphia in 1814.

Page 315.
GENUS *VULTUR.*

Besides the three species of Vultures which inhabit the United States, three others appear in the list, of these the Condor and King Vulture are South American, the latter reaching southern Mexico.

Vultur columbianus is a new name of Ord's based upon the "Buzzard" of Lewis and Clark. It is a synonym of the *Vultur californianus* immediately preceding,=*Pseudogryphus californianus.*

Page 315.
GENUS *FALCO.*

F. fulvus L.=*Aquila chrysætos L.*

F. leucogaster Gm.=*Haliætus leucogaster* Gm.; an Australian and Indian species wrongly attributed to North America.

F. leverianus Gm.=*Buteo borealis (Gm.).*

F. spadiceus Gm.=*Circus hudsonius (L.).*

F. sacer Gm.=*Hierofalco sacer* of Europe and Africa. Gmelin's "var B," which was attributed to N. America, may possibly have been intended for *Archibuteo sanctijohannis.*

F. obscurus Gm.=*Falco columbianus L.*

F. hiemalis Gm.=*Buteo lineatus (Gm.),* young.

F. uliginosus Gm.=*Circus hudsonius (L.).*

F. furcatus L.=*Elanoides forficatus (L.),* (1758). The name was changed to "furcatus" in the 12th. edition.

F. niger Wils.=*Archibuteo lagopus sanctijohannis* (Gm.). The *Falco niger* of Gmelin is a very different bird and is generally referred to *Aquila chrysætos* (L.).

F. pennsylvanicus Wils.=*Accipiter velox* (Wils.). The name *pennsylvanicus* was used for the "Slate colored" Hawk in vol. vi, p. 13 of the American Ornithology, and *velox* for the Sharp shinned Hawk in vol.

v, p. 116. In the latter part of vol. vi, p. 92, Wilson used *pennsylvanicus* for the Broad winged Hawk, but finding that he had already used the name, he changed it to *latissimus* in the last edition of the volume.

"BLUE H. F. CÆSIUS." This name was here proposed by Ord for a presumably undescribed species. No reference or description accompanies it, but from the fact that he called it the Blue Hawk and as the adult male of the Marsh Hawk is often known by that name, we presume this was the bird intended. This view is strengthened by the fact that Wilson did not figure or describe the adult male Marsh Hawk.

In a manuscript foot note Mr. Ord says, "name preoccupied," and this statement is correct, as Meyer proposed the name in 1810 (Tascheub. Deutschl. Vogelk., i, p. 60) for a European Hawk, i. e. the *Falco regulus* of Pallas, which latter name has priority.

F. obsoletus Gm.=*Buteo swainsoni* Bonap. ⎫ These Gmelinian names,
F. fuscus Gm.=*Accipter velox* Wils. ⎭
long in use, have been discarded by the A. O. U.

The other names included under this genus are of doubtful application, i. e.—*F. variegatus, cinereus, gentilis and novæ-terra.*

Page 315.
GENUS *STRIX*.

S. bubo L.=*Bubo virginianus.* (Gm.).

S. mexicana=*Asio mexicanus* Gm., a South American species.

S. albifrons Shaw.=Young of *Nyctala acadica* (Gm.).

S. otus L.=*Asio wilsonianus*, an American species.

S. nævia Gm.=*Megascops asio* (L.).

S. flammea L.=*Strix pratincola* Bp. At the time Mr. Ord's work appeared, the American Barn Owl was not distinguished from the European species.

S. passerina L.=*Nyctala acadica.*

S. hudsonia Wils.=*Surnia ulula caparoch* (Müll.).

S. brachyotus Gm. *Asio accipitrinus* Pall.

S. wapacuthu Gm. is based upon Pennant's "Wapacuthu Owl." The description of this bird agrees very well with *Bubo virginianus arcticus* (Sn.) except that it is included among the species *without* horns, so that the name can hardly be used for this species, and must be disregarded.

S. tolchiquatli and *chichictli* of Gmelin are unrecognizable.

S. funerea L. is *Surnia ulula caparoch* (Müll.).

Page 315.
GENUS *LANIUS*.

L. septentrionalis Gm. } the same: both=*L. borealis* Vieill. For many
L. excubitor L.   }
years the American *L. borealis* was confused with *excubitor*.

L. carolinensis Wils.=*Lanius ludovicianus* L.   Gmelin's *L. carolinensis*
=*Tyrannus tyrannus* (L.).

L. canadensis, nootka and *pileatus* are unrecognizable, though the first is
partly based upon a female *Thamnophilus cirrhatus* Gm. of South
America.

Page 315.
GENUS *PSITTACUS*.

P. leucocephalus.=*Chrysotis leucocephalus* (L.).   Cuba.

P. sordidus.=*Pionus sordidus* (L.).   Venezuela.

P. mexicanus Gm. is founded upon Germi's plate which seems to be a
"made up" bird, probably a Cockatoo which had been painted or dyed.
(Cf. Salvadori, Cat. Bds. Brit, Mus., vol. xx).

P. menstruus.=*Pionus menstruus* (L.).   Costa Rica to Peru.

P. ochrocephalus.=*Chrysotis ochrocephalus* (Gm.). Venezuela to Peru.

P. macao.=*Ara macao* (L.).   Southern Mexico to Amazon Valley.

P. aracango Gm.=*Ara macao* (L.).

Page 315.
GENUS *RAMPHASTOS*.

R. torquatus Gm.=*Pteroglossus torquatus* (Gm.).   The three other species given under this genus are unrecognizable.

Page 315.
GENUS *CORVUS*.

C. mexicanus Gm. is probably a Mexican Crow which does not reach
the United States.

C. argyrophthalmus Gm. and *zanoe* Gm. are unrecognizable.

C. corax L.   The American Ravens are now separated as subspecies,
principalis inhabiting north eastern N. America and *sinuatus* the south
western sections.

C. pica L.   The American Magpie is now separated as *Pica pica hudsonica* (Sab.).

Page 315.
GENUS *CORACIAS*.

C. mexicanus Gm., is unrecognizable. No true *Coracias* occurs in America.

Page 315.
GENUS *ORIOLUS*.

O. americanus Gm.=*Leistes guianensis* L., South America.

O. ludovicianus Gm. Brisson's plate, upon which this is based, has the appearance of being made from a partially albino *Quiscalus*.

O. mexicanus.=*Gymnomystax mexicanus* (L.). Mexico.

O. bonana L., *xanthornus* Gm. and *dominicensis* L. all belong to the genus *Icterus* and occur, respectively, in Martinique, South America and San Domingo.

Page 316.

O. capensis Gm.=*Sitagra capensis* (L.) a Weaver bird, wrongly attributed to America.

O. novae hispaniæ, costototl, griseus, melancholicus, viridis and *furcatus* are unidentified species of Gmelin's. The *O. viridis* of Müller is *Ostinops viridis*.

Page 316.
GENUS *GRACULA*.

G. barita Wils.=*Quiscalus major* (Vieill.). Gmelin's *G. barita* is of doubtful application.

G. ferruginea Gm.=*Scolecophagus carolinus* (Müll.).

Page 316.
GENUS *TROGON*.

Trogon curucui L. is a South American species.

Page 316.
GENUS *CUCULUS*.

C. ridibundus Gm. is probably a Mexican species of *Piaya*.

C. dominicus Lath. is probably referable to *Coccyzus americanus* (L.).

C. carolinensis Wils.=*Coccyzus americanus* (L.).

Page 316.

GENUS *PICUS.*

P. viridis Linn. is a European species.

P. tricolor Gm. is unidentifiable. The name was subsequently used by Vieillot for a South American species.

P. canadensis Gm. is a synonym of "*Dryobates villosus* [L.] var. *canadensis*" (Bodd.).

P. querulus Wils.=*Dryobates borealis* (Vieill.).

P. major L. is a European species.

ROCKY MOUNTAIN W. *P. MONTANUS.*" This is a new name, here proposed by Ord for a "Woodpecker" described as follows in the Narrative of Lewis and Clark's expedition, (vol. i, p. 398), "Among the woods Captain Clarke observed a species of woodpecker, the beak and tail of which were white, the wings black, and every other part of the body of a dark brown ; its size was that of a robin and it fed on the seeds of the pine." This was the Clark's Nutcracker *Picicorvus columbianus* (Wils.). *Picus montanus* Ord will therefore become a synonym of this species, which, in turn, has recently been shown* to be generically identical with *Nucifraga* of the Old World.

Page 316.

GENUS *ALCEDO.*

A. torquata L. This species is properly a resident of South and Central America and southern Mexico, but a specimen has been recently taken on the Rio Grande at Laredo, Texas (Auk, 1894) so that it may have just claims as a bird of the United States.

Page 316.

GENUS *SITTA.*

S. varia Wils.=*S. canadensis* L.

Page 316.

GENUS *TODUS.*

T. obscurus Gm. The true Todies are restricted to the West Indies. This bird is described from Rhode Island and seems to be a small Tyrant Flycatcher, perhaps *Sayornis phœbe.* The description is too meagre however to make the name of any value.

*Auk, 1894, p. 179.

Page 316.
GENERA *MEROPS* & *UPUPA.*

Merops cinereus Gm. ⎫
Merops californiensis. ⎬ **are** unidentifiable.
Upupa mexicanus Gm. ⎭

Page 316.
GENUS *CERTHIA.*

C. mexicana Gm. has not been identified; it is not the Mexican Creeper, *C. familiaris mexicana* (Glog.).

C. maculata Wils.=*Mniotilta varia*(L.).

C. caroliniana Wils.=*Thryothorus* **ludovicianus** (Lath.).

C. palustris.=*Cistothorus palustris* (Wils.).

Page 316.
GENUS *TROCHILUS.*

Of the Humming birds enumerated in the list only two occur in the United States, *Trochilus colubris* and *Selasphorus rufus.*

T. paradiseus and *cyanurus* of Gmelin have not been satisfactorily identified. The remaining species are now referred to other genera or are synonyms, viz.:

T. maculatus Gm.=*Lampornis gramineus* (Gm.). Northern South America.

T. punctulatus Gm.=*Lampornis violicauda* (Bodd.). **S. America.**

T. venustissimus Gm.=*Eulampis jugularis* (L.). **West Indies.**

T. mango.=*Lampornis* **mango** (L.). Jamaica.

T. holosericeus.=*Eulampis holosericœus* (L.). West Indies.

T. minimus.=*Mellisuga minima* (L.). Jamaica and St. **Domingo.**

T. exilis.=*Bellona exilis* (Gm.). **West Indies.**

Page 316.
GENUS *STURNUS.*

S. ludoviciana Linn. 1776.=*S. magna* Linn. 1758. **Now** known as *Sturnella magna.*

S. obscurus=*Molothrus ater* **obscurus** (Gm.).

S. prædatorius Wils. = *Agelaius phœniceus* (L.).

Page 316.

GENUS *TURDUS*.

T. plumbeus. = *Mimocichla plumbea* (L.). Bahamas.

T. hudsonius and *T. labradorus* of Gmelin are both based on specimens of *Scolecophagus carolinus* (Müll.).

T. rufus. = *Harporhynchus rufus* (L.).

T. melodus Wils. = *T. mustelinus* Gm. Wilson used Gmelin's name for the Veery (*T. fuscescens* Steph.) and proposed this new name for the Wood Thrush. Bonaparte discovered this mistake, but not having seen Stephen's desciption he added to the synonymy by proposing the name *Turdus wilsoni* for the Veery.

T. aurocapillus. = *Seiurus aurocapillus* (L.).

T. lividus Wils. (nec Licht) = *Galeoscoptes carolinensis* (L.).

T. aquaticus Wils. = *Seiurus noveboracensis* (Gm.).

T. solitarus Wils. = *Turdus aonalaschkæ pallasii* (Cab.) While Wilson's text relates to the Hermit Thrush, his plate is of the Olive Backed Thrush *T. ustulatus swainsonii* (Cab.).

T. mustelinus Wils. (nec Gm.). = *Turdus fuscescens* Steph. (sup. cit.).

Page 316.

GENUS *AMPELIS*.

A. americana. = *Ampelis cedrorum* (Vieill.).

Page 316.

GENUS *LOXIA*.

Three of the species included under this genus are not found in North America.

L. grisea. = *Spermophila grisea* (Gm.). South America.

L. canora. = *Phonipara canora* (Gm.). Cuba.

L. nigra. = *Melopyrrha nigra* (L.). Cuba.

L. virginica Gm. is of doubtful application, but is probably based on a moulting *Piranga rubra* (L.).

L. obscura Gm. is the young of *Habia ludoviciana* (L.).

L. flabellifera Gm. is perhaps based on the young of *Guiraca cærulea* (L.). See Cat. Bds. B. M., vol. xii p. 139. The following names have not been satisfactorily identified with any species: *L. mexicana, novæ hispaniæ, canadensis* and *hudsonica.*

Page 316.

GENUS *CURVIROSTRA.*

C. americana is now known as *Loxia curvirostra minor* (Brehm), the type of the genus *Loxia* being a Crossbill.

Page 316.

GENUS *EMBERIZA.*

E. mexicana Müll.=*Capodacus mexicanus* (Müll.) ; Gmelin's *E. mexicana* is doubtful.

E. atricapilla Gm.=in part, *Zonotrichia coronata* (Pall.).

E. cærulea Gm. is probably *Passerina cyanea* (L.) in winter plumage.

E. americana=Spiza americana (Gm.).

E. erythrophthalma.=Pipilo erythrophthalmus (L.).

E. oryzivora.=Dolichonyx oryzivorus (L.).

E. pecoris Gm.=*Molothrus ater* (Bodd.).

E. nivalis.=Plectrophenax nivalis (L.).

E. ciris.=Passerina ciris (L.).

E. graminea.=Pooecetes gramineus (Gm.).

E. hiemalis L. (nec Gm.)=*Junco hyemalis* (L.).

The following have not been satisfactorily identified, *E. leucouphala. E. ludovicia.*

Page 316.

GENUS *TANAGRA.*

T. mexicana.=Calliste mexicana L.

T. rubra.=Piranga erythromelas Vieill.

T. æstiva.=Musicapa rubra L.=*Piranga rubra* (L.).

T. anorea, and *grisea* of Gmelin are of doubtful application.

Page 316.

GENUS *FRINGILLA.*

F. cannabina L. is a European species.

F. cristata.=*Coryphospingus cristatus.* South America.

Page 317.

F. hudsonia Forst.=*Junco hyemalis* (Linn.).

F. arborea Wils.=*Spizella monticola* (Gm.).

F. melodia Wils.=*Melospiza fasciata* Gm.

F. palustrris Wils.=*Melospiza georgiana* (Lath.).

F. ferruginea Gm.=*Passerella iliaca* (Merr.).

F. carthaginensis, variegata, cutotol and *carolinensis* of Gmelin are unidentified.

Page 317.

GENUS *MUSCICAPA.*

M. forficatus. This name is given twice, once for the Fork-tailed Flycatcher and again for the Swallow-tailed. The first is doubtless an error for *M. tyrannus.* Both species belong in *Milvulus.*

M. ludoviciana. Gm.=*Myiarchus crinitus* (L.).

M. solitaria and *olivacea* belong in the genus *Vireo.*

M. cantatrix Wils.=*Vireo noveboracensis* (Gm.).

M. nunciola Wils.=*Sayornis phœbe* (Lath.).

M. rapax Wils.=*Contopus virens* (L.).

M. querula Wils.=*Empidonax acadicus* (Gm.). The *M. querula* of Vieillot however is *Contopus virens* (L.).

M. sylvicola Wils.=*Vireo flavifrons* Vieill.

M. cœrulea.=*Polioptila cœrulea* (L.).

M. canadensis and *pusilla* belong in *Sylvania.*

M. cuculiatus Wils.=*Sylvania mitrata* (Gm.).

M. melodia Wils.=*Vireo gilva* Vieill.

M. ruticilla.=*Setophaga ruticilla.*

M. striata Forst.=*Dendroica striata* (Forst.).

M. ferruginea Merr. is of doubtful application.

The other species all belong in the Family *Tyrannidæ* no true *Muscicapas* occur in America.

Page 317.

GENUS *ALAUDA*.

A. ludoviciana Gm. and *rufa* Wils.=*Anthus pensilvanicus* (Lath.).

A. magna.=*Sturnella magna* (L.).

A. alpestris.=*Otocoris alpestris* (L.).

Page 317.

GENUS *SYLVIA.*

S. icterocephala L.=*Dendroica pensylvanica* (L.).

S. cincta Gm.=*Dendroica coronata* Gm.

S. ludoviciana, aurocollis, canadensis, hudsonica & leucoptera have not been identified.

S. flavicolla Wils. and *S. pinus* Wils.=*Dendroica vigorsii* (Aud.).

S. solitaria Gm.=*Dendroica dominica* (L.).

S. citrinella Wils.=*Dendroica æstiva* (Gm.).

S. magnolia Wils.=*Dendroica maculosa* (Gm.).

S. autumnalis Wils.=*Dendroica castanea* (Wils.), young.

S. rara Wils. is the young of *Dendroica cærulea* (Wils.).

S. rubricapilla Wils. is a misprint for *ruficapilla;* the former spelling occurs in Wilson's Index.

S. pusilla Wils.=*Compsothlypis americana* (L.).

S. petechia Wils. (nec L.)=*Dendroica palmarum hypochrysea* Rdgw.

S. minuta Wils.=*Dendroica discolor* (Vieill.).

S. montana Wils. has not been found since Wilson's time and is a doubtful species.

S. parus Wils.=*Dendroica blackburniæ*, (Gm.), young.

S. maritima Wils.=*Dendroica tigrina* (Gm.).

S. marylandica Wils.=*Geothlypis trichas* (L.).

S. sialis.=*Sialia sialis* (L.).

S. calendula and *regulus* belong to genus *Regulus.* The latter is a European species; the American Golden-crowned Kinglet being now separated as *R. satrapa* Licht.

S. domestica Wils.=*Troglodytes ædon* Vieill.

S. troglodytes L.—*Troglodytes hiemalis* Vieill. *T. troglodytes* is the European species.

Page 317.
GENUS *PIPRA*.

P. cristata, picicitli and macatototl are not recognizable.

P. polyglotta Wils.= *Icteria virens* (L.).

Page 317.
GENUS *HIRUNDO*.

H. rupestris.=*Cotile rupestris* Scop., a European bird.

H. cinerea.=*Atticora cinerea* (Gm.), of South America.

H. oonalaskensis Gm. is not identifiable.

H. americana Wils.= *Chelidon erythrogaster* (Bodd.).

H. viridis Wils.= *Tachycineta bicolor* (Vieill.).

H. purpurea L.=*Progne subis* (L.).

Page 317.
GENUS *CAPRIMULGUS*.

C. americanus Wils.= *Chordeiles virginianus* (Gm.).

Page 317.
GENUS *COLUMBA*.

C. fusca, cærulea, hoiloti, nævia and **mexicana** are of doubtful application. The first may be *Scardafella* **squamata** of South America and *C. nævia* may be *Zenaidura* **macroura** (L.).

C. canadensis L.=*Ectopistes migratoria*, young, or female.

C. passerina. The true *Columbigallina passerina* (L.) is a West Indian bird, *C. p. terrestris* Chapm. is the Eastern U. S. race and *C. p. pallescens* (Baird) the Western form.

Page 317.
GENUS *PENELOPE*.

P. cristata L. is perhaps *P. purpurascens* from Guatemala.

P. cumanensis Gm. belongs in genus *Pipile*; habitat Guiana.

P. pipile. Probably the same as *P. cumanensis* Gm.

Page 317.
GENUS CRAX.

C. alector L. is a South American species, while *C. globicera* L. is found in Central America and southern Mexico.

C. pauxi L. belongs in genus *Pauxi;* it is a South American bird.

C. vociferans Gm. is not identifiable.

Page 317.
GENUS PHASIANUS.

P. mexicanus Gm.=*Geococcyx affinis?*

P. cristatus.=*Opisthocomus cristatus* Gm.

"COLUMBIAN P. *P. COLUMBIANUS.*" "The grouse or prairie-hen" of Lewis & Clark's Report, vol. 2, p. 180, is here named for the first time by Mr. Ord. The name now stands as *Pediocætes phasianellus columbianus* (Ord).

Page 317.
GENUS TETRAO.

T. albus.=*Lagopus albus* L., a European species.

"BROWN G. *T. FUSCA.*" A new species based on Lewis and Clark's narrative, and seems to refer to the Oregon Ruffed Grouse, generally known as *Bonasa umbellus sabini* (Dougl.). This is clearly pointed out by Dr Coues in his new edition of The History of Lewis and Clark's Expedition, vol. iii p. 872, foot note. He there proposes the adoption of Ord's name, as it has priority over that of Douglass, and writes the species *Bonasa umbellus fusca* (Ord).

Page 317.
GENUS PERDIX.

P. nævius, mexicanus and coyoclos are doubtful species.

P. hudsonica Lath.=*Porzana noveboracensis* (Gm.).

P. cristatus L. belongs in genus *Eupsychortyx;* it is a South American species.

In a mss. footnote Ord makes *virginianus, mexicanus* and *coyoclos* the same. *Californicus* and *cristatus,* he also indicates to be synonyms.

Page 318.
GENUS *CANCROMA.*

Cancroma cochlearia is a South American bird.

Page 318.
GENUS *ARDEA.*

A. americana belongs in genus *Grus.*

A. hoactli, spadicea, hohou, virgata, striata and *cana* are of doubtful application, though the first two **probably apply** to *Nycticorax nycticorax nævius* (Bodd.).

A. minor Wils.=*Botaurus lentiginosus* (Montag.).

A. gardeni Gm.= young *Nycticorax n. nævius* (Bodd.).

Page 318.
GENUS *TANTALUS.*

T. minutus L. is probably a young *Guara rubra* (L.).

T. mexicanus Gm. is probably *Plegadis autumnalis* (Hasselq.).

T. albicollis. A South American species now placed in *Geronticus.*

Page 318.
GENUS **SCOLOPAX.**

S. nigra, nutans and *candida* are of doubtful application.

S. gallinula.=*Gallinago gallinula* (L.). a European species.

S. melanoleuca, totanus and *vociferus.* Ord, in a manuscript note, says that these are identical. There seem, however, to be two species, *Totanus totanus* of Europe and *T. melanoleucus* of N. America; *vociferus* of Wilson being a synonym of the latter.

S. glottis.=*Totanus glottis*, a European species accidental in the United States.

S. calidris.=*Totanus calidris*, another European bird.

S. noveboracensis.=*Macrorhamphus griseus* (Gm.).

S. semipalmata (Gm.). belongs in genus *Symphemia.*

S. gallinago Wils.=*Gallingo delicata.* The true *G. gallinago* (L.) is a European species.

Page 318.
GENUS *TRINGA*.

T. striata, novæterræ, hiaticula and *variegata* are unidentified.

T. ochropus.=*Totanus ochropus* (L.), a European species, accidental in the United States.

T. icelandica and *cinerea* of Gmelin=*T. canutus,* as stated by Ord in a manuscript note. *T. rufa* Wils. is also a synonym.

T. borealis.=*Aphriza virgata* (Gm.).

T. bartramia=*Bartramia longicauda* (Bechst.).

T. semipalmata.=*Ereunetes pusillus* (L.).

T. cinclus L.=*Tringa alpina* (L.), in immature plumage.

Page 318.
GENUS *CHARADRIUS*.

C. apricarius L. is a European species. Wilson used the name for *C. dominicus.*

C. pluvialis L.=*C. apricarius* L.

C. hiaticula L. is a European species now placed in *Ægialitis.* Wilson used the name for *Ægialitis semipalmata* Bp.

C. calidris L.=*Calidris arenaria* (L.).

Page 318.
GENUS *HÆMATOPUS*.

H. ostralegus L. This is the European species. The American form is now known as *H. palliatus.* Temm.

Page 318.
GENUS *RALLUS*.

R. minutus Pall. is an Old World species.

R. cayennensis Gm.=*Aramides cayanea* Müll., S. American.

Page 318.
GENUS *PARRA*.

P. jacana and *nigra* are now known as *Jacana jacana* (L.) and *J. nigra* (Gm.).

P. chavaria.=*Chauna chavaria* (L.), one of the South American Screamers.

P. ludoviciana Gm. seems to be *Chettusia miles* Bodd., an Australian bird.

Page 318.
GENUS *GALLINULA*.

G. phorphyrio Wils.=*Ionornis martinica* (L.).

G. chloropus.=*Gallinula galeata* (Licht.).

G. flavirostris Gm.=*G. martinica* L.?

G. ruficollis Gm.=*Aramides ruficollis* (Gm.). Cayenne.

G. carthagena and *purpurea* of Gmelin are of doubtful application.

G. noveboracensis Gm. is now *Porzana noveboracensis* (Gm.).

Page 318.
GENUS *PHALAROPUS*.

P. glacialis Gm.=*Crymophilus fulicarius* (L.).

P. fusca and *hyperborea*=*P. lobatus* (L.).

Page 318.
GENUS *FULICA*.

F. atra L. is a European species. The American bird is *F. Americana* Gm.

F. mexicana is doubtful.

Page 318.
GENUS *PODICEPS*.

P. cornutus.=*Colymbus auritus* L.

P. minor Gm. *Tachybaptes dominicus?*

P. ludovicianus Gm.=*Podilymbus podiceps* (L.).

P. obscurus Gm.=*Colymbus auritus* L.

Page 318.
GENUS *RECURVIROSTRA*.

R. alba L. is of doubtful application.

Page 319.
GENUS *DIOMEDEA.*

D. spadicea Gm.—young of *D. exulans* L.

D. exulans L., & *Thalassogeron chlororhynchus* (Gm.) do not occur on the United States' coasts.

Page 319.
GENUS *ALCA.*

A. labradora Gm. is probably a Puffin; perhaps, as Dr. Coues suggests, a young *Lunda cirrhata* Pall.

Page 319.
GENUS *COLYMBUS.*

C. striatus Gm.=*Urinator lumme* (Gunn.) young.

C. septentrionalis L. & *stellatus* Brünn=*U. lumme* (Gunn.).

C. glacialis L. & *immer* L.=*U. imber* (Gunn.).

Page 319.
GENUS *STERNA.*

S. cayanensis Gm.=*S. maxima* Bodd.

S. minuta Wils.=*S. antillarum* (Less.).

S. fissipes L.=*Hydrochelidon nigra surinamensis* (Gm.).

S. aranea Wils.=*Gelochelidon nilotica* (Hasselq.).

S. plumbea Wils.=*Hydrochelidon n. surinamensis* (Gm.), young.

"BANDED-TAIL T. *S. PHILADELPHIA.*" This is a new species here described for the first time by Ord. It is however a true Gull and not a Tern, and is now known as *Larus philadelphia* (Ord).

S. simplex and *spadicea* are unidentifiable.

Page 319.
GENUS *LARUS.*

L. canus is a European species; the American bird is *L. brachyrhynchus* Rich.

L. fuscus L. is a European species.

L. ridibundus Wils.=*L. atricilla* Linn.

L. parasiticus belongs in *Stercorarius.*

L. cataractes & *keeask* both refer to *Megalestris skua* (Brünn.).

L. eburneus.=*Gavia alba* (Gunn.)?

"TOOTHED-BILL G. *L. DELAWARENSIS.*" Another new species which is here described for the first time.

Page 319.

GENUS *PROCELLARIA.*

P: obscura.=*Puffinus obscura*, habitat Indian Ocean.

P. melanopus and *brasiliana* of Gmelin are of doubtful application.

P. gelida.=*Puffinus gelidus* Gm. an Antarctic species.

Page 319.

GENUS *MERGUS.*

M. fuscus and *cœruleus* are doubtful.

M. albellus is a European species. Wilson confused it with the Butter-ball.

M. meganser L. is a European species. The American bird is known as *merganser americanus* (Cass.).

Page 319.

GENUS *ANAS.*

"WHISTLING SWAN *A. COLUMBIANUS.*" This species is based upon Lewis and Clark's narrative, vol. i, p. 398, and is here named for the first time. It is now placed in the genus *Olor.*

A. ferina is a European bird. Wilson employed the name for *Aythya americana* (Eyt.).

A. anser.=*Anser anser* (L.), a European species.

A. marila. The American bird is now subspecies *nearctica.*

A. mollissima. The true American Eider is *Somateria dresseri* Sharpe. This is a European bird. The Greenland form is *S. m. borealis* (Brehm.).

A. moschata L. Not found wild in North America.

A. bahamensis L. is *Dafila bahamensis;* not found in N. America.

A. viduata L.*=Dendrocygna viduata* (L.) a South American and West African species.

A. arborea L.*=Dendrocygna arborea* (L.) a West Indian species.

A. fuligula L. is a European bird. Wilson, however, used the name for *Aythya collaris* (Donov.).

A. spinosa Gm.*=Nomonyx dominicus* (L.).

A. crecca of Wilson and some others *=Anas carolinensis*. The true *A. crecca* is a European bird.

A. fulva belongs in *Dendrocygna*.

A. fuscescens, georgica and *novæhispaniæ* are of doubtful application. *

Page 319.
GENUS *PELICANUS*.

P. onocrotalus L. is a European species. Ord meant our *P. erythrorhynchos*.

P. carolinensis Gm.*=P. fuscus* L.

P. aquilus.=Fregata aquila (L.).

P. thagus Moll. is probably the *Pelecanus molinæ* Gray.

P. fiber L.*=Sula sula* L.

P. parvus Gm. is doubtful, but certainly a *Sula*.

P. graculus.=Phalacrocorax cristatus L., a European species.

Page 319.
GENUS *PLOTUS*.

P. surinamensis Gm.*=Heliornis fulica* Bodd., a South American bird.

Page 320.

With slight exceptions Ord's bird notes on this and following pages are a transcript from Wilson's Ornithology, many of them, however, being quoted from his own contributions to that work as editor.

The brief notes already appended to Ord's catalogue of Birds are

* Ord has added a note in lead-pencil at foot of Genus Anas, page 319, as follows: " Lewis's Red headed D. A. rufescens." This cannot refer to the "red-headed fishing-duck" of L. & C., vol. 2, p. 195, as the description expressly states it is the same as our eastern Merganser. On page 195 (sup. cit.) L. & C. describe a duck which is said to have "the head, the neck (etc.) of fine deep black with a slight mixture of purple about the head and neck." This is the only other duck mentioned by L. & C. to which Ord's lead pencil name can at all apply. Dr. Coues (1893 ed. L. & C., p. 889) identifies this duck as Aythya collaris (Donov.).

deemed sufficient to identify those of greatest interest. Owing to the completeness and accessibility of our ornithological literature, little comment seems necessary beyond the bare references aforesaid. By these it is hoped the critical reader may obtain some introduction to the necessary authors without our unduly encumbering this Appendix with details.

Page 324.

"Common Crow."

To these pertinent remarks on the relations of Crows to agriculture etc. the scientist of to-day can add but little, either of information or advice. Both the Crow and House Sparrow have demonstrated the divine right and ability to solve their own destiny without the advice of the United States government or of State legislatures. For discussion of Crow Roosts and Roosting Crows, see my paper in the American Naturalist, 1886, pp. 691 & 777.

Page 326.

"Purple Grackle."

Ord's (Wilson's) humane verdict on the economic status of our Blackbirds standsthe test of modern investigations in this important branch of ornithology.

Pages 327, 328.

"Downy Woodpecker."

While the general usefulness of our Sapsuckers is undeniable, it is a fact that some of them, especially the Yellow-bellied Woodpecker, do tap the healthy trees for the sap and that the insects thus attracted are incidentally devoured as well as the sap itself. See paper by the late Mr. Bolles, Auk, 1891, p. 270. Also Dr. Coues in Birds of the Northwest, and Proceedings of the Philadelphia Academy for 1866.

Page 329.

"Humming Bird."

Nineteen species of the *Trochilidæ* have been recorded in the United States.

Page 337.

"Wild Pigeon."

"The Present Status of the Wild Pigeon," (etc) is made the subject of a paper by Mr. Wm. Brewster in the Auk for October, 1889. The extinction of this bird over the greater part of its former habitat has been accomplished. Those remaining have "retreated to uninhabited regions, perhaps north of the Great Lakes in British North America." Mr. Brewster concludes "it is probable that enough Pigeons are left to re-

stock the West, provided that laws, sufficiently stringent to give them
fair protection, be at once enacted."

Page 341.

"Pinnated Grous."

The typical "Grouse plains" of New Jersey cover a very limited tract
between Woolmansie and Cedar Bridge, near the boundary line of Ocean
and Burlington Counties. The diameter of this area varies from three
to five miles. The pines and oaks here rarely attain a maximum height
of four feet. Turnbull mentions the extinction of the Heath Hen in
New Jersey as having occurred about 1869.

Page 357.

Of all the Reptiles enumerated in Ord's table of "Amphibia" and
which, it should be observed, he restricts to the "Zoology of the United
States," about ten per cent. are Mexican or South American, three or
four are exotic and two or more unidentifiable. Prof. E. D. Cope, after
careful inspection of the table, informs me that all of the newly named
species to which sufficient reference is made in the text to merit exam-
ination, are either synonyms or unidentifiable.

Note on Changes in Nomenclature.

Owing to unforseen delays in the publication of this work, the summary of changes in nomenclature here proposed, which was announced
on page 1 of the Appendix, to be given in this place, was published in the
American Naturalist, June 1894, pp. 523–526. To this the critical reader
is referred.

Errata of Reprint.

Page 291, (Genus *Mustela*); for "*vison*" read *vison*.
" " (Genus *Didelphis*); for "*opossum*" read *opossum*.
" 292, (Genus *Arctomys*); for "Prairie-dog" read Prairie-dog.
" " 13th line from foot, "Chikaree" is so spelt in the original.
" 294, 14th line from foot, for "favorite" read favourite.
" ", 11th line from foot, for "Indain" read Indian.
" 296, 23rd line from top, "*Lynx*" should not be italicized.
" 299, 11th line from foot, for : after "escape" read *.
" 300, 7th line from foot, for "comsidered" read considered.
" 307, 20th line from foot, for "thy" read they.
" 312, 19th line from top, for "*Hippopotamus*" read *Hippopotamus*.
" 317, (Genus *Hirundo*); for "Bock-swallow" read Rock Swallow.
" 318, (Genus *Gallinula*); for "*ssus horonsis*" read *noveboracensis*.
" 319, (Genus *Pelecanus*); for "Lesser G." read Lesser B.
" ", (foot note), 3rd line from foot, "*sixteen*" is so spelt in the original.
" 334, 17th line from foot, "e" in "*Wren*" should be italic.
" 344, 13th line from top; "k" in "*Woodcock*" should be italic.
" 346, 20th line from foot; for "smal" read small.
" 351, 11th line from top, for "Wigeon" read Whigeon.

Errata of Appendix.

Page 2, (middle); for "Page 299," read Page 290.
" 3, 16th line from foot, for "*nithmut*" read *without*.
" " 5th line from foot, for "*forent*" read *front*.
" 5, above "Arctic Walrus or Morse" insert Page 281. **Genus *Trichechus*.**
" " 5th line from top, for "*rosmarus*" read *rosmarus*.
" 6, 8th line from foot, for "Nillson" read Nilsson.
" 7, 2nd line from foot, for "Rich." read (Rich.).
" 8, 5th line from top, before "*Ovis bicrons* Say" insert —.
" 9, (middle); for "*Ovis cansek*" read *Ovis Cansek*.
" 11, 19th line from top for "certainty" read certainly.
" 12, 16th line from foot, expunge quotation marks after "*Lutreola vison.*"
" 13, 7th line from foot, for "synorym" read synonymn.
" " last line, for "Linn" read (Linn.).
" 16, 3rd line from top, for "Brazilian" read Brasilian.
" " 6th line from top, for "Canada" read Canadian.
" " (middle) for "*Arvicola pennsylvanica* Ord" read *Arvicola pennsylvanica* (Ord).
" 19, 13th line from top, for "*Sceiurus*" read *Sciurus*.
" 20, 22nd line from top, for "clasified" read classified.
" 21, 8th and 13th lines from top, for "Columbian" read Columbia.
" " 15th line from foot, for "*hedsonicus*" read *hudsonicus*.
" 22, 10th and 12th lines from top, for *hudsonius* read *hudsonicus*.
" 24, 18th line from foot, for "page" read **page.**
" 31, last line, for "species" read species.
" 32, 8th line from top, for "Nicolaus" read Nicholas.
" " 15th line from top, for "*Vatter columbianus*" read "Columbia V. *V. COLUMBIANUS.*"
" 33, 18th line from top, for "*anser terra*" read "*anser terror.*"
" 37, 16th line from top, for "*Mioditte*" read *Molotilte.*
" " 8th line from foot, for "*ludovicieus*" read *ludovicieus.*
" " 3rd line from foot, for "*ludovicieus*" read *ludovicieunus.*
" 38, 5th line from top, for "*hudsonius*" read *hudsonicus.*
" " 18th line from top, for "*natalivus*" read *natalivus.*
" " 19th line from top, for "*fuscescens*" read *fuscescens.*
" 39, 11th line from top, for "*Corpolarus*" read *Corpolarus.*
" " 11th line from foot, for "*leucophala*" read *leucophala.*
" " 4th line from foot, for "*onverea*" read *canora.*
" 40, 6th line from top, for "*palustrie*" read "*palustris.*
" " 7th line from foot, for "*coeculinus*" read *coeculinus.*
" " 6th line from foot, for *Vireo gilva* Vieill" read *Vireo gilvus* (Vieill).
" " 2nd line from foot, insert semicolon after "*Tyrannidæ.*"

52

INDEX TO WHOLE VOLUME.

[Note.—Page numbers under each entry follow their actual sequence in pagination, those of the Appendix (pp. 1 to 51 inclusive) following the original pagination of the Zoology (pp. 290 to 361 inclusive).]

53

Americana, **Spiza** 39
  ,Strix 315
  ,Talpa 14
Americanus, **Antilope** 292
  ,Bison 26
  ,Canis **291, 7**
  ,Caprimulgus 317
  ,**Coccyzus** 35
  ,**Dipus 292, 22**
  ,**Lanius 315**
  ,Lepus, 292, 22
  ,Manatus 5
  ,Merganser 48
  ,Mus 292, 16
  ,Mustela 201, 12
  ,Noctilio 3, 4
  ,Oriolus, 315, 35
  ,Sitomys, 16, 17
  ,Tapir 292, 26
  ,Ursus 291, 13, 29
  ,Vespertilio 291, 3
ammon, Ovis 292, 24
Ampelis Americana 316, 38
  cedrorum 38
  ,Genus, 316, 38
Amphibia, Class 357, 1
amphibius, Mus, 292, 16
Amphisbæna 357
  fuliginosa 357
  ,Genus 357
Anas acuta 319
  albeola 319
  Americana 319
  anser 319, 48
  arborea 319, 49
  Autumnalis 319
  Bahamensis 319, 48
  bernicla 319
  boschas 319
  Canadensis 319
  carolinensis 49
  clangula 319
  clypeata 319
  Columbianus 319, 48
  crecca **319,** 48
  cygnus 319
  discors 319
  ferina 319, 48
  fuligula 319, 48
  fulva 319 48
  fusca 319
  fuscescens 319, 48
  ,Genus 319, 48
  Georgica 319, 48
  glacialis 319
  histrionica 319
  hyperborea 319
  Labradora 319
  marila 319, 48
  mollisima 319, 48

Anas moschata 319, 48
  nigra 319
  Novæ Hispaniæ 319, 48
  obscura 319
  perspicillata 319
  rubidus 319
  ruficapilla 49
  spectabilis, 319
  spinosa 319, 48
  sponsa 319
  Stelleri 319
  strepera 319
  valisineria 319
  viduata 319, 49
Anguis **eryx** 357
  ,**Genus** 357
  lumbricalis 357
  maculatus 357
  ventralis 357
angulatus, Dicotyles, 6
annulatus, Coluber 357
anser, Anas 319, 48
  ,Anser 48
Anser anser 48
Ant-eater, Least 291, 4
  ,Striped 291, 4
Antelope, American 292, 294, 301, 306, 308, 24
  ,Barbarian 292, 24
  ,Cervine 306
  ,Prong-horned 292, 308, 23, 24, 30
  (Rupicapra) americana 25
Anthus pensilvanicus 41
antillarum, Sterna 47
Antilocapra americana 23, 24, 25
Antilocapridæ 24
Antilope Americanus 292, 24
  bubalis 306
  dorcas 292, **24**
  ,Genus 292, **24**
apella, Simia 291
Aphriza virgata 45
apricarius, Charadrius 318, 45
Aquatic Shrew 291, 14
aquatica, Zizania 333
aquaticus, Coluber 357
aquaticus, Scalops 14, 15
  ,**Sorex,** 291, 14
  ,**Turdus** 316, 38
Aquila chrysæetos 32
aquila, Fregata 49
aracango, Psittacus, 315, 34
Ara macao 34
Aramides cyanea 45
  ruficollis 46
aranea, Sterna 319, 47
araneus, Sorex 291, 14
arborea, Anas 319, 48
  ,Dendrocygna 49

www.ingramcontent.com/pod-product-compliance
Lightning Source LLC
Chambersburg PA
CBHW020543270326
41927CB00006B/704